Land Alienation and Politics of Tribal Exploitation in India

Suratha Kumar Malik

Land Alienation and Politics of Tribal Exploitation in India

Special Focus on Tribal Movement in Koraput District of Odisha

Springer

Suratha Kumar Malik
Department of Political Science
Vidyasagar University
Midnapore, West Bengal, India

ISBN 978-981-15-5381-3 ISBN 978-981-15-5382-0 (eBook)
https://doi.org/10.1007/978-981-15-5382-0

This Springer imprint is published by the registered company Springer Nature Singapore Pte Ltd.
The registered company address is: 152 Beach Road, #21-01/04 Gateway East, Singapore 189721, Singapore

Foreword

Since India's independence, considerations of economic development have repeatedly come in conflict with the interests of the tribal people, and the problem has become particularly critical in the wake of adoption of neo-liberal economic policies and programmes over the last few decades. Odisha, as we all know, is one of the states where the tribal question has assumed special importance for historical reasons. This research work, done by Suratha Kumar Malik, is an excellent analysis of this problem in the Koraput district of Odisha with special reference to the Narayanpatna movement as a counter to the government as well as corporate policies in regard to the tribals. The central issue underlying the tribal problem is, as the author has rightly argued, that of land alienation since it is land that gives identity to the tribal, defines the tribal and sustains the tribal. But in the colonial as well as in the post-independence era, every attempt has been made, despite legislative and constitutional provisions for safeguarding their interests, to take away land from the possession of the tribals, the only consideration being drive for profit, business and commerce. Malik's study addresses this question with deep insights, revealing how in the Koraput district the tribals have been subjected to brutal repression by the corporate lobby with the tacit support of the government. This has been possible especially for the reason, as the author has so convincingly explained, that there are at one level legal loopholes and at another level massive illiteracy.

All these, Malik has shown, have led to resistance movement on the part of the tribals, the political manifestation of which is the Narayanpatna movement that has emerged in recent times. This deserves special attention since the author has made a detailed analysis of the genesis and growth of this movement, its leadership, its political appropriation by the Maoists as well as its problems and difficulties. The fact that, this movement has sent a new message to the tribals as well as to the land grabbers is clearly evident.

Further, this study has viewed the problem from a normative angle too. At one level, he has explained that the Narayanpatna movement has a moral justification, and at another level, he has provided thoughtful suggestions in the form of alternative policy prescriptions for the redressal of the tribal problem.

This is a very timely study of the tribal problem which deserves attention of the concerned scholars as well as all sensible persons who want to understand how the tribal question has thrown up a major challenge to the neo-liberal perception of development in India.

Kolkata, India
March 2020

Sobhanlal Datta Gupta
Former Surendra Nath Banerjee
Professor of Political Science
University of Calcutta and editor of
Socialist Perspective (Journal)

Preface

Land is not only a tangible asset but is the mainstay of most of the rural folks as they are dependent on agriculture and allied activities. The tribals are emotionally attached to their land, and their economy is primarily agro-based. Due to non-tribals' entry into tribal areas, the tribal land is going to be alienated. Consequently, a large number of tribal cultivators have been rendered as landless labourers. The increasing trend in the number of landless labourers in tribal areas and decrement in the number of tribal cultivators simply argue the concerning issues with regard to tribal land alienation. The dominant discourse regarding land alienation of tribals is simply overshadowed by the problem of alienation of legal land holdings by non-tribals where the loss of tribal access to forest and land, through the process of forest reservations, land categorisation and displacement with the help of the state is not emphasised in the discourse. Shifting cultivation as the earliest form of agriculture continues to be predominantly practiced by the tribals though the shifting cultivation land is not settled with them, and they are being treated as encroachers in their own land. Earlier, every tribal family at least owned an ideal size of land holding to support his/her family even with the traditional and primitive way of cultivation, but now, the situation has changed and the tribals are becoming landless day by day. The tribals were forced to leave their land or sell it, due to heavy demographic pressure on tribal land and the pressure especially from the advanced sections of the society. The nature and causes of tribal land alienation actually differ from one state to another state. To prevent tribal land alienation, different laws have been enacted in all the states, but unfortunately, these laws were not implemented in their letter and spirit.

Due to inaccessibility, the tribal areas remained outside the land management system for a long time. For this reason, the tribals developed their own traditional system of land management. Land ownership in tribal areas comes under three distinct categories. These are (i) individual holdings, (ii) land belonging to clans and (iii) community land. Some of the tribal areas were also covered by the British system of land revenues, and other areas followed the system which is prevalent among the Indian princely states. These princely states had followed different land tenure systems, and there was no uniformity. Due to lack of regular land settlement system and absence of up-to-date record on land rights, the tribals remained in darkness, and the landlords, officers of the forest department and revenue officers exploited the tribals and their land.

The pressure increased on tribal land with the introduction of commercial preference of land as a resource. As a result of developmental processes and setting up of various irrigation, power, industrial and mining projects, the problem of land alienation further hastened. There were legal remedies to prevent the process of tribal land alienation, but the tribals could not take advantage of the legal remedies on account of illiteracy and poverty. Scheduling of the areas and the reorganisation of the states in post-independence period had severe entailments on the tribal land. Due to scheduling of areas, the areas that remained outside the Scheduled Areas, for quite some time, did not get the benefit of protective land laws. The instances of land alienation were much in tribal areas having rich in agricultural production and natural resources.

A large amount of tribal land has been alienated due to lacuna in the land laws, indebtedness of the tribals, acquisition of land for public purposes by the state and other public and private authorities, forcible eviction and encroachment of tribals from their own land by the government authorities for the developmental projects. The very common methods of tribal land alienation were through mortgage, sale, *benami* transfers, lease, fraudulent methods, collusive decrees and land grabbing. The landlords of tribal areas (mostly coastal people) had owned much of the tribal land for the money loaned to the tribals. The other form of tribal land alienation happens due to the non-tribals' marriage with a tribal woman, adoption of a non-tribal by a tribal or land purchased in the name of a tribal farm servant. Apart from alienation of *patta* land to private persons, the government has acquired substantial amount of tribal land for various developmental projects. It can be said that tribal land alienation happened due to inadequate preventive laws or simply lack of implementation of the already existing laws.

The Indian Constitution provides the broad frame to protect tribal interests in the land and property, and it would be prudent to highlight some of the provisions which unfortunately have not been translated to its potential. Thus, for example, in Article 46 of the Constitution, under the Directive Principles of the State Policy, it is mandated that the state shall *inter alia* protect the Scheduled Castes, Scheduled Tribes and other weaker sections from social injustice and all forms of exploitation. Interpreting this section, the Supreme Court has held that a law prohibiting the transfer of land belonging to a member of a Scheduled Tribe to a non-tribal is valid. The Constitution also provides for the specialised areas of administration—the Scheduled Areas and tribal areas in tribal-dominated populations. Despite of all these Constitutional protective mechanism, tribal land alienation still continues.

In the context of tribal land, one of the most radical enactments is the *Panchayats* Extension to the Scheduled Areas (PESA) Act, 1996. The PESA provides power to *gram sabha* in the area of management of natural resources, development planning and adjudication of disputes as per customs and traditions. The PESA also empowers the *gram sabha* to prevent tribal land alienation and to take suitable action to restore any alienated land. What is perhaps most critical in this regard is the manner in which the law has been adapted in the Scheduled Areas of the states. PESA is only an umbrella framework under which respective state *panchayat* acts have to be amended to incorporate the letter and spirit of PESA. A number of states, which have adapted PESA under a statutory timeline of one year as mandated in PESA, have left a lot of operational issues subject to rule-making powers and state prescriptions under their respective amendments. In this regard, it is still unclear, as seen in the manner in which such powers have been delegated at the state level, as to how to deal with the illegal alienation of tribal land and the nature and extent of powers entrusted with the *panchayats* and *gram sabhas* to deal with such issues. The rules under PESA in each state are required to be formulated to clarify the above issues especially with regard to the delegated powers of the *panchayats* and *gram sabha*.

There are radical-legal mechanisms already in place in each and every state to protect the tribal from being unlawfully dispossessed from his/her land. However, these laws have largely remained in paper. Thus, how much of the enabling provisions is being implemented in its letter and spirit remains a moot question. Various recommendations of the government-appointed commissions suggest that, in addition to the problem of implementation, a strong legal framework with strong jurisprudence is required in order to arrest tribal land alienation. A bulwark against rampant land alienation can be the recognition of communal land rights of the tribals. Again, this would require an in-depth and extensive survey leading to the communal rights of the tribals being identified, recognised and respected. Survey, settlement and updating of land records should be complete within a time frame. Special courts for the purpose of early disposal of tribal land alienation cases should be launched. A model law all over the country should be enacted by the government of India to provide protection to tribal interest in land. The problem of tribal land alienation is closely linked with lack of credit facilities of the tribals. Therefore, tribals should be provided easy loan and credit facilities so that their land cannot be loaned to non-tribals.

As far as tribal land alienation is concerned, Odisha remained no exception. In Odisha, tribals are the worst sufferers over the land question, where the tribal areas of the state are extremely poverty ridden and backward as compared to other states of the country. Though the tribal areas of Odisha are extremely enriched with natural resources, still 72% of tribal populations are poor and remain below the poverty line. The paradox of 'poor people' and 'rich resources' in the tribal areas of Odisha has been a challenge for the state. Earlier, the tribals in the state were not landless labourers. They had an ideal size of landholdings, but they had lost those landholdings over the period of time. The existence of the category as 'landless labourers' among the tribals of Odisha is a mark of land alienation. Through different causes and sources, tribal land alienation trend gained momentum over the years.

There are economic, social, cultural and political factors behind the dynamics of dispossession of the tribal communities of Odisha. The constantly shrinking economic base of the tribals of Odisha is the basic reason for tribal land alienation. To fulfil the daily basic needs, the tribals became exposed to cash transaction, and therefore, their non-monetised self-sufficient economy collapsed. The introduction of the state ownership of forest, forced the tribals to change their status, and from owner gatherers (gathering or collecting forest produce), the tribals were reduced to wage earners or encroachers in their own land and forest. The Odisha government through different developmental policies has displaced the tribals from their land and large-scale tribal land alienation happened due to these state facilitated processes. Therefore, the tribal communities of Odisha were forced to accept and bear the massive force of development.

The post-colonial state through its policies had facilitated the practice of land alienation both directly and indirectly. In Odisha, tribals have also lost their land rights through survey and settlement operations during the post-independence period. Due to the lack of regular and proper survey and settlement processes, land dispossession occurred on a massive scale. A huge amount of land has been alienated from the tribal communities of Odisha due to different reasons cited above.

The Planning Commission in a report indicated that in Odisha, due to development projects, the people who were displaced had lost control over their source of livelihood. Among the total people who had been displaced, 40% are tribals. Now, there are 18 large schemes in the Koraput district occupying 50,000 acres of land which accounts for 7.42% of the total area of the district. In the Koraput district alone, these 18 large schemes had displaced 10% of the tribals of the district from their livelihood. By the end of December, 1999, in Odisha, a total of 841,916.50 acres of tribal land were alienated. Koraput district had contributed the highest areas of alienated tribal land (28,901.55 acres), while Kandhamal district remained second in terms of tribal land alienation with 15,864.55 acres of alienated land. In south Odisha, sources also reflected that over the last two decades, hundreds of acres of tribal land have been sold illicitly with the open connivance of government officers. The tribals of Odisha are alienated from their land and being cheated mostly through *benami* (illegal) transaction.

The present decade has witnessed massive alienation of tribal land in Odisha. Encroachment by immigrants, loopholes in land laws, development projects, uneconomic size of land holding are some of the major causes for which tribals have to sacrifice their land. Further, it has been found out that, on one hand, demand for land from industrial perspective has increased manifold, and, on other hand, acquisition rate of land is low which may be largely on account of resistance by the tribals. Therefore, diversion of forest land in Odisha has shown a strong preference for mining activity. With little or no rehabilitation, tribals are displaced from their livelihoods and traditional habitats in the name of development. Tribal land alienation in the state of Odisha can be checked through social security measures for the tribals and with proper implementation of the existing land laws.

Koraput, being the tribal district under Fifth Schedule of the Indian Constitution, always remain in news for tribal discontent for different tribal issues, especially for the problem of tribal land alienation by non-tribals. The district has marked the highest tribal land alienation in the state. The outsider migrants, especially the non-tribals, have encroached and occupied large amount of tribal land through *benami* (illegal) transaction and fraud means, other than the government-assented land alienation. The tribals of Narayanpatna have started the movement against the non-tribals to get their land back from the outsider landlords which traditionally belongs to them. The state has forcefully arrested the movement after arresting all the activists and participants of the movement as Maoist sympathisers, in the name of restoring democracy, peace and security.

With the above backdrop, the present book entitled *Land Alienation and Politics of Tribal Exploitation in India: Special Focus on Tribal Movement in Koraput District of Odisha* examines the process of land alienation and tribal exploitation in India in general and Koraput district of Odisha in particular. An attempt has been made in this book to study the forms, underlying causes and the issues of land alienation in tribal areas of Odisha. This book also deals with the Narayanpatna movement which is based on tribal land alienation issues in the Narayanpatna block of Koraput district. I hope, this book will serve the academic pursuit of the readers at large.

Midnapore, India Suratha Kumar Malik

Acknowledgements

Acknowledging the contributions of different persons and institutions, first of all, I am grateful to Springer Nature, especially to Ms. Nupoor Singh and her entire team (Parimelazhagan Thirumani, Sushmitha Shanmuga Sundaram and Ashok Kumar) for their help and continuous cooperation at different crucial stages and for bringing the book in time. I am grateful to the anonymous reviewers of this book for providing their valuable suggestions. I am indebted to Prof. Sobhanlal Datta Gupta (Former Surendra Nath Banerjee Professor of Political Science, University of Calcutta) for writing the foreword of the book. As the present book uses the data from my Ph.D. work and from the major research project of the UGC, I must be grateful to my supervisor, late professor Tarun Kumar Banerjee and to UGC, New Delhi, for providing the grant to undertake the research work. I would also like to acknowledge the help of the subject expert and members of the mid-term MRP evaluation committee for their valuable suggestions during the mid-term presentation which helped me to do the research work methodologically. My heartiest thanks to Prof. Sumit Mukerji (Professor, Department of Political Science, University of Kalyani, West Bengal) for providing his suggestions at different times and as a subject expert for project fellow selection. Thanks to Prof. Tridib Chakraborty (Retd. Professor, Department of International Relations, Jadavpur University, West Bengal) and Dr. Amitava Chatterjee (Department of History, Kazi Nazrul University, West Bengal) for the evaluation of the project before submission to UGC, New Delhi.

I am thankful and indebted to the people of Narayanpatna block of Koraput district for their cooperation, help and support during the field work. I am also thankful to the administration, police, officers of the sub-collector office, officers of the land record room and revenue officers, and activists of the Koraput district who have directly or indirectly supported me in this juncture. Acknowledging the help and cooperation, I am thankful to the officers of the land acquisition office, Koraput, and the police personnel of Narayanpatna police station. I am really thankful to Raj Kishar Nag and Aruna Bakhya of Koraput for assisting me during the fieldwork. I am thankful to Rahul Kabiraj (UGC Major Research Project fellow), who has worked 2 years with me in the project. I am thankful to the teachers and able scholars of the Department of Political Science, Vidyasagar University, for their cooperation.

I am thankful to Professor Sibaji Pratim Basu (Dean, Faculty of Arts and Commerce, Vidyasagar University) for his help and valuable suggestions at different crucial times. I owe my deep sense of gratitude to the staff of central library, Vidyasagar University, staff of central library of J.N.U., the staff of Utkal University library and Ravenshaw University library for locating the required materials in the right time. A heartiest thanks to all of them for providing generous help to access the materials.

Last but not the least, I very humbly express my apt gratitude and affection to my family members and to all my beloved students who remained a constant source of inspiration and provided unstinted love to complete this job successfully.

Suratha Kumar Malik

Contents

About the Author

Suratha Kumar Malik has been an Assistant Professor at the Department of Political Science, Vidyasagar University, West Bengal, since 2012. He completed his postgraduate studies at the Centre for Political Studies, Jawaharlal Nehru University (JNU), New Delhi, and holds a Ph.D. from Vidyasagar University. He was awarded a Nirman Foundation Fellowship (Lord Bhikhu Parekh endowment) during his M.A. and was also awarded UGC-NET and junior research fellowships (JRF) during his M.Phil. at JNU. His research interests include dalit and tribal issues and politics, social–political movements, marginalization and identity politics, and Indian political thought and philosophy. He has published three books and more than a dozen of research articles in respected national and international journals as well as chapters in various edited books including Sage, Springer etc. He has presented papers at over thirty-five international and national seminars/conferences across the country and abroad, including at Imperial College London, and in Dubai and Malaysia. As the Principal Investigator (PI), he has completed the UGC Major Research Project recently. He was awarded 'Swami Vivekananda Excellence Award' in 2019 by Seva Youth Guild (Unit of Dakshin Kalikata Krira O Sanskriti Parishad), Kolkata (affiliated to NYKS, Ministry of Sports and Youth Affairs, Government of India). He is also the Programme Officer of National Service Scheme (Unit-VII) of Vidyasagar University, West Bengal.

Abbreviations

AAA	*Abad Ajogya Anabadi*
AIDSU	All India Democratic Students Union
ANM	Auxiliary Nursing Midwifery
BAMS	*Biplabi Adivasi Mahila Sangha*
BJD	*Biju Janata Dal*
BJP	*Bharatiya Janata Party*
BOR	Board of Revenue
BPL	Below Poverty Line
BSF	Border Security Force
CCP	Code of Criminal Procedure
CMAS	*Chasi Mulia Adivasi Sangha*
CMS	*Chasi Mulia Samiti*
COATS	Council of Analytical Tribal Studies
CPI (M)	Communist Party of India (Maoist)
CPI-ML	Communist Party of IndiaMarxist–Leninist
CPR	Centre for Policy Research
CRPF	Central Reserve Police Force
DFID	Department for International Development
DM	District Magistrate
DMVC	District Monitoring and Vigilance Committee
DNA	Deoxyribonucleic Acid
DPEP	District Primary Education Programme
DPP	Director of Public Prosecutions
DPSP	Directive Principles of State Policy
DSP	Deputy Superintendent of Police
EPW	Economic and Political Weekly
ERRP	Economic Rehabilitation of Rural Poor
FCA	Forest Conservation Act
FDC	Forest-Dwelling Communities
FIR	First Information Report

FRA	Forest Rights Act
GOI	Government of India
GOO	Government of Odisha
GP	*Ganatantra Parishad*
HAL	Hindustan Aeronautics Limited
HDI	Human Development Index
HINDALCO	Hindustan Aluminium Corporation
HLC	High Level Committee
ICAWPI	International Campaign Against War on the People in India
IDSA	Institute for Defence Studies and Analyses
IFAD	International Fund for Agriculture Development
ILO	International Labour Organisation
IPC	Indian Penal Code
IPCS	Institute of Peace and Conflict Studies
IRB	India Reserve Battalion
ITDPs	Integrated Tribal Development Programmes
KBK	Kalahandi-Balangir-Koraput
LAMPS	Large-sized Agricultural Multipurpose Cooperative Societies
LTAP	Long Term Action Plan
LTR	Land Transfer Regulation
MADA	Modified Area Development Approach
MDM	Mid-day Meal
MELA	Madras Estate Land Act
MESA	Municipalities Extension to Scheduled Areas
MFP	Minor Forest Produce
MGNREGA	Mahatma Gandhi National Rural Employment Guarantee Act
MMDRA	Mines and Minerals (Development & Regulation) Amendment Act
NALCO	National Aluminium Company
NBWs	Non-Bailabe Warrants
NEP	New Economic Policy
NGOs	Non-Governmental Organisations
NSCSTFDC	National Scheduled Caste and Scheduled Tribal Finance and Development Corporation
NSTFDC	National Scheduled Tribes Financial and Development Corporation
NTFP	Non-Timber Forest Produce
NTP	National Tribal Policy
NTS	National Talent Search
NUAC	*Nikhil Utkal Adivasi Congress*
OBCs	Other Backward Class
OGLSA	Orissa Government Land Settlement Act
OLCA	Odisha Land Ceiling Act
OLPBR	Odisha Land Pass Book Rules
OLRA	Orissa Land Reforms Act
OPLEA	Orissa Prevention of Land Encroachment Act
OSATIP	Orissa Scheduled Areas Transfer of Immovable Property

OTELP	Odisha Tribal Empowerment and Livelihoods Programme
PCRA	Protection of Civil Rights Act
PESA	Panchayats (Extension to Scheduled Areas)
PHC	Primary Health Centre
PLGA	People's Liberation Guerrilla Army
PoA	Prevention of Atrocities
PTGs	Primitive Tribal Groups
RCS	*Rythu Coolie Sangham*
RDI	Rural Development Institute
RDO	Revenue Divisional Officer
SCs	Scheduled Castes
SEZ	Special Economic Zone
SHGs	Shelf Help Groups
SMPTB	Special Multipurpose Tribal Blocks
SMVC	State Monitoring and Vigilance Committee
SOG	Special Operation Group
SP	Superintendent of Police
SPP	Special Public Prosecutor
SPTA	Santal Pargana Tenancy Act
SSA	*Sarva Shiksha Abhiyan*
STs	Scheduled Tribes
TAC	Tribes Advisory Councils
TDA	Tribal Development Agencies
TRIFED	Tribal Cooperative Marketing Development Federation of India Limited
TSP	Tribal Sub-Plan
UAPA	Unlawful Activities Prevention Act
UNDP	United Nations Development Programme
USA	United States of America
UTs	Union Territories
WFP	World Food Programme
WLPA	Wild Life Protection Act

Chapter 1
Introduction

1.1 Tribals of India: An Introduction

The Scheduled Tribes (STs) are divided into a number of groups and are heterogeneous in nature. These groups have historically identified by the British colonial state and later by the Indian state, as outsider to the conventional Hindu society due to their geographical isolation, typical culture and aboriginal way of life (Basha 2017: 78). They lived in forested and hilly areas, which is isolated from the settled plain areas and comparatively unprocurable. Throughout history, the tribals are involved in a variety of traditional occupations including hunting, gathering, collecting minor forest produce and shifting cultivation. Compared to the mainstream population, STs were believed to have much lower social and economic progress and variously depicted as primitive and backward. Engrafted within the category of 'tribes', there are two perspectives; the first perspective assumes the identity of the tribals descending from low social-economic development, whereas the second perspective describes tribes by their remoteness from the dominant culture and state, in a specific historical time.

As far as tribe is concerned, there are two narratives having basic contradictions that have featured the policies of the colonial state in British India and the state in independent India. 'Identity based isolation' is the first narrative, which describes tribals in terms of their geographical isolation and cultural traits as a distinctive group outside the Hindu mainstream society. 'Development through integration' is the second narrative, which seeks to improve their economic and social condition through integrating and assimilating them with the mainstream society. The second narrative that is 'development through integration' primarily guides the post-independence policy formulation. But the STs have considered the 'development through integration' narrative as both patronising and paternalistic averring that this does not attract tribal peoples' aspirations and development as per their own genius.

Article 366-(25) of the Indian Constitution defines Scheduled Tribes as tribes or tribal communities or parts of groups within such tribes or tribal communities as are deemed to be STs under Article 342 of the Constitution (Basu 1988: 971). Article

S. K. Malik, *Land Alienation and Politics of Tribal Exploitation in India*,
https://doi.org/10.1007/978-981-15-5382-0_1

342 vests the President with the power to declare by public notification tribes or tribal communities or parts of or groups within tribes or tribal communities as STs for a state or union territory (ibid.). Tribes should fulfil the following conditions for inclusion in the list of STs:-

- Indication of primitive traits
- Distinctive culture
- Geographical isolation
- Shyness of contact with the community at large
- Backwardness

The Constitution (Scheduled Caste) Order 1950 (as amended from time to time) mentions that no person professing a religion different from the Hindu or Sikh or Buddhist religion can be deemed to be a member of a Scheduled Caste (SC). There is, however, no religious bar for being treated as a Scheduled Tribe (Basu 1988: 971). The union has control over the administration of Scheduled Areas and the welfare of SCs/STs as per Article 339 (ibid.). According to this article, the president may at any time and shall, at the expiration of 10 years from the commencement of this Constitution, by order, appoint a commission to report on the administration of the Scheduled Areas and the welfare of Scheduled Tribes in the states. The order may define the composition, powers and procedure of the commission and may contain such incidental or ancillary provisions as the president may consider necessary or desirable. As per Article 339-(2), the executive power of the union shall extend to the giving of directions to a state, as to the drawing up and execution of schemes specified in the direction to be essential for the welfare of the Scheduled Tribes in the state (ibid.).

In relation to part A and part B states, as per Article 342, the President made two orders. The first two orders are: the Constitution (Scheduled Tribes) Order, 1950 and 1951. With respect to the part C states, the President also issued a third order, called the Constitution (Scheduled Tribes) Order, 1951 (Basu 1988: 972). As per the orders, 744 tribes were notified in 22 states of India. Due to state reorganisation, these orders were modified in subsequent years. In 28 states and 9 union territories, currently there are 750 tribes, which depicts the dispersion of tribes across the country. According to the census of 2011, the ST population in India is 104281034.[1] It is 8.6% of the total population of India. The STs make up 11.3% of the total population of rural areas and 2.8% of the urban population.[2]

The Constitution of India differentiates the Scheduled Tribes from other mainstream population and provides protective provisions along with three parameters. First, as opposed to individual representation in comparison to the mainstream population, the STs have both individual and group representation. Article 330 of the

[1]Census 2011, Office of the Registrar General and Census Commissioner, India, Ministry of Home Affairs, Government of India, p. 43. http://www.censusindia.gov.in/2011census/population_enumeration.html. Accessed 12 November 2018.

[2]ibid.

Indian Constitution provides for reservation of electoral constituencies in both Parliament and State Legislative Assemblies in tribal majority districts. Second, for the STs, the Constitution stipulates affirmative action provisions which provides 7.5% reservation in government jobs and government educational institutions. Third, Articles 244(1) and 244(2) of the Indian Constitution provides for Scheduled Areas in the Fifth and Sixth Schedules which carve out tribal majority areas from the geographical landmass of India. The Scheduled Tribes are the only minority group that have specially recognised rights to land in particular geographic areas as compared to the rest of the population

The Fifth Schedule of the Constitution deals with the administration and control of Scheduled Areas as well as of STs residing in any state other than the states of Assam, Meghalaya, Tripura and Mizoram. The states which currently come under Fifth Schedule Areas are—Telangana, Andhra Pradesh, Jharkhand, Gujarat, Himachal Pradesh, Chhattisgarh, Odisha, Maharashtra, Rajasthan and Madhya Pradesh (Basha 2017: 81). The north-eastern states like Mizoram, Meghalaya, Assam and Tripura also come under the Sixth Schedule which provides the broad framework for administration. Mizoram and Meghalaya are tribal majority states, whereas Tripura and Assam are tribal minority states. The Sixth Schedule provides for the creation of autonomous regions and autonomous districts which will be administered by the indigenous people as opposed to the state legislatures. The entire area of Meghalaya has come under Sixth Schedule as declared by the President.

As adopted in the Constitution, several laws to safeguard tribal rights to land were also enacted by the Indian Parliament and different state legislatures. These laws were meant to prohibit land transfer from tribals to non tribals in Scheduled Areas (Basha 2017: 81). States which have no designated Scheduled Areas, like West Bengal, Sikkim and Uttar Pradesh have also enacted legislations prohibiting transfer of tribal land, to non tribals (ibid.). Moreover, the Panchayats (Extension to Scheduled Areas) Act, 1996, and the Forest Rights Act, 2006 were also enacted by the Indian Parliament to safeguard the rights of tribals and other forest dwelling communities to forestland (ibid.). It aims to bring down the centuries of injustice upon forest-dwelling communities, mostly for STs, by discarding the nineteenth and twentieth centuries British forest laws. Other than the Forest Rights Act, a number of laws were also promulgated by the Indian Parliament and state legislatures to protect the Scheduled Tribes against atrocities.

Keeping in mind the geographical isolation and distinct identity of the tribals in one hand and their underdevelopment in comparison to the rest of the population in other hand, special constitutional and legal provisions were enacted. These provisions represented in retaining their distinctive tribal culture and identity and integrating and developing the STs simultaneously. Despite these special protective provisions, the Scheduled Tribes lag behind the general population on various social and economic indicators, i.e. health, literacy, poverty and landlessness. Landlessness, illiteracy and poverty are rampant amidst the STs. Though, tribals are the only group whose land rights are constitutionally protected, still, 9.4% of the STs are landless in comparison to 7.4% for the national average (Basha 2017: 82).

From 1951 to 1990, tribal population have been displaced from their habitats due to industrial development, construction of dams, creation of wildlife parks, mines and sanctuaries. The STs constituted for 40% of all people who have been displaced though their population constitute only 8.6% of the total population (Basha 2017: 82). Among these displaced persons, only 24.7% population were rehabilitated (ibid). Therefore, it can be said that the development-induced displacement burden of our country has disproportionately borne by the tribals. It simply raises a question, why these tribals despite of all Constitutional provisions, affirmative actions, land rights in their favour still continue to remain most displaced, landless, most impoverished and vulnerable?

1.2 Defining Tribe

From the Latin word 'tribus', the term 'tribe' is educed which means three and refers to the three divisions of the early people of Rome. It also means 'the masses' or 'the poor'. The word 'tribe' came along in English language in the sixteenth century which refers to a community having common ancestry. The word usually means a community affiliated with a particular territory, a social cohesive unit, and regards themselves as politically independent or autonomous. Each and every tribal group or community has a distinguishable cultural trait and distinct dialect. Tribe is defined as a collection of families bearing a common name, speaking a common dialect, occupying or professing to occupy a common territory and is not usually endogamous though originally it might have been so (Basha 2017: 78). R. N. Mukherjee views that a tribe is that human group, whose members have common interest, territory, language, social law and economic occupation (cited in Basha 2017: 79).

At the dawn of the twentieth century, for the first time, the British state attempted an organic definition of 'tribe', as a loose grouping of three different types identified on the basis of objective criteria and not simply in distinction from dominant Indian society. The Report on the Census (1901), identified tribes on the basis of three criteria: religion, profession and geographical location. Based on religion, the report referred to tribal communities as 'aborigines or animists'; on the basis of their geographical location, 'hill tribes, mountain tribes, or forest tribes'; and on the basis of profession, 'nomad and wandering tribes or wild tribes'. The 1901 Census defined 'tribe' as

> a collection of families or groups of families bearing a common name which as a rule does not denote any specific occupation; generally claiming common descent from a mythical or historical ancestor and occasionally from an animal, but in some parts of the country held together rather by the obligations of blood-feud than by the tradition of kinship; usually speaking the same language and occupying, professing, or claiming to occupy a definite tract of country.[3]

[3]Census1901.https://ruralindiaonline.org/library/resource/report-on-the-census-of-india-1901/. Accessed 14 November, 2018.

This definition of tribe for the first time included the geographical connection of the tribe and relationship to particular tracts of land. By the time of the 1911 Census, the British further came to define 'tribes' not as a 'collection of families' but as a 'social group' in distinction to 'caste'. According to the Census, unlike caste whose basis was 'economic or social', the basis of the tribe was political. Though the members of a tribe believed that they had a common origin, what held them together was 'community of interest' and 'need for mutual defence'.

The 1921 and 1931 Censuses made only minor changes to the classification of tribal communities, and the 1941 Census was disrupted by budgetary constraints during World War II. The twentieth century also saw the introduction of limited political reforms in British India in response to the increasing demands for political autonomy from British rule by the Indian freedom movement. The Montagu Chelmsford Report of 1918, which recommended diarchy (system of double government) for India, only mentioned the Scheduled districts to note that the reforms would not apply to them. This was because the tribal people were 'primitive', and there was no material on which to be found 'political institutions'.

The Government of India Act, 1919 divided the backward tracts into two categories: wholly excluded areas and partially excluded areas. Some areas were wholly excluded from the purview of elected provincial legislatures and provided within the jurisdiction of the Governor and his executive council. The provincial ministers have no power in these areas and were barred from any obligation regarding administration. The partially excluded backward areas were specially focused by the government to ensure the life and security of the primitive denizens, freedom to carry out and protect their traditional means of livelihood, security of land tenure for the tribals, and a fair and sensible exercise of their hereditary and patrimonial traditions and customs.

However, even under these new provisions, the rights of the tribal inhabitants were always subordinate to the rights of the state under its forests and land acquisition laws. The Indian Forest Act, 1927, which replaced the Indian Forest Act, 1878, allowed the state to 'acquire' land for the purpose of constitution of forests very much in the manner of the Land Acquisition Act, 1894. On a parallel trajectory, the British state continued to be preoccupied with the situation of the 'criminal tribes'. Following the enactment of the Criminal Tribes Act, 1871, the penalties against the criminal tribes had been stiffened between 1871 and 1911. In 1876, the Criminal Tribes Act was extended to the Bombay Presidency and in 1911, to the Madras Presidency covering all of British India. The introduction of the Criminal Tribes Act, 1911, was a turning point insofar as it recognised that crime had declined significantly among the tribes and that they had taken to a more settled life. Apart from protecting mainstream society from the criminal acts of the tribal people, for the first time, this act also included provisions for reforming the 'criminal tribes' and integrating them into mainstream society. The shift in British policy towards rehabilitation and integration of the 'criminal tribes' within mainstream civilised society continued in subsequent decades of the early twentieth century. The All India Jails Committee Report, 1919, urged the government to do more to rehabilitate and integrate the 'criminal tribes'. In 1924, a new Criminal Tribes Act was enacted which consolidated the legislative changes made in various provinces.

1.3 Conceptual and Theoretical Framework

Tribals or aboriginals living in isolated areas and leading an autonomous and insulated life, have spearheaded movement against the British in the past and against the Indian state in the post-independence period due to the latter's exploitation over the former. Tribal people, spread over large parts of India, organised hundreds of militant outbreaks and movements during the nineenth century which come under the purview of tribal movements or social movements. These movements were marked by immense courage and sacrifice on their part and brutal suppression and butchery on the part of the rulers. All these movements of tribals in India may be placed in the larger framework of the 'theory of social movements' for scientific discussion, conceptual clarity and for the purpose of analysis. It is pertinent to begin the present study on *land alienation and the politics of tribal exploitation in India: special focus on the tribal movement in Koraput district of Odisha*, with a discussion of the concept and theories of social movements.

The term 'movement' originates etymologically from the French word *movoir* which means to stir, impel or move: movement is also defined as an act of moving the body or part of the body or a series of actions and endeavours of a body of persons for a special object.[4] A movement is an act by people in a wide range to mobilise and radicalise people on a certain issue. It is a means to bring together people who share the same ideas and goals, make their cause popular and gather support. Movements are a passive way to bring about change and reach a goal by unity among like-minded people.

The early concept and use of 'social movement' were 'mechanistic' which aimed at social explanation but later the term became popular for different group activities towards political democracy. A movement entails self-generated, autonomous and independent action, an organisation and leadership. T.D. Weldon describes it as a 'hurrah word', like democracy, equality and liberty (Weldon 1955: 27). Three apparent advantages of the concept of 'movement' can be emphasised. In the first instance, it is culturally standardised; second, it is neutral in its ideology and in the third instance, it can be externalised forward or backward according to the time. Yet, anyone who attempts to write on social movements finds the concept ill-defined and fertile in its intension and references, which needs more investigation and clarity. The disquiets experienced in fine-tuning the term 'social movement' can be discussed under five categories: problems of type and concept, problems of generalisation, problems of depersonalisation, problems of comparison and the dangers of ambiguity. The term 'movement' has different meanings for different persons, which poses the

---

[4]Oxford Advanced Learner's Dictionary.

problem of what is the difference between 'movement' and the actions of different groups such as parties, pressure groups and unions.

In the words of Rudolf Heberle, all major social movements have the distinguishing characteristic of a more or less elaborate ideology or set of constructive ideas which have the aim of remaking the socio-economic and political orders, and upon which action programmes are based (Rudolf 1951: 2). For Herbert Blumer, whatever be its type, a social movement signifies either a collective effort to transform some given area of established social relations, or else a large unguided change involving, however unwittingly, large numbers of participants (Blumer 1957: 145). The general characteristics of the functional concept of 'social movement' may be summarised as follows: a social movement is a calculative corporate enterprise to boost and alter a situation in any direction by any means, not barring illegality, revolution and violence, which also needs a prescriptive dedication towards change by the active engagement of followers.

The views of T. K. Oommen regarding social movement were provided in the following paragraph which will help us to characterise social movement. Oommen views;

> The scholars who did research on social movements and revolutions initially viewed them either as pathological aberrations or anti-systemic eruptions, the conservative band. Their commitment appeared to get the system back to equilibrium while the radicals who did research on this theme constituted themselves into a demolition squad as it were, to squash the state system. They invariably opted for revolutionary transformation and structural change, rarely realising that no system ever undergoes total change. Neither the conservatives nor the radicals ever asked themselves what kind of research would be useful to those who lead movements, viewed in terms of the objective of movement activists, namely the reconstruction of society. However partial destruction, selective retention, judicious borrowing and gradual accretion are all necessary ingredients of authentic reconstruction. To wit, we have sociology *of* social movements but no sociology *for* social movements. Traditional wisdom in sociology views social movements as an exertion by the excluded categories for an egalitarian society. In this perspective, movements are defined as oppositional forces against the *status quo*. This perspective probably has greater validity, at a time when the state operates as a mere police state (Oommen 2004: 179-80).

1.3.1 Theories of Social Movements

Europe and the United States of America (USA) saw blow up of demonstrations and protests against the existing social practices and government policies in the 1950s. In the decade, the USA witnessed the feminist movement, civil rights movement, 'green' or environmental movement and anti-Vietnam war movement. Europe also witnessed the feminist movement and the anti-colonial movement, for example, in France, the pro-Algerian independence movement. In this backdrop, the question 'why social movements are born and grow' remain pertinent.

West European and American academic scholars have tried to understand the origin of social movement theories. The theories they have examined are as follows: resource-mobilisation theory, deprivation theory, structural strain theory, political process theory and new social movement theory. Regarding the birth and growth of social movements, there have been many theories, but the above theories on social movements are more prominent. The following sections provide a more detailed discussion of the theories of social movements.

1.3.1.1 Deprivation Theory

The basics of deprivation theory argues that social movements have their bases amidst people who feel divested of some resource(s) or goods. Persons who are lacking some services, goods, or comfort are more prone to organise a social movement to ameliorate their conditions (Morrison 1978: 203). As far as deprivation theory is concerned, there are two problems. First, since most people feel deprived, why a particular group organise social movement when other people are also deprived. Second, the reasoning behind this theory is circular—it sometimes argues that social movement is the only evidence for deprivation. If the only evidence for such is the movement, the reasoning is circular (Jenkins and Perrow 1977: 250).

1.3.1.2 Mass-Society Theory

According to this theory, individuals who feel detached or insignificant in society try to organise social movements. Therefore, organising social movement provide a sense of authority and empowerment to the organisers of the movement. The individual join the movement through associate or friend who is already a member of the movement (Kornhauser 1959: 27).

1.3.1.3 Structural-Strain Theory

The structural-strain theory highlights six components that promote the development of social movement (Smelser 1962: 132). These six elements of structural-strain theory were provided in the following points.

- Structural conduciveness—it means people believe that their society has problems.
- Structural strain—here, people feel privation.
- Growth and spread of a solution—it indicates the development of a solution to the problems which should propose and spread.
- Precipitating factors—the discontent person commonly expects an accelerator to become a social movement.
- Lack of social control—the entity should be open to change; it cannot be fulfilled if the social movement is suddenly suppressed.
- Mobilisation—people should be mobilised. It is the active component for the movement.

The theory incorporates deprivation for the underlying motivation, therefore, it is subject to circular reasoning. It happens with only denotation that there is deprivation or strain.

1.3.1.4 Resource-Mobilisation Theory

The theory heavily depends on and emphasises the value of resources in the development of social movement. Resources include: money, knowledge, labour, media, legitimacy, solidarity and the support (both external and internal) from power elite. It argues that social movement happens when individual with grievances can mobilise adequate resources to action. It explained why some deprived persons able to organise social movements while others are not on the basis of their emphasis on resources. The presumptions which the theory advocates include the following:

- In politically modern-pluralistic societies, due to ceaseless deprivation and grievances, there is incessantly possibility for protest.
- All the participants are rational intellectual; they consider the benefits and loss of their participation in the movement.
- All the members and participants are entered through different networks; they nurture social relationships through building commitment with collective identity.
- Movement organisation is contingent upon the aggregation of resources.
- The organisation which spearheaded the movement necessitate leadership and continuity of resources.
- Protest organisations and social movement entrepreneurs are the accelerators that translate collective dissatisfaction into social movements.
- The activities of the movement are shaped by the amount of resources.
- Movements formulate chances that determine their exertions to mobilise.

The theory is not an exception to criticism, as the critics view that this theory heavily depends on resources, particularly financial resources. Other than financial resources, time and labour is also required to make this theory success.

1.3.1.5 Political Process Theory

Many scholars regard that this theory is somehow similar to resource-mobilisation theory, but underline a distinct component that is ‘political opportunity’ which is important for development of social movement. This theory argues that for the formation of movement, there are three vital components essential, i.e. organisational strength, insurgent consciousness and political opportunities. Like resource-mobilisation theory, organisational strength argues that sufficient resources and strong leadership is essential in order to organise a social movement. The second component, ‘insurgent consciousness’ indicates to the ideas of grievances and deprivation. Accordingly, the members of the society experience that the system is unjust and they are being maltreated. This sense of feeling mistreated or abused arouse a sense of collective consciousness to resist against the injustice. The third component that is 'political opportunity' refers to challenge the vulnerability and receptivity of the existing political system. It solicits the emergence of social movements or issue of timing which are major advantages of this theory. Though some groups have resources to mobilise or insurgent consciousness, still they will not succeed because political opportunities are closed. Therefore, it argues that, this theory in order to be success, the above three components are quite essential. Critics of both 'resource-mobilisation' and 'political process' theory argue that neither of these theories develop culture movement. For this reason, culture theorists get an opportunity to expatiate the importance of culture in social movement.

1.3.1.6 Collective Action Theories

This theory propounds that purpose is the defining factor for any organisation to function, without any purpose, no organisation exist. Some organisations may fail to fulfil the purpose or interest of their members and others may lured into serving only the ends of the leadership. But the organisation which fail to fulfil the interest of its members gradually decease. Simply to play solitaire, there would be no point in forming the organisation. Obviously, there is no purpose in having an organisation which does not fulfil the purpose of individual. But individual will not be able to advance their single interest individually when a number of individuals have collective interest or action. So, when there are common goals and collective action, an organisation can perform better.

1.3.1.7 Relative Deprivation Theory

Gurr has led some designs on mass movements and agitation which comes under the doctrine of relative deprivation. It is identified as player's acknowledgement of incompatibility among their environment's attest value potentialities and value desires. People suppose they are fairly entitled the value prospects which are the goods and conditions of life. In the physical and social surroundings, the determinatives of value potentialities are to be looked extensively; it decides the possibilities of retaining or obtaining the norms, people desire to accomplish. Gurr comments: The aggression, frustration, and the related treat; aggression mechanisms, provide the basic motivational link between collective violence and relative deprivation (Gurr 1971: 12). With relative deprivation, he attaches three other points, namely; anomie, dissonance, and conflict (ibid.).

The person become violent who realise disappointment and deprivation. They are covetous of those who have more resources. They revolt or protest against the person who own more resources. They do not try to dissolve the problem, or to trace the origin of privation. Gurr considers 'deprivation' as mainly psychological; therefore, he does not focus on the social and economic part which are the real source of 'deprivation'. In the words of Gurr

> If such sense of deprivation is confined to an individual against another individual it leads to crime. When it is transformed to collective transformation- a deprivation of region, community or caste, it assumes the shape of collective activity. But it is not escorted with ideology for the social system; it lies to be a remonstration or agitation and rarely takes a form of social movement. Relative deprivation is an important but not an adequate factor for movements (Gurr 1971: 12).

The development of social sciences including economics, psychology and sociology are heavily influenced by deprivation theory. Psychological theory, for example, is much influenced by deprivation theory. Equity theory, frustration-aggression theory, reference group theory and social comparison theory which are parts of social psychology, are developed on the basis of relative deprivation theory. In the area and study of economics, the concept of measurement and relative deprivation is usually used. The study of economics centres on the quantification and measurement of relative deprivation applying multiple summary indexes i.e. the 'maximum index', the 'Gini coefficient' and the 'coefficient of variation'. In sociology, the fundamental causes of revolution and social movements are explained through relative deprivation theories.

1.3.1.8 Value-Added Theory

This theory determines whether collective behaviour will occur or not. It advocates that a particular compounding of determiners promotes and facilitates collective behaviour and collective outcomes. It forms a value-added process through determinants of collective behaviour. Value-added theory refers to the processes in which additional value is created at a particular stage of production or development and it originated and developed in the field of economics. It affirms that the determinants to collective behaviour combine according to a certain pattern. It requires the presence of the determinants in a predictable and logical order; particularly it asserts that there are six social determinants which are essential for the development of a social movement. These six conditions or determinants are—structural strain, structural conduciveness, precipitating factors, generalised beliefs, social control and mobilisation of participants.

1.3.1.9 Frame Analysis Theory

'Social movement framing theory' or 'frame analysis theory' tries to understand social movement actors and social movements or how ideas and events are composed. Social movements are analysed and understood through work or work culture. From the work of Erving Goffman (1986), the idea of frame analysis comes. It advocates that, in order to understand and organise the world around them, people frame experiences. Frame analysis works like a picture, where a picture excludes things while focusing attention on others. As frame analysis argues, on the basis of their previous experience and the social position they held, people interpret the world around them. According to Benford and Snow,

> Every social interaction that occurs is understood through a frame of reference within which people react, based on their perception of the situation and the way they perceive the people with whom they are interacting. In the study of social movements, collective action frames are used to bring people together and incite them to action. A social movement organisation is a formal group that functions as part of a broader social movement and that often provides the resources for the broader social movement (Benford and Snow 2000: 613).

In order to inspire people to act collectively towards some goal, social movements deploy collective action frames. Social movement analysis theory stresses on four domains: (a) the creation and use of collective action frames (b) framing processes (c) opportunities and constraints (d) the effect of framing on movement outcomes and other processes.

1.3.1.10 New Social Movement Theory

This theory advocates that in comparison to traditional social movements, contemporary social movements are playing collective and corporate action in different ways. In post-industrial and contemporary society, to analyse the role of new social movements, sociologists use new social movement theory. Understanding the applications, weaknesses and strengths of 'new social movement theory' is absolutely necessary for those who are interested in collective action and the sociology of social movements.

The theory indicates a new epitome of collective action and social movement activity. As distinct from traditional social movements, contemporary social movements are featured by goals, strategies and membership. The scholars and theorists of new social movement explicate that new social movements are developing from numerous channels in society. In our increasingly knowledge-based society, new social movements arise from the growing importance and ubiquity of information and also seen as an expressions of civil society's desire for structural change. In the post-industrial society, changing economic, social and political relationships are also seen as an inevitable outcome of new social movements. These are movements for alteration, based on the desire for structural reform, instead of revolution. It is characterised by self-limiting radicalism, and do not try to disassemble the already existing economic and political systems. Current social movement research is dominated by new social movement theory which allows for the study of micro-internal elements and macro-external elements. The theory began in the year 1950s, which emerged from the conflict and differences in post-industrial economy and society.

The theory argues that new social movements, such as environmental movements, anti-war movements, feminist movements and civil rights movements are different from traditional social movements, e.g. labour movements. New social movements deal with social and political conflict while traditional social movements are associated with class conflict. Traditional social movements engage with inequalities in terms of economic concerns. Basically, the members of new social movements belong to middle-class society. These are featured by loosely organised networks and it encourages members to engage themselves in the change of lifestyle and it tries for supporters rather than only members. New social movements are basically distinct from movements and protest groups. As they differ from protest groups which take a single issue, new social movements expect change on a global scale.

1.3.1.11 Culture Theory

'Culture theory' is based on both the resource-mobilisation theory and political process theory but expands them in two ways. Firstly, it signifies the movement culture and its importance. Secondly, it deals with the 'free-rider problem'. Both political process theory and resource-mobilisation theory, in their approaches, include a sense of injustice. The responsibility of culture theory is to bring this 'sense of injustice' to the front of the movement. Culture theory argues that social movements mobilise individuals, and in order to become successful, it should build up an injustice frame. An injustice frame is nothing but a collection of symbols and ideas. It exemplifies what the movement can do and how significant the problem is?

In addition to its emphasis on the 'injustice frame', the theory also deals with 'free-rider problem' which refers that people will not be prompted to take part in a social movement which will use up their personal resources, e.g. money, time, etc. The idea of free-riding comes when a person believes that without his/her participation, the movement will succeed, then he will avoid to participate in the movement but still reap the benefits without wasting his/her resources. The theory faces a problem when it wants to explain why people participate in movements when they believe that without their contribution, the movement can succeed. Culture theory advocates that other than social network being an important tool, the motivation for people to contribute to the movement comes from the injustice frame.

Given the above brief discussion of social movement theories, the purpose of the present study is to subject the contemporary 'Narayanpatna movement' in the Koraput district of Odisha to a detailed theoretical analysis. The Narayanpatna tribal movement is analysed within the framework of a popular social movement having all these characteristics and normative commitment towards change for an egalitarian democratic society. The Narayanpatna movement of Koraput district largely fits into the 'deprivation' and 'relative deprivation' theories and to some extent the 'mass-society' and 'structural-strain' theories of social movement. The movement of the tribals in Koraput district is based on the cause of land alienation, seeks to change the socio-economic structure generated by the centuries-old feudal land relationship between poor tribals and outsider-encroachers. The ideology, the organisation, the active participation of the thousands of tribal people and their ongoing demands have made the land movement no less than a major social movement which is highlighted in the present study through building a conceptual and theoretical framework of social movement.

1.4 Backdrop of the Study

The study of any movement, major or minor, requires analysis of the broader perspective against the background of which the movement takes place. For poor rural Indians, the greatest problem is the absence of a piece of fertile land, which is directly proportionate with rural chronic poverty and food insecurity. Without land security, efforts to explore resources for sustainable development in rural areas and especially in Scheduled Areas cannot be productive. In India, poverty and backwardness arise from the landlessness and marginal landholdings of the rural masses, especially the tribals. India is not an exception among the Asian countries where, among multiple factors, landlessness is the single most important factor resulting in food insecurity and starvation. More than 43% of rural households in the country are landless and suffer chronic poverty.[5]

After independence, many land reform laws were implemented to bring about some sort of equilibrium in the nature of land distribution among the rich and the poor peasantry. Though, after independence, a number of land reform legislations were initiated by the central government and different state governments, these were not implemented properly. The prime objective for which the Land Ceiling Act was enacted in 1974, namely, to ensure social justice to landless tenants, mainly tribals, has remained unfulfilled. Due to different reasons, the operation flunked to yield the anticipated results, i.e. poor land quality making it impossible to cultivate, lack of actual physical possession, and problem in demarcating the allotted land due to non-existence of the record of rights.[6] The land which was allotted to a beneficiary under the act, was impossible for the beneficiary to access, because it remained in the possession of the previous owner. Additionally, whatever land was collected under the *bhoodan yajna samiti* was reoccupied by the previous owners or remained undistributed. It can be said that what is reflected in government records about the sum of land that was transferred illegally is much less than the actual amount of such transfer.

The Forest Rights Act (FRA) 2006, which recognises the rights to the forest of the Scheduled Tribes and other forest dwellers offers the rights to those who have been in occupation of forestland (up to a maximum of 4 hectares) for at least 75 years or three generations. The act ensures that the *gram sabha* is the sole authority for determining the extent and nature of forest rights of individuals and community.[7] All these measures taken by the government failed to achieve their target due to lack of proper implementation. Despite all the efforts to arrest landlessness in tribal areas, encroachment and tribal land alienation are still continuing.

---

[5] Status Report on 'Land Rights and Ownership in Odisha (August 2008). UNDP. https://www.undp.org/content/dam/india/docs/land_rights_ownership_in_orissa.pdf. Accessed 26 September, 2019.

[6] ibid.

[7] The Scheduled Tribes and Other Traditional Forest Dwellers (Recognition of Forest Rights) Act, 2006, Ministry of Tribal affairs and Forestry, Government of India, p. 3. https://fra.org.in/document/FRA%20Rule_2012_complied%20version.pdf. Accessed 25 January 2019.

There have already been legal initiative to dilute the stringent land transfer regulations in the name of development scheme, industrialisation and special economic zone (SEZ) that may be prejudicious to the people concerned. Some new policies have been adopted by the government for the exploitation of natural resources which hampered the already existing land laws. In reaction, there have been continuous people's movements against land encroachment and alienation, but without any solution at the ground level. Intellectuals and civil society groups along with other tribal organisations have offered the suggestion that the government should take the initiative of arranging special land tribunals to expeditiously resolve the matters relating to land alienation, distribution and entitlement within a specific time. Special cells may also be set up in order to monitor the disposal of such cases. In cases of land encroachment, acquisition, mining and industrialisation related land alienation and development-induced displacement, the government should seriously review the issues and should provide justice to the weaker sections, especially in the case of landless tribals.

1.5 The Problem

> The fulcrum of rural life continues to rest on land. Land is the major economic aspect of any agricultural society, and especially for poor tribals. Land is not only a source of livelihood for the tribals, it is also connected with their sense of history and is a symbol of social prestige. For the tribals, the ownership of land or the assured possession of a few acres is not only the means of economic subsistence but is also a symbol of status, identity and dignity (Ambagudia 2010: 63).

Tribal people and their communities have historical relationship with their land and are the descendants of the original inhabitants of such land. The tribals have developed a holistic conventional knowledge of their natural resources, land and environment over many generations. To maintain this aboriginal identity of the tribals, Jaipal Singh, the founder leader of the *adivasi mahasabha,* and the tribal representative, had demanded some level of discrimination in the Constituent Assembly, when his turn came to address the land question in the tribal's life. The totality of tribal life process was built upon and evolve round on two major means of production, that is the twin pillars of tribal economy, i.e. the land and the forest. Their relationship with these two, particularly with the land, is something like their 'philosophy of life'. As a source of life and sustenance, land is handed down from one generation to the next. Land for tribals is a part of the larger socio-economic structure of their society and philosophy of life, though land for others may be only an object of agriculture.

Since time immemorial, tribal people have been living in most interior and inaccessible areas and utilising forest, land, and water for their basic survival. Their traditional customary rights define the nature of command over these resources. This sort of rights are recognised by the tribal communities who are ensconced in a specific eco-niche. As permanent power, the central government and the state governments have laid their claim over these resources, after independence. The unused or vacant land areas were claimed by the state. In context of tribal habitat, the rights to use these land and their traditional systems sometimes made untenable by the authorities. Tribal customary rights were not recognised by the state governments.

In India, inadequate or non-existent access to fertile land is one of the major problems of the tribal population. Rural poverty and underdevelopment in the country has its root in the absence of access to fertile land. Approximately, 98% of the land holders own just 75% of the land while 2% of landlords own 25% of the land which shows the skewed nature of the land distribution in India. About 43% of rural households in the country are landless. After independence, in order to bridge the gap between the poor landless and the rich landed peasantry, a number of land reform legislations were enacted but failed to achieve the desired results due to poor implementation.

1.6 Land as an Important Issue for Tribals

The distinctiveness of tribal tradition lies in affirming the centrality of land as the foundation for understanding the tribal people's culture, identity, personhood and religious ethos (Behura 1982: 1). Tribal people always understand themselves as an integral part of creation/land and not apart from it. Land is perceived as scared and co-creator with god and provides identity to the tribals. It is like the temple by which they become one with their ancestors, with the Supreme Being, with the spirits including other segment of the creation (ibid.). The whole religious system is centred and deeply rooted on the land itself. The rituals, religious practices, festivals, ceremonies and dance are all centred on land. Each and every tribal activities; including religious, ethical, social and economic life moves with land or soil.

Understanding the concept of land from tribal perspective provides an ethical basis of caring, sharing and responsible stewardship. Land, as per tribal world view, should be protected and preserved for the coming generations. Land cannot be commercialised and should be apportioned by all the denizens. It is not a mere piece of land to be exploited; it owns people, it provides identity to the tribal community. Without the land, there is no personhood and identity among the tribals (Behura 1982: 3). The land accommodates not only the village, the clan, and the tribe as one, but it also unites the spirits, ancestors, Supreme Being and creation as one family and for the tribals, land is conceived as mother (ibid.). As far as tribal attachment to soil or land is concerned, most of the tribals believe in the myths that they born from earth and their forefathers emerged from the bowel of the earth or from a big hole or from a stone. The tribals' experience of time and history is related to the land. When that land is encroached or alienated, for the tribal, it seems like the loss of everything, i.e. their identity, culture, self, economy and freedom. So, land alienation is a serious challenge for the tribals as far as their identity, culture, life and freedom is concerned.

Tribal life and livelihood depend on land. There backwardness and chronic poverty also related to their landlessness. After independence, regarding the land issues of the tribals, both the central government and the state governments have not performed well. In this regard, it is pertinent to quote Mohanty's article in the following paragraph.

> In recognition of the basic proposition that the Scheduled Tribes are the most disadvantaged in respect of land, which largely accounts for their perpetual poverty and makes them vulnerable to injustice and exploitation, attempts have been made by the union and the state governments to promote and protect their rights with regard to the control and use of land. Even after India's independence, with planned initiatives and policy measures, there has not been substantial improvement in the land holding status of the Scheduled Tribes where in some states, it has declined further (Mohanty 2001: 3857).

Though the tribals have launched movements against the exploitation and injustice in different times, but these movements were mostly unorganised, sporadic and fragmented, and were diluted or suppressed through various strategies by the dominant groups. However, many of these movements produced some perceptible changes in agrarian social relations and had enlightened the tribals.

The nature and pattern of land distribution in India is based on social hereditary. While the large landowners invariably belong to the upper castes, the cultivator belongs to the middle castes and the agricultural workers largely to the Scheduled Castes and tribes (cited in Mohanty 2001: 3858). Land being socially valuable asset, its improper and unequal distribution perpetuate deprivation and inequality in economic and social sphere. It also strengthens the basis of dominance of the privileged groups over the underprivileged. The remedy dwells in the idea of fair distribution. Land distribution by different methods as initiated in different times by the government through legislative measures was opposed by the rich landed peasantry and by the upper castes' vested interest. But when the magnitude of resistance of the marginalised and deprived people took the form of movement, then it provokes reform measures to absorb the revolutionary spirit. How the state action and reform measures followed peoples' collective resistance, were depicted by Mohanty in his article. In his words,

> In India, state action followed people's action, and people's action and empowerment rests on their agitation and collective resistance. The measures to promote and protect the interests of the deprived are not usually expected without persistent demands and protected struggles. Land reforms in India have been launched in response to compelling demands expressed through agitation, struggle and movements (Mohanty 2001: 3859)

The state passes legislation only to neutralise and pacify the tension. But, the measures need strong implementation which require political and bureaucratic will. The presence of strong social movement is essential in order to monitor the implementation of such measures. Without effort of mounting pressure from the side of the deprived people, the entrenched dominating privileged landowning groups would never like to give up their privilege and power.

In tribal areas, through exploitatory bureaucratic construction and land taxation policy, the British colonialism had made land alienable on a large scale. Through the help of the state machinery, by depeasantising the tribal people, the upper caste people dominating British administration had consolidated their landowning position. The tribals who were cleaning forests, cultivating land, without any experiences of landlessness, were forced to work as labourers in their own land and subjugated to different forms of exploitation and oppression. Land alienation through tenancy, debt mechanism and other dishonourable exercises continued unabated in tribal areas in spite of the proviso for prevention for land transfers from tribals to non-tribals. Slowly, it brings dissatisfaction and the boiling tensions among the tribals which resulted in rebellions and uprisings one after another. Agrarian problems were the chief motivating force behind the rebellions and movements, though many of these movements had social and religious issues in its content.

Many religious-minded rural Indians had contributed their small land holdings inspired by the *bhoodan* movement (started by Vinoba Bhave in 1951). From various states, more than 43% of land was collected through this scheme (up to March 1968). But most of the land donated under *bhoodan* scheme had been found either under dispute or unsuitable for cultivation (Mohanty 2001: 3862). Most of the donated lands under *bhoodan* scheme were found inferior in quality requiring significant investment to make suitable for cultivation. In some cases, it also found that persons who had donated land to *bhoodan yajna samiti,* denied later.

It seems that there are underlying ambiguities and loopholes in the legislative measures, lack of updated land records, slow proceeding at all levels of bureaucracy, the escaping attitude of the large landowners, the ignorance and illiteracy of the Scheduled Tribes population are the specified causes that embarrass fair distribution of land (Mohanty 2001: 3862). The dominant groups never accept the passing of the land to the Scheduled Castes and tribes and it became intolerable to them. The upper castes opposed the land allotment to the deprived sections (STs and SCs) by committing atrocities on members of Scheduled Castes and tribes. With the help of militant organised groups, like the *lorik sena* (formed by upper backward caste Yadavas in 1983), *bhumi sena and ranvir sena,* (private army of upper caste landlords mainly Bhumihars and Rajputs) the upper caste people have committed atrocities on SCs and STs. A number of *dalits* have been killed in Bihar by the *ranvir sena* for issue relating to land allotment (ibid.: 3863).

Therefore, the movement on the part of the landless tribals is a crucial need to counter the oppression of the upper caste/class elites. Regarding these movements, Mohanty's views are important to quote here. In the words of Mohanty;

> Though, these movements were not explicitly directed against the upper castes/class, it could combine the landless and poor tribal people in the rural settings providing a common forum against the propertied class and the local landed power holders who were mostly from upper castes (cited in Mohanty 2001: 3863).

1.7 Land Alienation in Tribal Areas

Land alienation in tribal areas happens in different forms and due to different reasons. Manipulation of land records is the first and foremost type of tribal land alienation. Land alienation problem immensely contributed by unsatisfactory state of land records in the tribal regions. The land which the tribals have cultivated for centuries was never enlisted and recognised with their names. Therefore, the land which was traditionally owned by the tribals is now alienated due to lack of *patta* or legal recognition. So, the tribals now are treated as encroachers in their own land which they have cultivated for centuries. The second factor which contributed for tribal land alienation is *benami* (illegal) transfers. In May 1975, the study team of the Union Home Ministry reported that large scale of tribal land were transferred or go out of hands of the tribals by way of collusive civil proceedings and *benami* (illegal) transactions etc., and the original land owners (tribals) were reduced to the level of share croppers (cited in Meena and Meena 2014: 53).

Mortgaging or leasing of the land is another form of tribal land alienation. The tribals mortgage their fertile land to get loans from the local moneylenders to fulfil various needs. The another form of depriving or stripping the tribals of their land is encroachment, which happens in all tribal areas by the new entrants especially where there were no proper land records. The non-tribals also get the tribal land in their name through manipulating the date of settlement of land disputes by bribing the local *patwari* (a government official who keeps records regarding the ownership of land). The practice of concubinage of the tribal women or marriage with a tribal women or man by non-tribal is another form to grab tribal land at no cost. Another method by which the non-tribals snatch the tribal land, is the fictitious adoption of the non-tribals by the tribal families. The lethargy in the rigorous implementation of the restrictive laws and provisions with regard to prevention of tribal land, also urges the non-tribals to occupy the tribal land.

All over the country, tribals were alienated from their land in various ways either by *benami* (illegal) transfers, mortgages, displacement of the tribals from their land by the state for various developmental projects, or demarcation of reserve forest areas in tribal regions. The large-scale tribal land alienation has threatened the right to life of the tribal population. However, the tribals are being deprived of their rights to forest and land as being the natural owners of forests and its adjoining land. The state should take initiative to protect the interest of the tribals as far as tribals' right to land and forest is concerned. In this regard, the Forest Rights Act 2006 is a landmark legislation to protect the interest of the forest dweller communities, but unfortunately the Forest Rights Act was not implemented in its letter and spirit.

Transfers of tribal land to non-tribals have been taking place in the tribal areas of the country for a long time. The problem has existed in varying degrees in the tribal areas of various states. Alienation of land not only deprives several tribal communities from their means of livelihood, but also sometimes leads to serious law and order problem. Tribal land has been acquired by non-tribals through loopholes in the law and through various illegal and fraudulent means—at times by way of oral transactions which have no legal sanction. Incomplete and unsatisfactory land records have merely aggravated the problem of land alienation. Land alienation in tribal areas is caused by rampant indebtedness among the tribals and by their deep-seated honesty and informal dealings. The non-tribals continuously alienating the tribal land owing to some loopholes and ambiguities in the already existing system of law. For irrigation, industrial, mining, power and for other projects, different state governments are also acquiring the tribal land. For that reason, tribal rights over land are going to be deprived. The tribal communities incurred loans from the moneylenders and rich farmers for non-productive purposes and mostly to meet daily basic needs. Borrowings are also the main source of meeting hospital expenditure among the tribal population. Some of the important factors responsible for land alienation in tribal areas are: (a) honesty and simplicity of tribals (b) poverty of tribals (c) absence of credit and banking facilities in tribal areas (d) unknowingness of land laws and forest acts on account of illiteracy are the reasons of tribal land alienation.

Unless tribal indebtedness is checked, there will be no permanent solution for the tribal land alienation problem. Several high power committees such as the Baua and Appu Committees have examined the issue and have made several recommendations to solve this problem. The committee suggested that production and consumption credit should be made available to tribals in an integrated manner at the field level with a view to ensuring that they keep away from moneylenders (cited in Meena and Meena 2014: 54).

1.8 Tribal Land Alienation in the Koraput District of Odisha

Of all the states of India, Odisha is considered as one of the more backward states, and the situation remains unchanged even after seven decades of India's independence. In terms of tribal population, Odisha has the third largest in the country, having 9.66% of the total tribal population. As per the census (2011), the state has 22.8% tribal population.[8] The total tribal population of Odisha is divided into 62 tribal communities, among which 13 communities are Primitive Tribal Groups (PTGs) and 44% of areas are declared as Schedule V areas of the state. Scheduled Tribes are the most marginalised sections of Odisha. Among the 30 districts of Odisha, Koraput being a tribal district (under the Fifth Schedule of the Indian Constitution) remains always in the news for tribal movements against the government and exploiters.

The tribals of Koraput have been lurching under famishment and in every sphere, they have been given an unfair bargain. Adding to their sufferings, are the increasing victimisation by moneylenders and landlords. With regard to the starvation and malnutrition-related deaths in the district, the government has initiated different welfare and developmental schemes. Unfortunately, nearly 80% of the money earmarked for these schemes is being filched due to lack of accountability. Nexus between the bureaucrats and the politicians leads to high corruption levels in the district, which contributes to the daily rising poverty index. The problems of poverty and unemployment are acute in the district and opportunities for health, education and transport exist in name only. Among the factors that lead to acute poverty;

[8]Census 2011, Office of the Registrar General and Census Commissioner, India, Ministry of Home Affairs, Government of India, p. 43. http://www.censusindia.gov.in/2011census/population_enumeration.html. Accessed 12 November 2018.

landlessness and migration in Koraput district are the most important ones and are increasing at an alarming rate with a sharp upward curve in their trend. Although the district of Koraput belongs to the Scheduled Areas of the Indian Constitution and is part of the Kalahandi-Balangir-Koraput (KBK) Long Term Action Plan (LTAP), the central issue (namely, the land problem of the tribals) remains unsolved even today. The present Narayanpatna tribal movement in the Koraput district has taken place against the background of these land issues, where the tribals are demanding the land which belonged to their ancestors, want back from the landlord encroachers.

In the history of Koraput, this is not the first movement by the tribals. Each decade has testified to some kind of violence, uprising and movement on the part of the tribals without any substantial solution. The tribal land problem of Koraput district of Odisha is a centuries-old problem, and the factors are complex, due to the negligence and non-performance of the government and revenue administration. It is pertinent to analyse the history of Koraput and its land revenue administration to realise the nature of the present-day land problems and tribal movement in Narayanpatna block of Koraput district.

The story of the land alienation problem and present movement anchor to the days of *zamindars* and kings to the present land administrative system. Land revenue administration in Koraput region was based on the ancient feudal system. The land was administered partly by the village system called *mustajari* and partly by the *ryotwari* system. There was an agreement between the tenants and the landlords in the '*ryotwari*' system and a revenue *naik* was appointed to look into the matter. In contrast, the *mustajari/gaonti* is an agent of the landlord for the collection of rent, and the system is like the *gaonti* system. They were remunerated by some percentage of the collections or by a piece of free land. The office of the *mustajari* was hereditary and chosen by an influential and important person from the village. As both the king and his *mustajaris* or *amins* were from the coastal areas, and were not tribals, they exploited the tribals through different means. Through their proximity to the king and administration, they displaced the tribals from their land. These outsiders forced the tribals from their land, and to some extent the exploiters practised the g*oti or bethi* system (system where the tribals work as unpaid labour).

The British, during their rule, aimed to exploit the forest resources and to collect revenues. The British government initiated many laws to increase the land revenues. The government never tried to simplify the system of collecting land revenues. The feudal estate was more powerful and the feudal system was reinforced under the terms of the permanent settlement of the British. With the permanent settlement, the British increased the land revenues, and there was more pressure on the tribals. As far as tribal rights over their revenue land was concerned, the British government did not attempt, or intend to lay down any principles in this regard. The Agency Tracts Interest and Land Transfer Act enacted on 14 August 1917 was the only act to safeguard the interests of the tribals. While the purpose behind the act was to prevent the transfer of land from tribals to non-tribals, it was not implemented properly in its letter and spirit. A new chapter in the history of Koraput (previously the princely state of Jeypore) was begun with the formation of the new district of Koraput. On 1 April 1936, the district was incorporated into the new province of 'Odisha' (as the state was formed on 1 April 1936 on the basis of the Odia language). For the first time in 1938, survey and record of rights operations were carried out in the district on a small scale, but were immediately suspended for the Second World War (1939–1945).

Under the 1935 Government of India Act, Koraput was demarcated as a 'partially excluded area'. Under this provision, the enactments passed by the provincial and federal legislatures could not automatically come into force in this district without being specifically extended. Koraput was declared as a Scheduled Area under the Constitution of India which came into force on the 26 January 1950. Now, the enactments passed by the state and union legislatures would automatically come into force in this area unless specifically barred by the government or the legislature.

From 1951 to 1964, the survey and settlement process continued in the Koraput district (Kumar et al. 2005: 52). But due to the adoption of a faulty system of survey by the government (the plain table survey method was adopted instead of the chain survey method, which is costly), hill slopes greater than 10 ° remained unsurveyed. These hilly land with slopes greater than 10 ° are the traditional agriculture land of the tribals, and are not recorded in the name of the tribals (ibid.). The existing *amin, mustajar,* feudal heads and landlords benefited from their better knowledge and proximity to the surveyors of the district, and recorded the majority of the land in their names. The tribals were alienated from their ancestral revenue land. The land donated in favour of the *bhoodan yagna samiti* has been reoccupied by the donors themselves and were not recorded in favour of the *samiti* during the settlement operation for redistribution among the landless. The lack of land-to-land rehabilitation policy in the cases of the National Aluminium Corporation (NALCO) and Hindustan Aeronautics Limited (HAL) and four mega-dams (Kolab, Machhkund, Indrabati and Chitrakonda) added to the existing landlessness and the land alienation process of the tribals in Koraput district.

Another wave of land alienation in Koraput started in 1970. The non-tribal 'men of affairs' and landlords of Andhra Pradesh migrated to Koraput district in 1970 due to the armed revolution in Srikakulam (Bannerjee 1986: 214). After settling there, they joined hands with the outsider coastal people of Odisha and unitedly encroached the tribal land. Against this backdrop, the tribals are now being duped by non-tribals and exploited by forest officers, landlords and outsider encroachers. Non-tribe outsiders, landlords, businessmen and mostly the *shundis* (the liquor vendors of the area) are trying to exploit the tribals and get small piece of their land by keeping the tribals indebted through alluring them with liquor.

The tribal movement in Odisha has an unequivocal historic pattern and the present state of agitation is not new. The indigenous people of Odisha have never adjourned or retired from their relentless rebellions against the land-grabbers. The tribals of Odisha have challenged the British, the *zamindars,* and formed alliances against the exploitative kings and against the *dikus* (exploitative outsiders). The tribal movement in the state has systematically targeted the foreign interventions via confiscation of their land which jeopardised their economic situation. Ghurye in his book *The Scheduled Tribes* (1963) quotes J. H. Hutton's observation that All these rebellions were defensive movements: they were the last resort of tribesmen driven to despair by the encroachments of outsiders on their land or economic resource (Ghurye 1963: 16).

Against this backdrop of land alienation, the *Chasi Mulia Adivasi Sangha* (CMAS) (the tribal organisation which spearheaded the movement in Koraput district) organised a popular movement in Koraput district against the outsider-land encroachers. CMAS' activities were highlighted by the media which had shaken the state government for six years (2009–2014). The fundamental question that arises here is why the indigenous tribals are landless today, despite the constitutional safeguards and laws in their favour. In other words, what are the 'politics' behind land alienation, tribal exploitation, and tribal resistance in the Koraput district of Odisha in particular and in India, in general?

The Narayanpatna movement by the CMAS is unique in its character of addressing the centuries-old land problems and encroachment. The agitation among the tribals in the Narayanpatna block of Koraput district has incurred a great deal of attention and has shaken the Odisha government and administration. Regarding the cause of the movement, the tribals argue that the land belonged to them and they have been cheated by the landlords for centuries. Therefore, they are reoccupying the land from the landlords of the area forcefully and unitedly through the movement. Due to the movement, around 3,000 acres of private land were reoccupied by the tribals of Narayanpatna. They have also redistributed the occupied land among the landless tribals of the area. The administration on its part has not tried to solve the basic issues of the tribals and has declared the movement as Maoist-inclined. The state has also declared the CMAS as a frontal organisation of the Maoists and has banned the organisation. It has forcefully stopped the Narayanpatna movement by arresting almost all the members and leaders of the organisation.

1.9 Review of the Literature

The tribals occupy a very important position in the planned economic development of the country at the micro-level. Unfortunately, competent socio-economic studies on the tribals are very scarce at the national level in general and on the state of Odisha in specific. A review of the literature available regarding the problem of tribals in general and the tribals of Odisha in particular are provided below.

Tribal Movements in India (3 vols) edited by K. S. Singh analyses different tribal uprisings and movements in India, where the tribal uprisings and movements in Odisha are well discussed. It also discusses that the reason behind tribal uprisings in Odisha, was their apprehensions that alien rule intended to assess their land, punish their leaders for the religious rites performed by them. For these, the tribes fight with the upper castes, the landlords and land grabbers and these all are outsider encroachers to the tribal land. The book provides a historical account of the Odisha people's movement against the British.

Changing Land System and Tribals in Eastern India in the Modern Period, edited by Tarasankar Banerjee, discusses the present-day discontent of the tribals, and looks into the operation of the British Indian laws and particularly the changing land system after the introduction of the permanent settlement which ushered a new era in eastern India in which the tribals found themselves mostly at the receiving end. The impact of the changing land system was multi-dimensional. It affected slowly the social structure, manners, customs, religion, etc. of the tribals in Assam, Bengal, Bihar and Orissa in the long run. Philip Viegas's work, *Encroached and Enslaved*, discusses the impact of land alienation on the socio-economic structures of the tribals of Odisha. He shows the nature and extent of tribal land alienation and the processes inherited with it.

B. C. Ray's *Tribals of Orissa: The Changing Socio-economic Profile,* vividly describes the tribals of Odisha and their socio-economic conditions and status in the changing circumstances. In his book *Changing Tribal Life in British Orissa,* K. Majumdar describes the policy of the British government towards the tribal people of Orissa, i.e. the *Kandhas*, and their reaction. Such anti-people developmental policies of the state even today need to be scrutinised, and for that reason, Majumdar's work has relevance even today. S. N. Tripathy, in his outstanding work titled Watershed Approach for Socio-Economic Development of KBK Tribals (Orissa) in S. N. Chaudhury (ed.), *Tribal Development since Independence,* elaborately discusses an alternative approach for socio-economic development in the KBK districts of Odisha. He mentions that tribals which constitute about 23% of the total population, are backward, marginalised and poverty-stricken population. The KBK districts ('KBK districts' basically refers to the undivided districts of Kalahandi, Bolangir and Koraput or the eight newly organised districts of Odisha, namely, Kalahandi, Naupara, Bolangir, Sonepur, Koraput, Nawrangpur, Malkangiri and Rayagda) which are among the most backward districts of India, account for 19.27% of the population of the state and over 30.59% of geographical area of the state and tribals constitute 38.72% of the total tribal population of the state. Several socio-economic indicators highlight the backwardness of the KBK region, which is one of the poorest regions of the country. The low level of income in the region, large-scale unemployment, poverty, and ultimately the distress migration of tribals have been due to the lower growth rate in the agricultural sector. Such migrant tribals fall prey to exploitative contractors and suffer as bondage labourers, social isolation and identity crisis.

The Adivasi Question: Issues of Land, Forest and Livelihood, edited by Indra Munshi deals with the Santal Pargana Tenancy Act (SPTA) passed in 1949, which furnishes a theoretical account of land systems in the Santal Parganas. According to the act, any transfer of tribal land is illegal, with exceptions mainly relating to gifts to a daughter or sister, grant to a widowed mother or wife or transfer in favour of a daughter married to a '*gharjawae*' (resident son-in-law). Munshi has also discussed the 'Samatha Judgment' (1997) which stated that mining operations in tribal areas should be conducted through the cooperation of tribals. Twenty percent of the net profit should be spent on education, health and communication services and no private mining should be allowed. Following this judgment, all state governments were asked to consider revisions in their mining rules in Scheduled Areas, rather than violating the law. The book also highlights that in Odisha, though there were tribal movements, they were confined within small geographical boundaries. In the post-independence period, neither the SCs nor the STs have organised themselves against the dominant upper castes, landlords and outsider migrants. Most of the positions in the Odisha administrative and bureaucratic structure are occupied by the forward castes, and the major political parties in the state are under their control.

Gandham Bulliyya's 'Public Policies and Legislations on Land and Forest Rights of Tribals in Orissa', in R. M. Sarkar (ed.), *Land and Forest Rights of the Tribals Today,* discusses the tribal land alienation problem in Odisha. Bulliyya mentions that a chunk of tribal land has been alienated and displaced in the name of establishing mega projects. Tribals have been displaced from their own settlements because of their ignorance, illiteracy and low resistance capacity, and were paid miserable amounts of compensation. Due to river valley projects, the state has lost nearly 63 km^2 of dense forest that include 25 km^2 in the Rengali project, 25 km^2 in Koraput river valley projects and 13 km^2 in Keonjhar. The other factors apart from displacement which account for tribal socio-political marginalisation and land encroachment are mining and industries. Multi-purpose irrigation and hydro-electrical dams have caused heavy disruption in the area, including Hirakud, Machkund, Balimela, Rengali, Upper Kolab and Upper Indiravati.

Nilkanta Panigrahi and Rashmirani Balabantaray in their article Displacement, Tribal Communities and Social Justice: Some Experiences in Post-Globalisation Period in Orissa, in M.C. Behera and Jumyir Basar (eds.), *Resources, Tribes and Development* have mentioned that the era of globalisation has widened the inroads of capital flow. One of the areas in which capital inflows have become significant is investment in mega projects which are associated with problems of displacement hitting the resources-rich tribal regions particularly hard. Tribal peoples have been displaced from their land, their homes, their livelihoods and their communities to make way for projects. The state of Odisha, particularly the southern belt, i.e. undivided Koraput, Bolangir and Kalahandi (KBK) districts is endowed with 1,733 million tonnes (70%) of the total bauxite of the nation. In the post-liberalisation period, this mineral resource has attracted foreign investment, which has brought the state into the international arena. Koraput district has five hill systems rich in bauxite minerals. The Panchapatmali hills were leased out to NALCO in 1986 and Maliparbat to HINDALCO; both are included in Koraput district. These mining projects have an adverse impact on the life and livelihood of tribal people. This can be categorised as impact on the livelihood and both the physical environment and the social environment, affecting people directly and indirectly. The tribal people in Odisha have raised their voice against such mega development investments. They have questioned the development process by asking development for whom and at whose cost? Such development projects are a reason why the tribal people of the state have raised their agonised voices against the state in contemporary times.

Dip Kapoor and Tejwant Chana, in the article "Adivasi Social Movements in Orissa: Development, Marginalisation and Dispossession" in Roy Singh and K. Debal (eds.), *Dissenting Voices and Transformative Actions: Social Movements in Globalized Era* discuss *adivasi* (tribal) exploitation in Odisha historically, since the British period. They assert that the systematic process of penetration and colonisation of *adivasi* space was initiated by the British in 1885, when the government first restricted customary rights of the tribal over the forest land. The New Economic Policy (NEP) of 1991 has exacerbated the process of *adivasi* land alienation. In the case of Odisha, *adivasis* account for 42% of 'displaced persons', as Odisha's rich mineral deposits are now open for economic exploitation by the national and multi-national corporate interests. About 95% of the mining activity takes place on *adivasi* land, while one-third of *adivasis* have been rendered landless through such avenues for capitalist development in Odisha.

Jagannath Ambagudia, in his work "Scheduled Tribes and the Land Question: The Root of Discontent and Protest in Scheduled Areas of Orissa", in Sisodia Yatindra Singh and Tapas Kumar Dalapati (eds.), *Development and Discontent in Tribal Area,* examines the importance of the land question, which assumes great significance in India, particularly, because of socio-economic necessities and constitutional commitments. These constitutional commitments are primarily designed to protect tribal rights in different spheres. These are essential for the economic and social empowerment of tribal communities. There is a need to protect tribal rights to land. This is due to the close relationship between land and tribal life. Ambagudia exclusively discusses the tribal land situation in the state of Odisha, where, as mentioned earlier, 44% of the land in the state constitutes Scheduled Areas. Out of 12 districts, 6 districts including Koraput, Malkangiri, Mayurbhanj, Nabarangpur, Rayagda and Sundargarh have been declared in their entirety as Scheduled Areas while parts of the remaining districts have been declared Scheduled Areas. The districts which have been wholly declared as Scheduled Areas have more than 45% tribal population as a proportion of the district population. This is not to argue that districts which have more than 45% tribal population are wholly declared as Scheduled Areas, as Gajapati (50.78%) and Kandhamal (51.96%) have been declared as partial Scheduled Areas. The Government of Odisha has enacted a number of legislative measures to address the socio-economic necessities and constitutional commitments. To protect the tribal rights over land, the Orissa Scheduled Area Transfer of Immovable Property (by Scheduled Tribe) (OSATIP) Regulation, 1965, was passed. The main provisions of these regulations are the following: First, transfer of immovable property by a member of STs to non-tribal people without consent of the authority is invalid. Second, *suo moto* action may be taken for identification and restoration of the illegally transferred land. To put it differently, the transfer of tribal land may be made with the prior permission of the competent authority (collector or sub-collector, among others), which ultimately dilutes the measures and the tribal communities remain at the mercy of such competent authorities. The Government of Odisha has also implemented the PESA Act, 1996. Tribals are facing the problem of land alienation despite the protective legislative measures adopted by the state.

N.K. Behura and Nilkanta Panigrahi in their book *Tribals and the Indian Constitution* argue that British rule in India strongly influenced the land management and revenue politics, which were basically exploitive in nature. The book elaborately discusses the problems in the Odisha context. The OSATIP Regulation, 1956, and the Orissa Scheduled Areas Transfer of Immovable Property (Scheduled Tribes Regulations) Amendment, 1965, are two important measures taken by the Odisha government. In the first half of the nineteenth century, after the confiscation of a few princely states like Banki (1840), Kandhamal (1840) and Angul (1847), the British had introduced the *mustajari* revenue system in Odisha. The undivided Koraput district had two types of land administration system, *ryotwari* and *mustajari.* In Koraput, the land administration started with the Salabansi kings of Nandapur in the fourteenth century A.D. and was subsequently handed over to the *rajas* of Jaipur. The district followed a similar pattern of land policy to that prevalent in Madras Presidency. The Madras Estate Land Act, 1908, largely influenced the Koraput land administration system. The maintenance of a record of rights in the district by the government started only during the 1940s. The tribals of Koraput district were induced by moneylenders and other non-tribal people and being alienated from their land holdings at cheaper prices. S.N. Tripathy in his article "An Analysis of Tribal Movement in Contemporary Odisha", in S.N. Chaudhury (ed.), *Social Movements in Tribal India,* remarks that for the last few decades, and more particularly since the 1990s, the issue of human rights violations and rights to life and livelihood of tribal peoples has been a central concern.

Binay Kumar Pattnaik in the article "Tribal Resistance in Orissa: Studies in New Social Movements" in Kamal K. Misra and N. K. Das (ed.), *Dissent, Discrimination and Dispossession: Tribal Movement in Contemporary India,* mentions that Odisha has witnessed several resistance movements such as the Hirakud hydro project resistance, Baliapal protest movement, Gandhamardan movement, the Gopalpur protest movement, *Chilika Bachao Andolon* (movement for safety of Chilika lake) and the tribal resistance movement at Lower Suktel Dam. Apart from these resistance movements that have swept the state of Odisha, other micro-social movements that shook India in past decades have been based on mobilisations of people as a result of development-induced displacement. K. Gopal Iyer in his article "Women's Participation in Protest Movements in Kalinganagar and POSCO", in S.N. Chaudhuri (ed.), *Tribal Women: Yesterday, Today and Tomorrow,* observes that in tribal-populated regions, women are more related to the land than their male counterparts. Thus, the proliferation of mining companies in the region is the root cause of the exploitation of tribal women. The land which kept them occupied is taken away by the mine owners, who acquire these land in the name of development without opening up any avenues of employment for the women.

S. N. Tripathy in his article "Problems of Distress Migration of Tribal Women in the KBK Districts of Orissa: an Analysis", in S. N. Chaudhuri (ed.), *Tribal Women: Yesterday, Today and Tomorrow,* discusses how tribal women accompany the male migrants of Kalahandi, Bolangir and Koraput, the poverty-stricken, drought-ravaged, tribal-dominated districts of Odisha where food security and livelihood options are conspicuously absent. Gurukalyana Rout, in his work "Legacy of *Adivasi* Exploitation and Misgovernance in Post-PESA Act Orissa", in Nupur Tiwari (ed.), *Tribal Self-Governance: PESA and Its Implementation,* examines the new post-PESA Act rules and regulations of the Government of Odisha, which direct that if a tribal person possesses less than five acres of unirrigated land or less than two acres of irrigated land, then he/she cannot transfer the land to non-tribals. But notwithstanding this restriction, tribal land alienation still prevails.

L. K. Mahapatra, in his article "The Jharkhand Party in Orissa", in K.S. Singh (ed.), *Tribal Movements in India* (vol 2), describes how during the period from 1951 to 1959, the Jharkhand Party, which was leading the *adivasi* movements in the northern hill districts of Odisha, faced constant threats from two other organisations, the *Ganatantra Parishad* (GP) and the *Nikhil Utkal Adivasi Congress* (NUAC). Towards the end of the year 1950, Mr. Ranjit Singh Bariha had laid the foundation for the *Nikhil Utkal Adivasi Congress*, which in the succeeding year was able to abolish the Jharkhand movement of Odisha. He points out that the organisation of the Jharkhand Party in Odisha resembled Bailey's 'movement' model.

Yatindra Singh Sisodia and Tapas Kumar Dalapati in their edited book *Development and Discontent in Tribal India* (2015a) argue that development is a continuous and a multi-dimensional process which involves reorganisation and reorientation of the entire economic and social system. In India, the tribal communities are at different levels of this socio-economic development. There are tribes that are still dependent on the forests for their livelihood, with their primitive technology, limited skills and traditional ritual practices. On the other hand, there are several communities in India that have been totally assimilated into the national mainstream. However, low productivity from the land, a dispersed habitation, shrinking shifting cultivation, a weak cooperative/marketing infrastructure, and land grabbing by non-tribals leading to dispossession and marginalisation are all common phenomena across the tribal areas. The book explains the broad trends in development and discontent emanating across tribal groups. Due to alienation from the fruits of development processes, these groups fall easy prey to alternative ideologies and create law and order problems in their hinterland.

S. K. Chaudhary's book *Livelihood for Tribals in Naxal Hit Areas* (2012), argues that the *adivasis* of central and eastern India are the poorest of the poorest people in India. More than 90% of these *adivasis* particularly in states like Chhattisgarh, Jharkhand, Odisha, Madhya Pradesh and West Bengal are rural, and therefore, are forced to depend on agricultural practices and collection of forest products. Those who are able to cultivate pieces of land on their own or on a communal basis can acquire foods for only 2–3 months. In the remaining months of the year, they work as agricultural labourers or collect forest products. The livelihoods of the *adivasi* people are closely intertwined with the forests. The relations of *adivasis* with the forests are reciprocal and natural. They collect a variety of forest products from the forest land to sustain their living; notable among which are saal seeds, tendu leaf, harra, mahua flower/seeds, tora, tamarind, mango kernels, bamboo, gums, etc. This struggle has led to various reconstructions of identities leading to exclusive community claims and counter-claims. The claims have today extended to territoriality with its concomitant conception of ethnic state and state-governed territorial boundaries. The book in general speaks of humanistic and constitutional need in terms of livelihoods for Tribals in Naxal-hit Areas.

1.10 Significance of the Study

The rationale of the present study is that, after seven decades of India's independence, land remains a central issue in relation to the poverty and backwardness of the tribals, as far as their socio-economic conditions vis-a-vis conflict and cooperation among other social groups are concerned. In a globalised and competitive era, due to industrialisation and liberalisation, tribes are suffering the most due to displacement, encroachment of land, and exploitation by outsiders making them landless and vulnerable. This problem at an all-India level is considered as an important aspect of this study. However, a general, comprehensive socio-economic study of land alienation, encroachment and redistribution leading to a popular movement with special reference to Koraput district of Odisha has been wanting. No post-colonial study truly reflects this issue.

Accordingly, an attempt has been made in the present study to examine the socio-economic conditions of the tribals in general, the tribal land situation as far as land alienation and encroachment are concerned, and the plans and policies of the central government as well as the Odisha government relating to tribal land. The study focuses specifically on the tribal movement in the Koraput district of Odisha, generalising the inferences with regard to land alienation and tribal exploitation at the all-India level.

1.11 Methodology of the Study

The study depends on both primary and secondary sources. Chapter 5, "Narayanpatna movement in the Koraput district of Odisha" and Chap. 6, "role of the state and different political parties towards Narayanpatna movement", are wholly based on primary sources that consist of the data collected from field work in Koraput district on the land alienation process and the movement. The primary sources include the oral statements of participants and interested observers in the Narayanpatna block of Koraput district where the movement took place. The land data were collected from the land offices and record rooms (office of the sub-collector, Koraput district).

The secondary sources include books, journals, articles, government reports and newspaper sources relating to the land alienation and tribal exploitation issues in different states and the activities carried out during the movement in Koraput district of Odisha. The present work is both a historical and a contemporary study of tribal land alienation and exploitation in India and the land movement in the Koraput district of Odisha. It uses both analytical and descriptive methods where the situation/event is described through analysing the data collected from the field. The research applies both quantitative and qualitative approaches where close-ended questions are used for quantifying the data and open-ended questions are used for qualitative analysis. As far as the limitations of the study is concerned, the field work on Narayanpatna movement is limited to the Narayanpatna village and its nearby villages like Gatigura,

Mundigura, Podapadar, Bhaliaput, Balipeta, Jhaliagura etc. within the Narayanpatna block of Koraput district. Though the anti-liquor and land movement in Koraput was started by the CMAS in both the blocks of Narayanpatna and Bandhugaon, I have only studied the Narayanpatna movement under the leadership of Nachika Linga, because the Bandhugaon fraction later collapsed. During the interview with the people, in maximum cases, the respondents asked not to disclose their names, and for that reason, the names of the respondents are not disclose in this study. Though the appendix section provides some questions for leaders of the movement, the researcher did not get a chance for the interview of any leaders during his fieldwork, because the Narayanpatna movement happened in 2009, (though Nachika Linga, the chief leader of the movement surrendered to police in 2014) and the researcher has conducted his fieldwork in 2015, and at that time, all the leaders of the movement were in jail as reported from the field.

References

Ambagudia, J. (2010). Tribal rights, dispossession and the state in Odisha. *Economic & Political Weekly, XLV*(33), August 14.

Ambagudia, J. (2015). Scheduled tribes and the land question: The root of discontent and protest in scheduled areas of Orissa. In Y. S. Sisodia & T. K. Dalapati (Eds.), *Development and discontent in tribal area*. Jaipur: Rawat Publication.

Banerjee, T. (Ed.). (1989). *Changing land system and tribals in Eastern India in the modern period*. Calcutta: Subarnarekha.

Bannerjee, T. K. (1986). Girijan Movements in Srikakulam: 1967-70. In A. R. Desai (Ed.), *Agrarian struggles in India after independence*. New Delhi: Oxford University Press.

Basha, P. C. (2017). Tribal land alienation: A sociological analysis. *International Journal of Advanced Educational Research* 2(3), 78–85. May.

Basu, D. D. (1988). *Shorter constitution of India* (10th ed.). New Delhi: Prentice Hall of India.

Behura, N. K. (1982). Forest and tribal world view. *Journal of Social Research, XXV*(1), 1–8.

Behura, N. K., & Panigrahi, N. (2006). *Tribals and the Indian constitution*. Jaipur: Rawat Publication.

Benford, R. D., & Snow, D. A. (2000). Framing processes and social movements: An overview and assessment. *Annual Review of Sociology, 26*.

Bulliyya, G. (2006). Public policies and legislations on land and forest rights of the tribals in Orissa: An overview. In R. M. Sarkar (Ed.), *Land and forest rights of the tribals today*. New Delhi: Serials Publications.

Census. (1901). https://ruralindiaonline.org/library/resource/report-on-the-census-of-india-1901/. Accessed 14 November, 2018.

Census. (2011), Office of the Registrar General and Census Commissioner, India, Ministry of Home Affairs, Government of India, p. 43. http://www.censusindia.gov.in/2011census/population_enumeration.html. Accessed 12 November, 2018.

Chaudhary, S. K. (2012). *Livelihood for Tribals in Naxal Hit Areas*. New Delhi: Surendra Publications.

Ghurye, G. S. (1963). *The scheduled tribes*. Bombay: Popular Prakashan.

Goffman, E. (1986). *Frame analysis: An essay on the organisation of experience*. Boston: Northeastern University Press.

Gurr, T. R. (1971). *Why men rebel*. New Jersey: Princeton University Press.

Herbert, B. (1957). Collective behaviour. In J. B. Gittler (Ed.), *Review of sociology: Analysis of a decade*. New York: Wiley.
Iyer, G. K., (2015). Women's participation in protest movements in Kalingnagar and POSCO. In S. N. Chaudhury (Ed.), *Tribal women: Yesterday, today and tomorrow*. Jaipur: Rawat Publications.
Jenkins, J. C., & Perrow, C. (1977). Insurgency of the Powerless: Farm Worker Movements (1946–1972). *American Sociological Review*, *42*(2), 250–259.
Kapoor, D., & Chana, T. (2010). Adivasi social movements in Orissa: Development, marginalisation and dispossession. In S. Roy & K. Debal (Eds.), *Dissenting voices and transformative actions: social movements in globalized era*. Delhi: Manohar.
Kumar K. et al. (2005). *Scheduled Tribes' land in Odisha: A Socio-economic and legal study.* Bhubaneswar: Supported By World Bank, Washington. https://www.researchgate.net/publication/232062518_A_socioeconomic_and_legal_study_of_scheduled_tribes'_land_in_Orissa Accessed 30 October, 2019.
Kornhauser, W. (1959). *The politics of mass society*. New York: Free Press.
Mahapatra, L. K. (2015). The jharkhand party in Orissa. In K. S. Singh (Ed.), *Tribal movements in India,* Vol. 2, New Delhi: Manohar.
Majumdar, K. (1998). *Changing tribal life in British Orissa*. New Delhi: Kaveri Books.
Meena, S., Meena, N. P. S. (2014). Historical perspectives of different tribal groups. *India International Journal of Interdisciplinary and Multidisciplinary Studies* (IIJIMS), *1*(10), 48–57.
Mohanty, B. B. (2001, October 6–12). Land distribution among scheduled castes and tribes. *Economic and Political Weekly*, *36*(40), 3857–3868.
Morrison, D. E. (1978). Some notes toward theory on relative deprivation, social movements, and social change. In L. E. Genevie (Ed.), *Collective behavior and social movements*. Peacock: Itasca.
Munshi, I. (2012) (Ed.). *The Adivasi question: Issue of land, forest and livelihood.* New Delhi: Orient Blackswan.
Oommen, T. K. (2004). *Nation, civil society and social movements*. New Delhi: Sage.
Panigrahi, N., & Balabantaray, R. (2014). Displacement, tribal communities and social justice: Some experiences in post globalization period in Orissa. In M. C. Behera, & J. Basar (Ed.), *Resources, tribes and development*. Jaipur: Rawat Publication.
Pattnaik, B. K. (2014). Tribal resistance in Orissa: Studies in new social movements. In K. Misra Kamal & N. K. Das (Eds.), *Dissent, discrimination and dispossession: Tribal movement in contemporary India*. New Delhi: Manohar.
Ray, B. C. (1989). *Tribals of Orissa: The changing socio-economic profile*. New Delhi: Gian Publishing House.
Rout, G. (2015). Legacy of adivasi exploitation and miss-governance in post-PESA act Orissa. In T. Nupur (Ed.), *Tribal self-governance: PESA and its implementation*. Jaipur: Rawat Publication.
Rudolf, H. (1951). *Social movements: An introduction to political sociology*. New York: Appleton-Century-Crofts INC.
Singh, K. S. (Ed.). (1980). *Tribal movements in India* (Vol. I), II, III, New Delhi: Manohar.
Sisodia, Y. S., & Dalapati, T. K. (2015). (Ed.), *Development and discontent in tribal India*. New Delhi: Rawat Publication.
Smelser, N. J. (1962). *Theory of collective behavior*. New York: Free Press.
Status Report on 'Land Rights and Ownership in Odisha (August 2008). UNDP. https://www.undp.org/content/dam/india/docs/land_rights_ownership_in_orissa.pdf. Accessed 26 September, 2019.
The Scheduled Tribes and Other Traditional Forest Dwellers (Recognition of Forest Rights) Act, 2006, Ministry of Tribal affairs and Forestry, Government of India, p. 3. https://fra.org.in/document/FRA%20Rule_2012_complied%20version.pdf. Accessed 25 January, 2019.
Tripathy, S. N. (2009). Watershed approach for socio-economic development of KBK tribals (Orissa). In S. N. Chaudhury (Ed.), *Tribal development since independence*. New Delhi: Concept Publication.
Tripathy, S. N. (2015a). An analysis of tribal movement in contemporary Orissa. In S. N. Chaudhury (Ed.), *Social movements in tribal India*. Jaipur: Rawat Publication.

Tripathy, S. N. (2015b). Problems of distress migration of tribal women in the KBK districts of orissa: An analysis. In S. N. Chaudhury (Ed.), *Tribal women: Yesterday, today and tomorrow.* Jaipur: Rawat Publications.

Philip, V. (1991). *Encroached and enslaved: Alienation of adivasi land and its dynamics.* New Delhi: Indian Social Institute.

Weldon, T. D. (1955). *The vocabulary of politics.* Harmondsworth: Penguin Books.

Chapter 2
Paradigm of Tribal Development in Post-independence Era

2.1 Introduction

The colonial period in India began with the British colonisers entering India in the seventeenth century for trade and commercial enterprises. They observed economic and cultural diversity and heterogeneousness in livelihood. So, they categorised the Indian population into certain dwelling and occupational groups and started implementing various laws, acts and policies for the development and benefits of these people in general and tribals in specific. The post-independence state though tried for the development of the tribals but follows the colonial legacies as far as tribal issues and policies are concerned. The following sections historically brief the paradigm of tribal development in post-independence period, respectively. Before discussing the tribal development paradigm in post-independence era, it's pertinent to have a look on the policies and development of tribals during the British period.

The history of the tribal polices that interest in forestry was noticed in 1806 with the reservation of teak forest in Malabar during the British period (Dash 2002: 354). In 1865, the Forest Act of 1865 was ordained that empowered the free movement of tribal forest dwellers on the forest (ibid.). In 1878, another act was made which was particularly concerning with removing uncertainty about the absolute proprietary right of the state. This act was designed to make easy state control over forest resources. These policies went against the tribal as well as non-tribal forest dweller communities. In reaction to these policies, people did not cooperate with the forest department and the tribals and forest dwellers stirred up and had gone for revolts against the loss of rights to control over the natural resources. Then came the Indian Forest Act, 1927 which recognised 24 yielding and privileges of the forest dwelling tribal people and labourers in respect of cultivation, collection of firewood, timbers for household, consumption of raw materials for crafts etc. (Mohapatra 2002: 393).

The rulers of the colonial period realised the difficulties in administration for widespread tribal areas irrespective of the acceptance of policy of isolation or segregation. British rulers realised that isolation would protect the tribals against the aggression and exploitation which they found on the increase. As isolationists, the

S. K. Malik, *Land Alienation and Politics of Tribal Exploitation in India*,
https://doi.org/10.1007/978-981-15-5382-0_2

British in position asserted certain contiguous and thickly populated tribal belts as excluded and partially excluded areas. The policy of isolation was supported by the anthropologists of that time who advocated for tribal reserves. Pledging to isolation, the British anthropologists suggested for the establishment of the 'national park theory' within the framework of policy of isolation and the creation of excluded and partially excluded areas, where some legislation were enacted (Mann 1993: 77). The basic idea behind the policy of isolation was to preserve tribals away from the people coming from more advanced communities. The protection and preservation of tribal life and culture were guaranteed by the Scheduled District Act of 1875 that provided for special tribal administration. This excluded the tribal areas from the operation of common laws of the country. This expulsion from the jurisdiction of provincial government was also suggested by Montague–Chelmsford Report of 1918. According to government of India Act 1919, the tribal areas were divided into wholly excluded areas and area of modified exclusion (ibid.: 78).

In 1930, the Simon Commission was sent to India to evaluate the reforms initiated by the Montagu–Chelmsford Report of 1918 and instrumentalised by the Government of India Act, 1919. The act for the first time recognised that perpetual isolation of the tribals from mainstream Indian society was not the long term solution for protecting tribal communities from exploitation. Instead, to stand on their own feet and in order to make them self-reliant, the administration should educate these people. The Commission's observations reflected the beginning of a debate about the future of the excluded areas, between British anthropologists like Verrier Elwin and W. Grigson on the one hand, and leaders of the Indian National Congress and Indian anthropologists like G.S. Ghurye, on the other. The Congress opposed exclusion of the tribes, regarding it as a cynical attempt by the British to cling onto power in India, and is harmful to the tribes whose best interests lay in assimilation with mainstream Indian society. British anthropologists and later tribal activists like Jaipal Singh, however, believed that some sort of isolation—whether temporary or even permanent—was in the best interests of the tribes, because it allowed them to assert their autonomy from the mainstream.

Nevertheless, the Government of India Act, 1935, retained the classification of 'excluded areas' and 'partially excluded areas' created by the Government of India Act, 1919. The British Parliament justified the decision for creating the excluded areas on three main grounds. The first ground was one of culturally distinct primitive identity of the tribals, the second ground was that of protection from exploitation by the mainstream population and the third ground was development of the tribes, all of which supported the continuation of a policy of isolation of the 'hill tribes'. The leaders of the Indian National Congress in its All-India Congress Committee meeting in Faizpur adopted a resolution which repudiated these provisions for exclusion in the Government of India Act, 1935 and remarked that it is another attempt to divide the people of India and to obstruct the growth of uniform democratic institutions in the country.[1] The Congress resolution noted that these provisions were intended to leave a larger control of disposition and exploitation of the mineral and forest wealth in those areas with the British state and to keep the inhabitants of those areas apart from the rest of India for their easier exploitation and suppression.[2] The Congress resolution articulated an alternative narrative of 'development through integration' that characterised the Indian government policies throughout the post-independence period.

This 'integration narrative' is expounded by Z. A. Ahmad in 1937, in a paper called, *The Excluded Areas under the New Constitution*, which views that,

> The British policy of divide and rule had preserved the tribal people in a state of underdevelopment, denying them education and medical facilities in order to prevent them from developing a political and economic consciousness. The British had inflicted economic wrongs on the tribes via special forest laws, land laws, excise laws and a number of other enactments, all of which were hitting at the very root of the economic life of these people, virtually reducing them to the position of chattel slaves or serfs of tea planters and other European adventurers. Moreover, the British had actively strengthened the tribal chiefs and moneylending classes to safeguard their own interests, vesting them with enormous powers at the expense of the tribal communities. And finally, British government had failed to take measures to provide extra funds to these areas for the economic and social development of the peoples and impeded development of local self-government (cited in Pati and Dash 2002: 37).

Ahmad proposed an extensive list of policy alternatives for the tribal areas, which involved political, legislative and administrative integration of the tribal communities with the rest of the Indian population; reform of land laws to protect tribal land rights, material development of tribal areas through provision of economic and social infrastructure, including health and education facilities. It is clear that protecting tribal rights to land was central to the Congress agenda, but the Congress was not prepared to recognise the sovereignty of the tribal peoples to land in both the excluded and partially excluded areas. The Congress was consistent in its philosophy of 'development through integration' in their approach towards the tribals.

With India's independence, it was decided to put all the tribal communities in a separate Schedule of the Constitution of India. These 25 'excluded and partially excluded areas' were drafted in Fifth and Sixth Schedule. The areas resided by Scheduled Tribes were termed as Scheduled Areas. In the Indian Constitution, Part C (para 6) of the Fifth Schedule, specially defined these areas. States except Meghalaya, Assam, Tripura and Mizoram were administered under Fifth Schedule of the Constitution and the remaining states were under Sixth Schedule. Articles 244[2] and 275[1] are specially meant for Sixth Schedule areas that were later on reformed as Scheduled Districts.

---

[1] 50th Session of All-India Congress Committee, Faizpur (1936). Viewable in 'Excluded Areas under the new Constitution. https://archive.org/stream/in.ernet.dli.2015.276455/2015.276455. Accessed 6 November, 2018.

[2] ibid.

2.2 Tribal Developmental Policies During Post-independence Period

In the post-independence period, the British policy of isolation was switched to the integration model of tribal development. Various customary programmes were started in the tribal areas for bringing about social and economic change among the tribal people. Our first Prime Minister Mr. Jawaharlal Nehru, who was concerned about formulating a tribal policy made a herculean contribution to the tribal development policies. Based on his integrationist model, Nehru gave the policy of Panchsheel (Rath 2006: 86). The main characteristics of the policy were

- We should try to encourage in every way the tribals' own traditional arts and culture and the tribals should provide freedom to live life and develop according to their own choice.
- For development and administration work, we should build up and train a group of their own people.
- We should work through and not in discord with their cultural and social institutions and should not over administer the tribal areas.
- Tribal peoples' right on land and forest should be respected.
- We should not evaluate our developmental policies on the basis of the amount of money we spent in these areas, rather on the basis of the quality of human development and character that is developed.

A new forest policy was excogitated after independence (in 1952) that boosted the formation of forest development committees in different states of India to hitch the commercialisation of forest resources (Mann 1993: 36). The report of the committee on 'Forest and Tribals in India' (1982), which was developed under the chairmanship of B. K. Roy Burman, an Indian anthropologist, stated that, there is a symbiotic relationship between the tribal social organisation and forest economy in the specific historical context of our country (Dash 2002: 357). The Committee highlighted that,

> Tribals are not only forest dwellers but also they have evolved a way of life which, on the one hand is woven round forest ecology, and forest resources are protected against degradation by man and nature. The symbiosis between the tribal communities and forest management should be established through forestry programmes, conservation and reorganisation of traditional skill of labour (ibid.: 358).

Just after Independence, tribal development policies were framed in different successive Five Year Plans by Planning Commission for making target of the tribals to incorporate them into the mainstream societies or thereby making their own destinies of 'self-development'.

2.2.1 First Five Year Plan (1951–1956)

In this period, the government introduced schemes on education and welfare programmes for providing direct benefits to Scheduled Tribes which were drawn under the state and central sectors for the economic, educational and social progress of this community. The report of Scheduled Areas and Scheduled Tribes Commission (1960–61) shows that in the first five year plan, out of the sixteen sectors identified for the allocation of the amount, education, agriculture and public health were given special attention for development. In tribal areas, 4000 schools, 653 forest labour cooperatives and 312 multipurpose cooperatives were set up. For economic upliftment, Rs. 3.6 crores were spent, and towards development of communication and roads, Rs. 6.5 crores were expended (Mohanty 2002: 91).

2.2.2 Second Five Year Plan (1956–1961)

The second five year plan was initiated with an indicative change in the approach to the schemes of development. In the expenditures on economic activities, the amount was raised to Rs 16.86 crores in the second plan (Mohanty 2002: 92). Forty-three Special Multipurpose Tribal Blocks (SMPTB) were established in the Scheduled Areas. To assess the performance of these SMPT Blocks, the government of India appointed a committee in 1959 with Verrier Elwin, the well-known anthropologist as chairman. After Elwin Committee, the Dhebar Commission (1960–61) was appointed to study the tribal development. The Dhebar commission's recommendations have gone a long way to strengthen the defensive shell and giving *panchayati raj* a tribal bias (ibid.: 93). The commission's recommendations on planning and development were more precise for solving the problem of land alienation, indebtedness, promotion of education, protecting tribal interest in forest, and sectoral development. The Dhebar commission also recommended for institution of tribal cultural research and training institutes in states for conducting training for official and non-official development functionaries and participants taking part in research studies (ibid.: 94).

2.2.3 Third Five-Year Plan (1961–1966) and the Plan Holidays (1966–1969)

To involve tribal people in the process of development and to improve the conditions of tribal areas, 415 tribal development blocks were set up in the plan period. Priorities were in order of economic upliftment, health, education, communication and housing. The retrospect of the tribal development programme was taken up by a study team under the chairmanship of Shilo Ao (1969) (Joseph 2008: 111). The team made a review of the steps undertaken for tribal development during the course of first three five-year plans. The findings of this team had made it clear that it was necessary to adopt a flexible policy for tribal development (ibid.). Although, the accomplishment under the programme had helped in bringing about psychological change in the outlook of the tribals', it is necessary to have a development policy.

2.2.4 Fourth Five-Year Plan (1969–1974)

For the encompassing and inclusive development of tribal areas with a focus for the development of the tribal populations (economic development), 489 tribal development blocks were set up at the beginning of the fourth five-year plan period. A number of new programmes were introduced. In addition to intensifying programmes, land colonisation schemes were started and several tribal colonies were established. Sectoral planning with schematic budget was also inaugurated during this plan period. Emphasis were given on the conditions of rural poor, and some of the backward tribal regions also received greater regard. Individual family programmes were enclosed and new programmes of the Tribal Development Agencies (TDA) were taken up by the Ministry of Agriculture (Patel 1998: 12). Total six TDAs were started in the country in which two started in Madhya Pradesh only (ibid.).

2.2.5 Fifth Five-Year Plan (1974–1978)

In this plan, the following three categories were given attention:

- Area of tribal concentration
- Primitive Tribal Groups (PTGs)
- Dispersed tribals were given attention.

The fundamental approach towards tribal development adopted in the fifth plan was to carve out larger areas of tribal concentration which included the Scheduled Areas that is contiguous tribal development blocks and other backward regions having 50% tribal concentration (Patel 1998: 13). All such blocks in the states were brought under a separate Tribal Sub-Plan (TSP). The tribal sub-plan had two objectives:

- Promotion of development activities to enhance the standard of living of the tribals.
- Provision of legal and administrative support for tribals. The TSP laid underline an accountability, non-divertability and utilisation of allotted funds for the welfare and development of tribals.

This period also marked the beginning of group-based programmes like Large-sized Agricultural Multipurpose Cooperative Societies (LAMPS), in order to bring the tribals into cooperative movement and eliminate moneylenders, forest contractors and middlemen.

2.2.6 *Sixth Five-Year Plan (1980–1985)*

During the sixth five–year plan period, it was marked and identified that areas having tribal density which were exterior to the TSP area, were still excluded from the TSP strategy. During the sixth plan, it was thus resolved that clusters having 50% Scheduled Tribes and 10,000 minimum population should be treated under TSP and should modelled for Modified Area Development Approach (MADA) (Pati and Dash 2002: 35). The purpose of MADA was to empower at least 50% of ST families. Under this plan, a total of 75% of the tribal population was covered. Substantial achievements during this plan period were as follows:

- Establishment of 245 MADA pockets and 72 primitive tribal projects.
- About 200,000 hectares of tribal land was brought under soil conservation.
- Electrification of 9000 tribal villages.
- Drinking water supply to cover over 80,000 villages.

2.2.7 *Seventh Five-Year Plan (1985–1990)*

In this plan period, the target remained to be a mix of family-cum-area development. Under the poverty line, about 40 lakhs Scheduled Tribe families were targeted to be benefited by delivering financial and economic aid. (Padhi 2005: 77). By the end of the year 1987–88, a total 184 Integrated Tribal Development Programmes (ITDPs) were functioning and the ITDPs covered 313.21 lakh tribal populations (ibid.). The main attainments of this plan period were as follows:

- In 1987, for State Tribal Development Cooperative Corporations (STDCC), it was suggested to set up the Tribal Cooperative Marketing Development Federation (TRIFED) as an apex body. The primary task of the TRIFED was to provide remunerative prices for the forest and agriculture produces of tribals.
- Expansion of educational development schemes for Scheduled Tribes.
- Formation of the National Scheduled Caste and Scheduled Tribe Finance and Development Corporation (NSCSTFDC) in 1989 with the objective of credit support for employment generation.[3]

[3]Draft National Tribal Policy 2006, p. 259. www.tribal.nic.in. Accessed 16 January, 2019.

2.2.8 *Eighth Five-Year Plan (1992–1997)*

The major targets and strategies of this plan were to make the tribal sub-plan strategies more result-oriented, and special schemes were formulated during this period for the educational development of the Scheduled Tribes, particularly in the field of women education and reducing the dropout rates among the ST students at primary level. It also aimed at providing economic assistance to the tribals to upgrade the productivity level to take above the poverty line and to make grow the economic and educational infrastructure. Therefore, several attempts were made to balance the gap among the other downtrodden segments of the society with the STs. The PESA Act, 1996 was enacted during this plan period to make the tribal enable and endue to conserve and preserve their traditional rights over natural resources and to have control over their own circumstances (Dixit 2006: 187). The following were conceived by the eighth five-year plan:

- Collection and marketing of Minor Forest Produce (MFP) through TRIFED.
- A new policy on minor forest produces in relation to Scheduled Tribes to be articulated.
- The review of the functioning of diverse cooperative institutions including Large Area Multi-Purpose Cooperative Societies (LAMPS). It laid significance on elimination of exploitation of tribals, tribal land alienation and non-payment of minimum wages to tribals.

2.2.9 *Ninth Five-Year Plan (1997–2002)*

The ninth Five-Year Plan aimed to empower the Scheduled Tribes by creating and enabling the socio-economic environment for the tribals where the tribals will come up with freely, and will lead a life of dignity and self-confidence when compared to the other segments of the society. Hence, a major shift was visualised in this period, so as to envisage their advancement through a process of empowerment. This process essentially encompassed three essential components, these are as follows:

- Social justice
- Economic empowerment
- Social empowerment.

Other than the *Sarva Shiksha Abhiyan*, the plan laid stress on reliance creation through quality education and strengthening infrastructure and resources in the tribal sub-plan areas. The main achievements of this plan period were as follows:

- Emphasis were given towards tribal area development, integrated waste land development project in tribal sub-plan areas, and assistance to tribal families by launching income generation schemes.

- Funds were provided for improvement of infrastructure such as roads, staff quarters, education and hostel facilities, community centres, drinking water facility, rural electrification and irrigation projects.
- The National Scheduled Tribes Financial and Development Corporation (NSTFDC) was set up for financing economically viable projects for the Scheduled Tribes.

2.2.10 *Tenth Five-Year Plan (2002–2007)*

This plan concentrated on tracking the unresolved issues and problems on a time-bound basis. The National Scheduled Tribes Finance and Development Corporation (NSTFDC) was set up in 2001 under which 14.64 lakh STs benefited. Remunerative prices and marketing assistance to STs for surplus agricultural produces and collecting Minor Forest Produces (MFP) were provided by the Tribal Cooperative Marketing Development Federation of India Ltd (TRIFED) with the objective of defending them from middlemen and private traders and from their exploitation.

A special specific scheme was plunged in 1998–99, and was enforced throughout this plan period for focusing the protection, survival and development of the Primitive Tribal Groups (PTGs). Through this scheme, it also tried to put up support for the tribals and tribal intended services including land, housing, cattle rearing, agriculture inputs, nutritional services, health and income-generating schemes. The Forest Rights Act, 2006 was ordained to reanimate the traditional and customary rights of the Scheduled Tribe people over the natural resources including the forest (Dixit 2006: 188).

2.2.11 *Eleventh Five-Year Plan (2007–2012)*

The eleventh five-year plan does not provide any special plan or programmes for STs. Rather, through an area-based approach, it focused on the socio-economic empowerment of the tribal by continuing the already existing programmes and schemes of the former plan. In each and every states, the higher education department and elementary education department have ordered for peculiar and special inducements for the tribal students that include school and college uniforms, textbooks, abolishment of tuition fees, etc. Through the District Primary Education Programme (DPEP), special and extra care were provided to the tribal students. These special programmes include Mid-day Meal (MDM), Kasturba *Gandhi Balika Vidyalaya*, National Talent Search (NTS) Scheme, etc. For all Scheduled Tribe students, whose parent's annual income is up to one lakh, were provided with scholarships to help the students to study professional courses and also general courses.

This plan also encourages tribal languages through textbooks, and appointment of tribal teachers who were well skilled in the tribal language. This plan recommends to look after the socio-cultural discrimination faced by the disadvantaged groups. It promotes health care of the tribal people and setting up Auxiliary Nursing Midwifery (ANM) training centres in tribal blocks. Under housing schemes, the plan embraces houses for tribal and Primitive Tribal Groups (PTGs). Finally, this plan has laid stresses on poverty eradication in rural and tribal areas which focuses on sustainable development, education, employment access to forest resources and agricultural production and subsidies.

2.2.12 *Twelfth Five-Year Plan (2012–2017)*

The target of this plan was to achieve all-round betterment of the conditions of the tribals. Government started focusing on administrative strengthening of the implementation of programmes or schemes in the tribal areas. The administration, in order to inspire the officials to work in remote backward tribal areas, have adopted a clear cut policy by determining their incentives and tenure for a specific prescribed period. The plan gives emphasis on some important issues like acquisition of tribal land and displaced tribal population which needs to be addressed. In order to upgrade the skills of the tribal youth, the scheme of vocational training centres in tribal concentrated areas was spread out under the plan which depends upon the market potential, present economic trends and the educational qualifications of the tribal youths.

The Tribal Affairs Ministry opened the programme of grant-in-aid during this plan period, to help the organisations working voluntarily for the tribals' welfare and to the NGOs for running mobile clinics in tribal villages and establishing 10 or more bedded hospitals in tribal concentrated areas. To ensure the extension of benefits covered under "Mahatma Gandhi National Rural Employment Guarantee Act" (MGNREGA) in tribal blocks, government focuses on effective monitoring, social audits and their reviews in a strict manner.

In this plan, government introduced the entrepreneurship among tribal youngsters through 'start up' and 'stand up' programme. The government focuses on research, information, mass education and tribal festivals to promote tribal culture, capacity building and awareness generation among the tribals. In keeping with the objectives of more exclusive growth, steps were taken to reform the Tribal Sub-Plan (TSP).[4]The plan advises a supreme body directed and headed by Chief Minister to assure efficient institutional and organisational model for execution at state level, and to appraise or evaluate the Tribal Sub-Plan (TSP) by some specific nodal departments.

[4]www.planningcommission.nic.in, https://niti.gov.in/planningcommission.gov.in/docs/plans/planrel/fiveyr/welcome.html. Accessed 19 February 2020.

2.3 Draft National Tribal Policy, 2006

In 2006, the draft national tribal policy was prepared by the Ministry of Tribal Affairs, Government of India and in later period, there were further revisions in the draft policy in order to incorporate certain legislative and policy changes. Smt. Renuka Singh Saruta, then union minister of state for tribal affairs, on 15 July 2019 has provided the following information in the *Lok Sabha* (house of the people). She added that,

> A High Level Committee (HLC) was constituted on 14.08.2013 to prepare a position paper on socio-economic status of STs and suggest a way forward. The Committee submitted its report on 29.05.2014 which contains 108 recommendations cutting across various central ministries/departments as well as state governments. The recommendations were forwarded to central ministries/departments of government of India and state governments to furnish their views/comments which are still awaited.[5]

However, it is pertinent here to have a detail discussion on the draft National Tribal Policy (NTP) (2006), as far as tribal development in post-independence period is concerned. The draft NTP was articulated in order to address the issues concerning the tribals like—lower literacy levels, poor infrastructure, economic restraints, continuous menaces of dispossession from their home ground, lessening control over natural resources, excluded from mainstream and deprived from the allocation of wealth and opportunities. It also aims at addressing each of these problems in a concrete way.

The draft NTP attempts to increase the literacy rate of the tribals which is still low in comparison to the national literacy rate. The forest dwelling tribal people have passed a kind of knowledge about their surrounding pertaining to medical system, agriculture, ethno-veterinary, environmental conservation and so on, which the draft national policy on tribals seeks to conserve and promote (Draft National Tribal Policy 2006: 11). The policy largely tries to boost modern health system and seeks to mix the tribal traditional indigenous system of medicine with the Indian systems of medicine like *Siddha* and *Ayurveda* (ibid.: 12). It specifies that displacement of tribal people is kept to the minimum. The policy seeks to formulate anti-alienation land laws so as to scrutinise the loopholes of diverse state laws and bring them in conformity with the PESA Act. It also seeks to amend the Indian Registration Act in order to identify the transferee whether or not a member of Scheduled Tribe (ibid.: 6).

This policy seeks to develop the Primitive Tribal Groups (PTGs) who are the most vulnerable among the tribal population. It envisages developing both the categories of PTGs, i.e. those who are isolated from the surrounding and placed in isolated ecologies niches and those who are located in the fringes of mainstream population. It seeks to develop them economically, and to preserve their ecosystem, life styles and traditional skills of both the groups of PTGs.

As per the Human Development Index (HDI) report, in comparison to the rest of the population, regarding all parameters, the *Saharia* (tribe) population have much

---

[5]https://pib.gov.in/PressReleasePage.aspx?PRID=1578780. Accessed 23 March 2019.

lower HDI. Hence, this policy assures to enhance all the indicators among the tribal population and especially the HDI among the *Saharia* tribes. It intends to check dropout rate of tribal children particularly among girls by providing them various facilities like stationery, scholarship, etc. It targets to operate the *Eklavya* model resident schools from classes sixth to twelfth by the end of the Eleventh plan.[6]

It also assures to stop teacher absenteeism by providing employment to the local tribals. This policy seeks to establish Primary Health Centre (PHC) in most of the tribal regions to arrange safe drinking water, good hygiene and sanitation among STs, to eradicate the endemic disease. It aims to develop livelihood standard of *Saharia* tribal community through different livelihood schemes like vocational training, establishment of Industrial Training Institute (ITI), encouraging traditional arts and crafts or agro-forest-based activities. It also encourages marketing of these which include minor forest products to generate income through National Scheduled Tribes Finance and Development Corporation (NSTFDC), through Banks, through Tribal Cooperative Marketing Development Federation of India (TRIFED), etc. By providing income generating employment through different schemes, it aims to check migration in the tribal areas which is related to other problems such as school dropout, health etc.[7]

The draft policy also stimulates the NGOs to work in the tribal areas to reduce the dependence of tribals exclusively on government. It intends proper functioning of various acts and laws meant for the Fifth and Sixth Scheduled Areas so as to assure their development and security. While dealing with the scheduling and de-scheduling of tribes, this policy aims to follow the criteria developed by 'Lokur committee'. The Draft National Tribal Policy apprises to establish more tribal research institutes, particularly in the states predominantly inhabited by tribals.

2.4 Constitutional Framework Governing Scheduled Areas and Scheduled Tribes

From the very outset, the Constituent Assembly was preoccupied with the situation of the tribal communities and the excluded and partially excluded areas. The Advisory Committee on Fundamental Rights and Minorities, constituted to represent the interests of all minorities was tasked with preparing a scheme for the administration of the tribal and excluded areas. The committee's preoccupation with the tribal communities, however, did not extend to the 'criminal tribes', while they experienced legislative reform during this period, but did not receive any special constitutional protections like the 'hill tribes'. In line with the Congress' position, the advisory committee recognised that the solution to the problem of the excluded areas was 'development', not 'isolation'.

[6]Draft National Tribal Policy 2006, p. 10. http://www.indiaenvironmentportal.org.in/files/tribal.pdf. Accessed 16 January, 2019.

[7]ibid, p. 13.

The committee recommended that the development of these areas should not be left to the provincial governments with their limited financial resources and competing claims, instead, the centre should play an active role in making schemes for these areas and ensuring their implementation by the provinces. Within the Constituent Assembly, the debates on the tribal question are characterised broadly by the narratives of both ‘identity-based isolation’ and ‘development-based integration’, with much greater emphasis on the latter. The narrative of integration encapsulates provisions for political representation and affirmative action for tribal communities in the form of reservations in government jobs and educational institutions. On the other hand, the narrative of identity intertwined with geographic location, resulted in the creation of relative autonomy of tribal peoples in the Fifth and Sixth Scheduled Areas.

As ultimately adopted, Article 244 (1) of the Constitution read with the Fifth Schedule provided for the administration of variously described ‘tribal majority’ and ‘backward’ areas in ten states within peninsular India. The President of India can by order declare any area to be a Scheduled Area. According to the Fifth Schedule, these areas are to be administered by the Governor of the state, in consultation with the Tribes Advisory Councils to be appointed by the Governor. For the ‘good governance’ in the tribal areas, the Governor is empowered to modulate the acts of the Parliament and laws of the state.

2.5 Constitutional Provisions for Tribals

The Constitution of India is the fundamental law of the country, which came into effect on 26 January 1950. It has tried to spell out the hopes, dreams and ambitions of the people of India, which emerge very powerfully in its preamble (Mathew 2004: 1). Scheduled Tribe is one of the categories for which the Indian Constitution has special safeguards and provisions. These safeguards are based on the principle of equality and justice within the framework of social, economic, political and historical processes, because historically, the Scheduled Tribes were alienated from their resources, exploited and discriminated by the dominant groups and excluded from society and the benefits of development. The Constitution of India guarantees the development of STs. In the Constitution, various provisions were made for the development of the tribal groups and these provisions can be categorised in terms of social, economic, political, administrative and legal domains.

2.5.1 *Social Domain*

- **Exceptions in the Constitution for Scheduled Tribes**

Constitution provides equality before the law. There is a prohibition of discrimination on grounds of caste, religion, race, sex or place of birth under Article 15[1]. For the empowerment of the tribals and other marginal sections of the society, there is provision for exception in the Article 15[4] and 16[4].

- **Safeguards for a Dignified Life**

Article 17 guarantees the prohibition against untouchability. Article 19 provides protection of certain rights regarding freedom of speech, freedom to assemble, to form associations, etc. Free profession, propagation and practice of religion, freedom of conscience, entry into Hindu temples and entry into Hindu religious institutions by the tribals are ensured by Article 25. While Article 38 of the Directive Principles of State Policy (DPSP) of the Indian Constitution directs the state to ensure a social order for promotion and welfare of the people.

- **Educational and Cultural Safeguards**

To reserve seats for the tribals in educational institutions and to make special and specific provisions for the Scheduled Tribes, Article 15[4] authorises the state to enact laws and policies. Special arrangements for the Scheduled Tribes for providing opportunity in matters of public employment are guaranteed by Article 16. The economic and educational interests of the people in general, and Scheduled Tribes in particular, are provided by Article 46 of the DPSP of the Indian Constitution. The article further protects the tribals and the marginalised segments of the Indian society from different types of exploitation and social injustice.

2.5.2 Economic Domain

For the administration and governance of Scheduled Areas and promoting the development and welfare of the tribals, there is a provision for grant-in-aid from the consolidated fund of India under Article 275[1]. Being consistent with efficiency of administration, Article 335 ensures the demand and claim of the STs in the appointments of posts and services.

2.5.3 Administrative Domain

A minister in charge of tribal welfare for the states of Madhya Pradesh, Jharkhand, Chhattisgarh and Odisha are provided with Article 164(1). Article 338[A] provides for the National Commission for STs. To report on the welfare of STs and regarding the administration of the Scheduled Areas, there is a provision under Article 339 for the appointment of a commission. Parliament may by law include or exclude from the list of STs and the provision was ensured by Article 342. Any states other than Meghalaya, Assam, Mizoram and Tripura, the control and administration of the Scheduled Areas are ensured with the Fifth Schedule of the Indian Constitution under Article 244 [1].

2.5.4 *Positive Discrimination*

The positive discrimination measures, known as the provisions of reservation, are seen as the main means of empowerment of the STs.

- Reservation in the educational institutions
- Reservation of services and posts in the government
- Reservation of seats in the legislature.

In direction with the provisions of Article 15[4] of the Indian Constitution, which provides for special provisions for the Scheduled Tribes, now the central government is providing 7.5% reservation for Scheduled Tribes in colleges and universities and jobs in public sectors. There is provision for reservation of seats for the Scheduled Tribes in different state assemblies and also in the Parliament under Articles 330 and 332. The 73rd Constitution Amendment Act, 1992, further provides reservation for weaker sections in the local governance unit [Art. 243(D)].

2.6 Legal Measures

The overall goal of the Constitution of India is to promote equality, justice and dignity for every citizen. It aims to protect and safeguard the interest of Scheduled Tribes especially. In the post-independence period, legislations have been enacted to ensure rights, dignity and justice to tribals and special care for their preservation, protection and promotion. The following are some of the legal measures which have been adopted by the Indian state to protect the interest of the tribals and to provide them social justice.

2.6.1 *Scheduled Castes and Scheduled Tribes (Prevention of Atrocities) Act, 1989*

To prevent atrocities against the Scheduled Tribes and Scheduled Castes, the Scheduled Castes and Scheduled Tribes (Prevention of Atrocities) Act, 1989 was enacted by the government of India. For checking the cases like atrocities, and basically when the Indian Penal Code (IPC) and the protection of Civil Rights Act failed and found to be inadequate to arrest such cases of atrocities on SCs and STs, the said act was enacted. The preface of the act mentioned that the act was enacted:

> to prevent the commission of offences of atrocities against the members of Scheduled Castes and Tribes, to provide for special courts for the trial of such offences and for the relief and rehabilitation of the victims of such offences and for matters connected therewith or incidental thereto.[8]

Salient Features

- The rules of the act are generally divided into three categories and covers a list of issues or problems regarding atrocities against Scheduled Caste and Scheduled Tribe people.
- Provisions associated with criminal law is covered under the first category.
- Relief and compensation for the atrocity victims come under the second category.
- The third category includes the effort of monitoring and supervising of the act, it provides for setting up authorities with special power or special authorities.

With the above provisions, the act also furnishes a framework for supervising and monitoring the reaction and response of the state against the atrocity cases. According to the provision of the act, there should be monthly reports from the office of the District Magistrates (DM), and there should be quarterly review meetings by the District Monitoring and Vigilance Committee (DMVC) and there should be half-yearly reviews by the State Monitoring and Vigilance Committee (SMVC) with a 25-member board chaired by the Chief Minister. In every quarter, the Director of Public Prosecutions (DPP) will review the pursuance of every Special Public Prosecutor (SPP). In every year, by 31 March, the annual reports should be sent to the central government.

2.7 Land Alienation Prohibition Laws

After the adoption of the Constitution, the first major legislative reform was introduced to safeguard tribal rights on land. Noting the centrality of land to tribal identity, economy, and culture, and the need to protect the Scheduled Tribes from exploitation and displacement, during the 1950s–1970s, the Parliament and legislatures of all states with Fifth and Sixth Schedule Areas enacted legislation to safeguard tribal rights to land by prohibiting transfer of land in the Scheduled Areas from tribals to non-tribals. States like Sikkim, West Bengal and Uttar Pradesh that do not have any designated Scheduled Areas under the Fifth and Sixth Schedules also enacted legislations prohibiting the transfer of land from tribals to non-tribals. These protective laws for the land rights of tribals were however arrayed against numerous displacing laws, including the land acquisition, forests, and mining laws. The Centre for Policy Research (CPR) in its study has shown that there are 102 land acquisition laws in India, including 15 central and 87 state laws (Padhi 2005: 81). Moreover, the effects of the land alienation prohibition laws are also countered by the effect of land reform

[8] http://legislative.gov.in/sites/default/files/A1989-33_2.pdf. Accessed 12 June 2018.

laws, which protect the rights of non-tribals who have settled in tribal areas for a certain period of time. Since the non-tribal population is more sophisticated than the tribal population, when laws protect land rights of both, the non-tribal population is able to use laws more effectively to displace the tribal population.

2.8 *Panchayats* (Extension to the Scheduled Areas) Act, 1996

On 24 December 1996, the *Panchayats* (Extension to the Scheduled Areas) Act, 1996, also popularly known as PESA act was implemented. The notion behind this act was to extend the 73rd constitutional amendment of 1993 to the Scheduled Areas to empower the tribals to get control over the natural resources and to preserve and maintain their customary and traditional rights through *panchayats* and *gram sabhas* (Shrama 2001: 305). This act recognises the prevailing traditional practices and customary laws of the local people besides management and conservation of natural resources through *gram* panchayat. It encourages the organisation of people through *gram sabha.* By this act, the *gram sabha* is empowered:

- To sanction and approve the projects and programmes of socio-economic welfare in tribal areas before taken by the village *panchayat* for their implementation.
- To mark and identify the actual donees of poverty alleviation programmes and other financial benefitted schemes.
- To provide certification of utilisation of funds by the *panchayats* for the above programmes. These powers make the *gram sabha* a powerful body in implementation of projects for social and economic development of tribal communities.

Prospects of the PESA Act, 1996

This act opens up range of prospects for safeguarding and promoting the interest of tribes (Hasnain 1983: 73). Some of the major prospects are as follows:-

- The act has a constitutional mandate and a binding law to put a legal and moral pressure on the government and its machinery to implement it.
- There is a qualitative change in the very notion of tribal development. There is no more distribution of funds but a paradigm shift which consists in its basic assumption.
- Development is projected as collective. The approval of plans, programmes and projects for social and economic development is the responsibility of entire village.
- The idea of empowerment is based on decentralisation. The higher level of *panchayats* does not interfere with the lower.
- There is a provision for accountability to monitor all kinds of financial transactions to avoid any irregularities.

- *Gram sabha* is supreme and is endowed with the power to have control over water, minor minerals, drinking water, minor forest produce, alienation and restoration of tribal land, market and over the system of debt.
- There is recognition of traditional way of settling disputes. This avoids the bureaucratisation of justice.
- Women empowerment gets a boost as the act ensures one third (33%) of women participation in the *panchayat.*

With the new *panchayat* act, the tribals hope that their dreams of a dignified life will be fulfilled. They are hopeful that the new act will bring them equality and justice. They hope that their alienated land will restored to them. They want to have control over the resources and their management. They believe that the new act will provide them a mechanism to be masters of their own destiny without falling prey to the bureaucratic set up of government. But the PESA Act 1996, despite many provisions, has its own inbuilt 'policy level struggles'. There lies, in the process of empowerment, a clash of interests. Vested interests at every place either in bureaucracy and political party or in the village itself, try their best to throttle the process of tribal empowerment. A battle between entrenched vested interests and new social forces seems to be emerging at the grassroots. Bureaucrats are uncomfortable about the powers of the *panchayat*. There is also lack of awareness and understanding among elected functionaries and officials.

2.9 Scheduled Tribes and Other Traditional Forest Dwellers (Recognition of Forest Rights) Act, 2006

The Scheduled Tribes (Recognition of Forest Rights) Bill, 2005 is revised as the Scheduled Tribes and Other Traditional Forest Dwellers (Recognition of Forest Rights) Act, 2006. It recognises the rights of the Scheduled Tribes and other forest-dwelling communities on forest land that include the protected forest, reserved forest, wildlife sanctuary and national parks. The Scheduled Tribes and the forest-dwelling communities who have been living in such forest areas for more than 75 years or three generations but their rights were not recorded, are entitled to get their rights over the forest and occupations under this act. The act further furnishes a framework for recognising and recording the rights of the Scheduled Tribes and other forest-dwelling communities with regard to forest-based resources. It attempts to ensure the food security and livelihood of the Scheduled Tribes and other forest dwelling communities while strengthening the conservation regime (Dadibhavi 2000: 199).

From the preamble of the act, certain key features egress, that include

- The FRA is a rights vesting statute.
- It admits that the Indian state has flunked to acknowledge the rights of the tribals and other forest-dwelling people as they have been residing in the forest historically.

- As far as the Indian forest law is concerned, for the first time, a major change in the approach to the forest eco-system has been formulated.
- The preamble of the act distinctly acknowledges that the tribals and other forest-dwelling communities are not only an essential component, but are very indispensable to the endurance and preservation of the forest and its ecosystem.
- Through this act, the state has admitted the fact that its development intercessions have resulted large-scale displacement of the tribals and other forest dwellers from their habitat, which needs to be rectified.

Undoubtedly, the act is another milestone in order to provide justice for the forest living communities and especially the tribals. This act is a forward step in preserving the traditional right and livelihood of the tribals and forest-dwelling people. This act needs to be developed in consonance with the objectives of a final policy formulation for the tribals.

Although the act provides for the management of local level by *gram sabhas,* it is totally silent about the administration of *Panchayati Raj* Institutions (PRIs) at district and tahsil level. The act is also silent on the role of traditional tribal institutions including those related to forests. The act does not envisage any provision for ensuring their role in forest management. The act fails to dilute the overarching control of the state. This is evident from the precondition that only for livelihood purposes, the right to forest can be exerted and not for commercial intentions.

2.10 The Post-colonial State's Treatment of the Scheduled Tribes and Scheduled Areas

Although both the 'development through integration' narrative and the 'identity based isolation' narrative directed the formulation of the constitutional provisions for safe-guarding the rights of the STs, but in the post-independence era, we find that the 'development through integration' narrative dominated policymaking with respect to the tribal population. The Report of the Backward Classes (Kalelkar) Commission, 1955, classified the Scheduled Tribes and de-notified (ex-criminal) tribes along with Scheduled Castes, women, and other socially, economically and educationally backward classes as backward classes (Rath 2006: 155). It also identified certain 'backward' districts and recommended their classification as Scheduled Areas. The Committee recommended various measures for the removal of social, educational and economic backwardness, all of which were aimed at the integration of all the backward classes, including the Scheduled Tribes and de-notified tribes in society.

A few years later, in 1959, the Renuka Ray Committee on social welfare and welfare of backward classes, again defined 'backward classes' to mean the Scheduled Castes, Scheduled Tribes, de-notified communities, and Other Backward Classes (Rath 2006: 156). Again, the commission expressly recommended that the major objective of all social programmes that were targeted to benefit the 'backward classes' including the STs and de-notified communities was their eventual integration into a normal community (ibid.). The broad priorities for the STs included their economic development, communications, education and public health. The principles guiding the welfare services included not 'imposing things on tribals' but rather helping them to evolve in accordance with their own genius and through their own social and cultural institutions.

Following a directive in the Constitution, in 1960, a commission was constituted to report on the administration of Fifth Schedule areas, in particular; the functioning of the Tribes Advisory Councils, the application of laws to Fifth Schedule areas, and the exercise of the Governor's powers in these areas (Rath 2006: 156). This commission is known as the 'Dhebar Commission', after the name of its chairman, which recommended consideration of some factors while declaring Scheduled Areas. The factors which the commission has recommended are: (a) the compactness and reasonable size of the area (b) prevalence of tribals in the population (c) marked disparity in the economic standard of the people (d) the underdeveloped nature of the area. This Commission for the first time in post-independence period, reiterated the 'identity based isolation' narrative based on geographic location, but at the same time, included the 'backwardness' criteria that had been enunciated by the Kalelkar and Renuka Ray committees, respectively (ibid.: 157).

The Dhebar Commission recommended that the benefit of the Fifth Schedule should also be extended to the Union Territories (UTs). It recommended the inclusion of additional areas of 58,897 square kilometres along with a tribal population of approximately 4500,000 to the Fifth Scheduled Areas (Rath 2006: 157). The Commission noted its disappointment with the functioning of the Tribes Advisory Councils (TACs) and in line with Jaipal Singh's recommendation in the Constituent Assembly, it recommended the creation of TACs in all states and UTs with powers to advice and review all matters pertaining to tribal areas. This was more in relation to legislation for protecting tribal rights to land and against exploitation by moneylenders. Finally, the commission recommended special financial allocations by different state governments to the Scheduled Areas. While the recommendation with respect to special financial allocations by state governments to the Scheduled Areas was later implemented as part of the Tribal Sub-Plan (TSP).

The 'Lokur Committee Report' or the 1969 report of the advisory committee on the revision of the list of SCs and STs has noted that the Constitution has not expressly prescribed any principles or policy for drawing up lists of STs. Primitiveness and backwardness were the tests applied in preparing the lists in 1950 and 1956 that were notified by the President pursuant to Article 342 (Rath 2006: 158). In submitting the revisions to those lists, the Lokur Committee noted that they had adopted the following five criteria: (a) indication or denotations of primitive traits, (b) geographical isolation, (c) distinctive culture, (d) backwardness and (e) shyness of contact with the community at large. Correspondingly, they had excluded from the lists those tribes whose members had largely integrated with the mainstream population. Thus, despite reference to the 'identity' narrative in the identification criteria of the STs, 'development through integration' remained the goal of the government's policy objective regarding the tribal communities in the first two decades of the post-independence era.

In line with the 'development through integration' narrative, in 1978, the Government of India created a multi member commission for Scheduled Castes and Scheduled Tribes, to conduct studies on the social and economic conditions of both the backward communities (Rath 2006: 158). In 1992, under the chairmanship of Ram Dhan, the first National Commission for Scheduled Tribes and Scheduled Castes was establish following a constitutional amendment in 1990 (ibid.). The commission was charged with monitoring and investigating all legal and constitutional safeguards for Scheduled Tribes, and to enquire into specific complaints regarding the violation of these safeguards and rights. The commission was further empowered to advise and participate in the socio-economic welfare of tribals, and to assess their advancement. The commission was also given the responsibility in dispatching other functions associated with the development, welfare and protection of the tribals.

However, following this, there was a growing realisation on part of the Parliament and the executive that there is a need to attend separately to the needs of the Scheduled Tribes from those of the Scheduled Castes and Other Backward Classes (OBCs). This resulted in the creation of a separate department for tribal affairs within the Ministry of Welfare in 1985, and then in the Ministry of Social Justice and Empowerment in 1998, followed eventually by the creation of a separate Ministry of Tribal Affairs in 1999 (ibid.). Even as these changes were happening, in 1994, the Ministry of Rural Development constituted a select committee of experts led by Dileep Singh Bhuria. This committee considers the extension of the provisions of the 73rd and 74th Constitutional amendments which introduced elected local governments in the form of *panchayats* and municipalities in rural and urban areas, and also for Scheduled Areas. The Bhuria Committee recommended the enactment of the Panchayat Extension to Scheduled Areas (PESA) Act, and the Municipalities Extension to Scheduled Areas (MESA) Act. In 1996, Parliament accepted the Bhuria Committee's recommendation to enact the PESA, but MESA has still not been enacted. The government should take initiative to pass the MESA Act to provide justice to the tribals.

2.11 Conclusion

Through the Constitution, India acknowledges and arranges the special protective measures for her indigenous tribal peoples and also recognises the tribals' social, cultural, and economic identity which distinguish them from the mainstream society. However, in spite of these special provisions, the Scheduled Tribes continue to be the most vulnerable and impoverished sections of the Indian population. Despite the centrality of land to the identity, economy, and culture of the tribals, the Indian state has failed to protect the tribal land. Indeed, given that, the Constitution guaranteed to all citizens the fundamental right to move freely throughout the territory of India, it is not clear how such a limitation could have been imposed by law while considering non-tribals entry into the tribal area which is the major factor for tribal land alienation. Thus, even though the Indian Constitution was progressive for its time, both generally in its recognition of rights for all its citizens, and also in terms of its recognition of protections for minority rights, including those of the Scheduled Tribes, the incoherence and contradictory nature of the provisions diluted their effectiveness in safeguarding the rights of the STs.

Among the two narratives, both the 'identity-based isolation' and 'development through integration' narratives qualified the making of the constitutional securities for the tribals. But the post-independence planning and policy formulations for the STs were primarily guided by the latter. Notwithstanding, the tribals have regarded the 'development through integration' narrative as both paternalistic and patronising and alleged that this narrative does not seem to capture the aspirations of the tribal people to 'develop according to their own genius'. In order to have a coherent strategy for the uplift and protection of the tribal people, we, therefore, need clarity on how the 'identity-based isolation' and 'development through integration' narratives can be integrated into policy discourse and law-making, to facilitate the design of laws and policies that can safeguard the rights of tribals and help them develop according to their genius. Needless to state, the processes of law-making must happen in consultation with the tribal communities and not be a paternalistic imposition on them by the state, because they are not only a minority, but also a very special minority.

A contrary legal framework comprising of colonial and post-colonial forest, mining and land acquisition laws have further diluted the constitutional protections for the STs. The land alienation prohibition laws only prohibit the transfer of tribal land to non-tribals. But, in the Scheduled Areas, there is nothing to prevent the state from getting the land for its own purposes. The state with the exercise of its power of 'eminent domain' gets the tribal land and forest land. The Samata judgement, which has been observed more in the breach, prohibited the grant of mining leases in the Scheduled Areas to private companies, but not by state mining corporations. Based on the intensity of dams and mining activities in the Scheduled Areas, we can easily infer that land acquired in the Scheduled Areas for the purpose of construction of dams and mining has displaced and impoverished millions of Scheduled Tribes. While 90% of all mineral wealth generated in India comes from the Schedule Areas, but, this wealth is not channelised appropriately for the benefit of the tribal people. This is especially worrying when we find that there are huge shortfalls in expenditure in the special financial allocations made for the welfare of the Scheduled Tribes and Scheduled Areas.

All of the above is not to say that the struggle for safeguarding the rights of tribal people has been a failure. The decriminalisation of criminal tribes, the special constitutional provisions for tribal representation, affirmative action for the tribals, recognising the land rights of tribals, creation of the tribal sub-plan for special financial allocations for tribal population, creation of the National Commission for Scheduled Tribes, Ministry of Tribal Affairs, the enactment of the PESA Act, 1996, the FRA 2006, and the creation of the District Mineral Foundation under the MMDR Act, 2015 are some of the important constitutional, legislative and administrative steps that have the potential of going a long way to redress the historic injustices against the tribal communities in India. But, only the effective and coordinated functioning of all these mechanisms can truly safeguard the rights of tribals in India.

References

Dadibhavi, R. V. (2000). Management of common property resources: A review and some policy issues. *Journal of Rural Development, 19*(2), 199–217.

Dash, J. (2002). *Impact of forest policies in the indigenous people.* New Delhi: APH Publishing Company.

Dixit, N. K. (2006). *Tribals in India.* New Delhi: Vista International Publishing House.

Draft National Tribal Policy (2006). (pp.1–23). http://www.indiaenvironmentportal.org.in/files/tribal.pdf. Accessed 16 January, 2019.

Hasnain, N. (1983). *Tribal India today.* New Delhi: Harnam Publication.

http://legislative.gov.in/sites/default/files/A1989-33_2.pdf. Accessed 12 June, 2018.

https://pib.gov.in/newsite/PrintRelease.aspx?relid=181758. Accessed 18 July, 2018.

https://pib.gov.in/PressReleasePage.aspx?PRID=1578780. Accessed 23 March, 2019.

https://tribal.nic.in/DivisionsFiles/mj/4-preventionofAtrocities.pdf. Accessed 10 March, 2019.

Joseph, V. (2008). *Tribal development during the five year plan.* New Delhi: Sarup & Sons.

Mann, R. S. (1993). *Culture and integration of Indian tribe.* New Delhi: M.D. Publication.

Mathew, P. D. (2004). *Constitution of India simplified.* New Delhi: Indian Social Institute.

Mohanty, P. K. (2002). *Tribes in India: Ongoing challenges.* Delhi: Kalpaz.

Mohapatra, L. K. (2002). *Customary rights in land and forest and the state.* New Delhi: APH Publishing Company.

Padhi, K. (2005). Tribal development in India: A study of human development. *Orissa Review*, February–March, pp. 71–78.

Patel, M. L. (1998). *Agrarian transformation in tribal India.* New Delhi: M.D. Publication.

Pati, R. N., & Dash, J. (2002). *Tribal and indigenous people of India: Problems and prospects.* New Delhi: APH Publishing Company.

Rath, G. C. (2006). *Tribal development in India: Contemporary debates.* New Delhi: Sage Publication.

Session of All-India Congress Committee (50th). Faizpur (1936). Viewable in 'Excluded Areas under the new Constitution. https://archive.org/stream/in.ernet.dli.2015.276455/2015.276455. Accessed 6 November, 2018.

Shrama, B. D. (2001). *Tribals affairs in India: A crucial transition.* New Delhi: Sahyog Pustak Kutir.

www.planningcommission.nic.in, https://niti.gov.in/planningcommission.gov.in/docs/plans/planrel/fiveyr/welcome.html. Accessed 19 February, 2019.

Chapter 3
Land and the Tribals of India: Problems and Prospects

3.1 Introduction

Uniqueness of the tribals and their traditions revolve around the centrality of land and land is vital for understanding tribals' identity, culture and religion (Behura 1982: 1). As an integral part of the land, the tribals are always identified with it. It provides an identity to the tribals, and through the land, the tribal people become one with their ancestors, with the spirits, with other segments of the creation and with the Supreme Being. The totality of tribals' lives and activities moves with the land. The meaning of tribal life and their religious, ethical, social and economic activities are directly and indirectly related to the land/soil. Without a piece of land, the tribals has no meaning to their life, culture and identity and land is conceived as mother of the tribals. When that land became encroached or alienated, for the tribals; it seems to be loss of everything, i.e., their identity, culture, self, economy and freedom. So, land alienation is a serious challenge for the tribals. To preserve this primordial identity of the tribals, Jaipal Singh, the tribal representative and the founder leader of the *adivasi mahasabha,* demanded some level of discrimination in the Constituent Assembly, when his turn came to address the land question in the tribal's life.

The problem of tribal land alienation has always been a matter of anxiety to the policymakers, planners, activists and for the academicians. This is so because, despite progressive and protective legislations, tribal people all over the country are perpetually threatened over their land rights. The process of alienation of tribal land began with the stabilisation of the British rule in India. This process was accelerated for the development of transport, establishment of individual rights over agricultural land, commercialisation of agriculture and the spread of English judicial system. Now, the menace has become more intensified than ever due to the onslaught of infrastructural development, commercialisation, industrialisation and the outsiders' migration to tribal areas. The traditional mode of securing their livelihood is seriously threatened without any appropriate alternatives in sight. Therefore, the tribals became the worst sufferers over the land question. At present, the existence of landlessness among them is a sign of land alienation, whereas they were not landless labourers

S. K. Malik, *Land Alienation and Politics of Tribal Exploitation in India*,
https://doi.org/10.1007/978-981-15-5382-0_3

earlier. On account of different factors, the process of land estrangement has gained momentum over the times. Viegas has rightly pointed out that the dynamics of the process of dispossession involves an intricate of social, cultural, economic and political forces (Philip 1991: 77). Unfortunately, the rate of tribal land alienation in the country is alarming, despite the Constitutional protections (Fifth Schedule of the Indian Constitution) and numerous laws prohibiting transfer of tribal land to non-tribals. A report by the Land Reforms Division regarding tribal land alienation states that:

> 3.75 lakh cases of tribal land alienation have been registered so far, covering 8.55 lakh acres of land, of which 1.62 lakh cases have been disposed in favour of tribal covering a total area of 4.47 lakh acres. Another 1.54 lakh cases covering an area of 3.63 lakh acres have been rejected by the courts on various grounds.[1]

In the Scheduled Areas, the *panchayats* and particularly the '*gram sabha*' *have* powers to preclude tribal land alienation. Under the *Panchayat* (Extension to Scheduled Areas) Act (PESA) 1996, the *gram sabha* can take steps to restore the already alienated land of the Scheduled Tribes. For the above purpose, the PESA rules need to be spelled out regarding the special powers and the procedures which the *gram sabha* are enthroned. Special courts and judicatures need to be set up with special regulations to be framed by the Governors for any appellate procedure against such an action.

With the above background concerning the issues of tribal land alienation and encroachment, the present chapter analyses the land alienation process and reviews the laws ordained for the safeguard and promotion of land rights of the tribals of India. The chapter is divided into three parts. The first part deals about the introduction of the chapter and the issues involved with tribal land alienation. The second part highlights the land problems of the tribals briefly. The third part examines the extent of tribal land alienation and explains the situation in all India contexts as far as the tribal land issues are concerned.

3.2 Land Issues and the Tribals

Land distribution in India closely followed social hereditary. The agricultural workers largely belong to the Scheduled Castes and Scheduled Tribes, the cultivator belongs to the middle castes and the large landowners always belong to the upper castes. Land as a social asset maintains the hierarchical structure and strengthens the basis of dominance due to its unequal distribution. In socio-economic spheres, the uneven distribution of land perpetuates the inequality and deprivation. Therefore, the idea of just distribution of land affects such hierarchical socio-economic relations. For that

[1] *Draft National Land Reform Policy*, Department of Land Resources, Ministry of Rural Development, Government of India, 24 July 2013, p. 9. https://www.slideshare.net/fundsforngos/draft-national-landreformspolicyjuly2013.

reason, the vested interest of the upper castes has opposed the legislative measures towards land distribution.

> Land reforms in India have been launched in response to compelling demands expressed through agitation, struggle and movements. As far as the land reform policy being a political issue, the state passes legislation only to appease and liquidate the agrarian discontents. But the existence of strong protest movements are always essential in order to get implement of such policies rigorously. The entrenched dominant landowning privileged groups would never like to surrender their power and privilege without exertion of mounting pressure from the deprived people (Mohanty 2001: 3859).

The British government made land alienable on a large scale especially in tribal areas through its land revenue policy and elaborate exploitatory bureaucratic structure (Mohanty 2001: 3859). During the British period, the upper caste elites who were dominating each sphere of British administration alienated the tribals from their land and consolidated their landowning position through the state machinery. The tribals were repressed to various forms of oppression and subjugation and were forced to work as labourers in their own land.

Gradually, it generated strong discontentment, and the simmering tensions culminated in rebellions one after another. In spite of the fact that many of these uprisings had social and religious contents, agrarian problems were the principal mobilising force (cited in Mohanty 2001: 3859).

The '*bhoodan* movement'[2] appealed too many conscientiously oriented rural Indians as they have contributed their small holdings for the landless. Up to March 1968, near about 43% of land collected from different regions and states (cited in Mohanty 2001: 3862). But, the land collected under the scheme had been founded either under dispute or unsuitable for cultivation and in some regions, it was also reported that many persons who were donated land to *bhoodan samiti* declined later (ibid.). As highlighted by a number of researches that:

> The donated land were by and large of inferior types requiring substantial investment to make them worthy of cultivation. The inherent loopholes and ambiguities in the legislative measures, slow proceeding at all levels of bureaucracy, lack of updated land records, the ignorance and illiteracy of the Scheduled Tribes population and the escaping attitude of the large landowners are the major reasons that hinder fair distribution of land by allowing the bulk of land owners to avoid expropriation (cited in Mohanty 2001: 3862).

Even a slow process of passing of the land to the Scheduled Castes and tribes and its resultant upliftment becomes intolerable and non-acceptable to the dominant groups. They resist the allotment of land by committing atrocities on members of Scheduled Castes and Scheduled Tribes through well-organised groups, like the *Ranvir Sena, Bhumi Sena and Lorik Sena (*formed by the upper caste *Bhumihars*, *Rajputs*, rich *Kurmis* and *Yadavas* in Bihar and other regions of the country) (Mohanty 2001: 3863). In Bihar, a number of dalits have been killed by the *Ranvir Sena* alone owing to issue relating to land allotment (cited in Mohanty 2001: 3863).

---

[2]Acharya Vinoba Bhave started the *Bhoodan* movement in 1951 at Pochampally Village in Telangana.

Forest-and land-based resources, especially the land, are fundamental to the cultural and social existence of the tribals. Most of the tribals live in forested and mountainous regions of central India and northeast India. The tribal region in central India actually covers about 100 districts in eight states and stretching along Purulia (West Bengal) in the east to Banswara (Rajasthan) in the west. This vast tribal population cover 68 million hectares of geographical land mass which accounted for more than 55 million people and approximately 70% of the total tribal population of India (cited in Kumar et al. 2005: 10). The colonial state has marked that tribal land alienation is a serious administrative and political issue which contributes to tribal rebellions and unrest, and therefore, the British government had passed special policies and laws to preserve tribals' right over the land. After independence, through the Fifth and Sixth Schedule, the protection of land rights of the tribals was also integrated in the Indian Constitution.

Legally, tribal land alienation indicates the loss of private or *patta* land. But this approach doesn't have any sense while applying in the common land ownership system of the tribals. Other than the northeast India, communal ownership of land in tribal areas were not legalised by the British administration or by the post-independence Indian state. Tribal land dispossession in case of reserve forests or forest land diverted for various purposes did not figure out in the formal discourse on tribal land alienation.

However, besides alienation of private or *patta* land of the tribals, the state has made diversion of tribal land for different purposes which played significant role in making the tribal landless. These include diversion of land for development projects, large-scale plantation programmes, encroachment, notification of forests, etc. Therefore, it is necessary to take into account these processes, in order to comprehend the restraints on tribal access to land, along with alienation of private or *patta* land by the tribals.

The issue of tribal land alienation has always been a matter of great concern to planners, policymakers, academicians and activists. This is so because, despite progressive and protective legislations, tribal people all over the country are perpetually threatened over their land rights. The process of alienation of tribal land began with the stabilisation of the British rule in India. This process was accelerated by the development of transport, establishment of individual rights over agricultural land, commercialisation of agriculture and the spread of English judicial system. Now, the menace has become more intensified and compounded than ever on account of the onslaught of urbanisation, industrialisation, commercialisation and the development of infrastructure. Without any appropriate alternative livelihood for the tribals, the traditional livelihood system of the tribals is severely jeopardised. As far as land question is concerned, the Scheduled Tribes are the biggest and worst sufferers in the country. As landless labourers, the tribal communities did not have a tradition earlier. At present, the existence of landless category amidst the tribals is a perceptible indication of land alienation. Through different sources and patterns, this process of land dispossession among the tribals has gained momentum over the years. The process of dispossession of land within tribal areas implies the complex interaction of economic, social, cultural and political factors (Philip 1991: 77).

The constantly shrinking and fragile economic base are the main reasons behind tribal land dispossession. For the fulfilment of their daily basic needs, the Scheduled Tribes got exposed to cash transactions and therefore, their non-monetised self-reliant economy gets collapsed. Earlier, the tribals were mostly dependent on forest and forest products. But, from the status of owner gatherers, the tribals are now brought down to encroachers or wage earners in their own land with the notification of state ownership of forests. Due to developmental programmes of the central government and different state governments, tribals in large scale have been displaced from their land and habitat. Thousands of poor tribals without any economic possession have been evicted and lost their land and livelihood owing to many projects of the government at different times. With the so called development model of India, displacement caused by large projects has actually ensued the transfer of resources from the marginal section to the more privileged segments of the Indian society (Pradhan and Behera 2007: 6). The development programmes can also reduce access to land by the tribals. In other words, the tribal communities were forced to bear the massive burden of development.

3.3 State Policy and Tribal Land Alienation

The legacies of the colonial government regarding forest policy were inherited by the government of Independent India where the National Forest Policy, 1952, underlies continuity of the colonial policy. This colonial policy strengthened the state's claim for total control over forest production and protection. The policy considered shifting cultivation as the major threat to state forestry. But, it affected the rights of the Scheduled Tribes who were dependent on forest products and resources. Therefore, the tribal communities in different times have challenged the state's policy regarding the denial of tribal rights. In 1957, in Madhya Pradesh, the *Khanwar* tribes had withstood with the forest laws and resisted against revenue collection and the laws which breached their traditional rights. They vehemently opposed the commercial use and external control of tribal land and forest and their slogan was '*jangal zamin azad hai*' that means land and forest are nature's gift. The other form of conflict between the tribals and the state arises from the 'contractor system'. This system is the routine method of leasing forest in India. The tribals have opposed to this 'contractor system'. The state's involuntariness to substitute the 'contractor system' has afforded the militant movements and left extremism in different tribal regions of India. The consequences of this kind of exploitation have resulted in the Naxalite movements in tribal-dominated areas.

The Universal Declaration on the Rights of Indigenous Peoples has urged the international community to think on indigenous rights. It says indigenous people have the right to participate fully in the political, economic, social and cultural life of the state while maintaining their distinct political, economic, social and cultural characteristics.[3] In 14 June 1992, the United Nations Conference has adopted the Rio de Janeiro declaration, which promulgates that indigenous peoples' culture, identity and interest should be recognised by the states and the state should enable and support the indigenous peoples' participation for achieving sustainable development. They are the posterity of the original denizens who lived in forest for hundreds of years and have an historic relationship with the forests and land. Therefore, the indigenous people have acquired a holistic conventional knowledge of the natural resources, environment, animals, plants and on their land through many generations. The Rio declaration stated that:

> They shall enjoy the full measures of human rights and fundamental freedoms without hindrance or discrimination. Their ability to participate fully in sustainable development practices on their land have tended to be limited as a result of factors of social, economic, and historical nature.[4]

The International Labour Organisation (ILO) in its convention No. 169 (1989) on '*adivasi* (aboriginal) and indigenous peoples' suggested that governments must consult with indigenous and *adivasi* peoples within their countries on development projects and other activities affecting them.[5] It also directed the sates to respect the land rights of the *adivasis* and indigenous people. These land rights of the aboriginal tribals are considered the right to refuse deracination other than exceptional situation. In the name of development, with little or no rehabilitation, tribals have been consistently displaced from their livelihoods and natural habitats.

In India, a study found that, till 1990, 85 lakhs tribal people were displaced, among them 65% remained without rehabilitation.[6] Different other studies and statistics put the figure near about 2 crores.[7] Tribals are diminished from the status of owner gatherers to encroachers or wage earners and large section of the Scheduled Tribes are being pauperised due to this trend of development. This has increased the insecure forms of tenancy and landlessness among the tribals of the country. In 2004–05, the official figures reveal that most of the tribals (approximately 70%) were either had less than 1 acre of land or landless.[8] Furthermore, tribal households with marginal and small land holdings have been enhancing steadily with time.

Loss of tribal access to land or tribal land alienation happens through different routes and forms. Considering the conditions of Scheduled Tribes, the Xaxa

[3] *The State of India's Indigenous and Tribal People* (2009). Asian Indigenous & Tribal Peoples Network, 31st March.

[4] *The State of India's Indigenous and Tribal People* (2009). Asian Indigenous & Tribal Peoples Network, 31st March.

[5] ibid.

[6] ibid.

[7] ibid.

[8] ibid.

Committee in its report had identified the following routes or forms to tribal land alienation:[9]

- Development caused displacement which facilitates tribal land alienation—large areas of land were gained by private parties or state in the name of developmental projects, with very less or modest benefit for the tribals.
- Common ownership lands or community lands of the Scheduled Tribe communities are not recorded in their name during the survey and settlement process. These huge lands are recorded as government land. In many states, the tenancy laws only recognise individually owned registered land.
- For the settlement of expatriates and refugees, the state is acquiring land in tribal areas which resulted in tribal land alienation.
- Tribal land alienation, forced migration and displacement also happen due to the creation of national parks and sanctuaries in tribal regions.
- *Benami* transactions and illegal land transfers occurred owing to the numbness of revenue officials and department, manipulation of land records and permission granted to alienate tribal land in different times as per law and legal procedures. Different state governments' laws are ameliorated from time to time to incorporate the provisions which facilitate tribal land alienation.

Among the different ways by which tribal land alienation occur, development-stimulated land alienation is one among these factors. There are also other causes of land alienation which are not directly associated with acquisition of land for development projects. These include *state-assented* land alienation. It happens through unrecorded, *benami* (illegal) purchases, informal tenancies, long-term leases, gift by tribals, manipulation of records, *usufructory* agreements and loopholes in land laws. The state-acquiesced land alienation admits the government or revenue officials' indirect or direct engagement in land alienation process. This kind of land alienation occurs mostly on account of faulty settlements and survey processes, lack of land records, inexact surveys, permits granted for buying or conversing tribal land and due to lack of execution of the existing policies and laws. Among the above factors of tribal land alienation, some factors are considered as legal, but other cases are mostly illegal, unofficial and unrecorded. These kind of alienations are considered as *benami* (illegal), although the *benami* category does not cover the scope and ambit of tribal land alienation depicted above.

A huge section of these land alienation are done by oral or unwritten transactions, and altogether in absence of the consent of the tribals (seller). These lands were possessed and controlled in forcible manner, or absorbed by the powerful and rich, with dynamic collusion of the administrative authority and revenue officials, without being the knowledge of the tribals. How far-flung the situation is, can be estimated from the data from Ministry of Rural Development (annual report 2007–08). It is approximated that in the year 2007–08 alone, for restoration of alienated land, 5.06

[9] *Report of the High Level Committee on socio-economic, health and educational status of tribal communities of India,* (May 2014). http://www.indiaenvironmentportal.org.in/files/file/Tribal%20Committee%20Report,%20May-June%202014.pdf. Accessed 22 February 2019.

lakh cases were registered, which covers 9.02 lakh acres of land.[10] As most of the land alienation cases are without any record, it can be safely taken for granted that the above data from the Ministry of Rural development only divulges the proverbial tip of the iceberg regarding the circumstances of land alienation among the tribals.

Historically, there is no record of individual dealings of land transfers or land alienation from tribals to non-tribals and has been badly documented. Nevertheless, there are some studies which have attempted to appraise the magnitude of this land alienation phenomenon at different state levels. A study in Andhra Pradesh by the Tribal Cultural Research and Training Institute projects that almost 80% of land has been alienated and shifted to non-tribals through encroachment and sale alone.[11] Incase of Odisha, debt mortgaging through unofficial and informal ways by private transactions were found the most suitable methods of tribal land alienation. But, the magnitude, scope and extent of tribal land alienation through this process are still unknown.

3.4 Extent of Tribal Land Alienation in Different States of India

The Sixth Schedule and the Fifth Schedule of the Indian Constitution postulated rigorous safeguards as far as tribals land is concerned. In every state, to protect the transfer of land from tribals to non-tribals, various laws and policies have been adopted. Despite these provisions, the trend of tribal land alienation in the country is alerting. In its annual report (2007–08), The Ministry of Rural Development, Government of India indicates that The state governments have accepted the policy of prohibiting the transfer of land from tribals to non-tribals and for restoration of alienated tribal land to them. The states with large tribal population have enacted laws for this purpose.[12]The report further submits that:

> Reports received from various states indicate that 5.06 lakh cases of tribal land alienation have been registered, covering 9.02 lakh acres of land, of which 2.25 lakh cases have been disposed of in favour of tribals covering a total area of 5.00 lakh acres. 1.99 lakh cases covering an area of 4.11 lakh acres have been rejected by the courts on various grounds.[13]

The Ministry of Rural Development has reported land alienation in different states. On the basis of the report, land alienation situation has been analysed in different states in the following sections.

---

[10]Annual Report (2007–08), Government of India, Ministry of Rural Development, p. 276. https://rural.nic.in/sites/default/files/anualreport0708_eng.pdf. Accessed 12 November 2019.

[11]ibid.

[12]ibid.

[13]ibid.

3.4.1 Andhra Pradesh

In Andhra Pradesh, the tribals' lands were illicitly possessed by the non-tribals, in spite of the fact that 'the Andhra Pradesh Scheduled Areas Land Transfer Regulation, 1959', which was ameliorated by the regulation 1 of 1970, forbids transfer and sale of Scheduled Tribes' land to non-tribals in different Scheduled Areas. A tribal woman, Karam Devudamma of Chinnabhimpalli of East Godavari district, on 2 September 2008, filed a petition before the High Court of Andhra Pradesh where she averred that the Revenue Divisional Officer (RDO) bought the tribal land for building the Polavaram irrigation project and the petition was acknowledged by the High Court.[14]

From the report, it is apparent that in the Scheduled Areas of Andhra Pradesh, the trend and degree of tribal land alienation are more frequent which remain a case of public concern. The tribal protective laws or anti-land alienation laws in the state have failed to arrest tribal land alienation. The report further substantiates the data that in Scheduled Areas of the state, 48% of lands were occupied by the non-tribals. Therefore, it can be safely assumed that whatever the legal means are available to prevent tribal land alienation were never implemented in its letter and spirit. The report also highlights the broad gap within formulating the laws and their rigorous implementation.

3.4.2 Assam

In the state of Assam, the government has failed to arrest the alienation of tribal land. With the cooperation and nexus among the revenue officials and the land-grabbers, lands of the tribals have been either transferred or illegally occupied by the non-tribals. The All Assam Tribal *Sangha* mentions that till 4 May 2008, within the 47 tribal blocks of Assam, approximately 800,000 *bighas* of tribal land were illegally possessed by the non-tribals.[15] Approximately, 325 *bighas* of tribal lands in Sonapur tribal area of Kamrup district are illicitly transferred or invaded by the non-tribals. The *Dimoria Bhumi Suraksha Samiti,* in a report, has indicted that many non-tribals have possessed Scheduled Tribes' land. The tribals' lands have been transferred or occupied by the non-tribals mostly through illegal means.

As per some survey record, in Sonapur tribal areas, the list of the names of the non-tribals who occupied the land of the tribals illegally were provided below. Under *patta* No.53, Abhisekh Agarwal (a non-tribal) has illicitly bought four *bighas* of Scheduled Tribes land. Under *dag* No. 60 and *patta* No. 7, B. K. Agarwal (a non-tribal) has bought three *bighas* of land from the tribals illegally at Byrnigaon. At Sarutari village, he also have bought seven *bighas* of land from the tribals under *dag*

---

[14]The Times of India (Daily English Newspaper, Hyderabad Edition) (2008). 3 September, p. 6.

[15]Tribal land encroached by people of suspected nationalities (2008). *The Sentinel*, 6 May. http://www.indiaenvironmentportal.org.in/content/245398/tribal-land-encroached-by-people-of-suspectednationalities/?page. Accessed 22 January 2019.

No. 48/49 and *patta* No. 5. In 4 June 2002, at Dimoria, it was reported that Anisuj Jaman (a non-tribal) has illicitly bought four *bighas* of tribal land under *dag* No. 111, *patta* No. 102. Under *dag* No. 34/38/41 and *patta* No. 01, RK Himmat Sinka (a non-tribal) who resides in Tokobari (Guwahati) has bought 109 *bighas* of land from the tribals in an illegal manner. At Sarutari village, the person named Kakali Saikia (a non-tribal) has illicitly bought six *bighas* of tribal land. At Tamulikuchi, 13 *bighas* of tribal land were illegally bought by Santi Dutta (a non-tribal). At Nazirakhat, N.N. Dutta (a non-tribal) has also bought four *bighas* of land from the tribals under *dag* No. 159 and *patta* No. 134.[16]

3.4.3 Jharkhand

In the state of Jharkhand, tribal land alienation is large scale and the tribals are the victims of this massive land alienation. In the state, there are laws for the prevention of land alienation. For example, the 'Santhal Parangan Tenancy Act, 1949' and the 'Chotanagpur Tenancy Act, 1908' are the laws against land alienation. But despite this anti-land alienation laws, tribal land alienation in Jharkhand is as usual. As per the data of the Ministry of Rural Development 'Annual Report (2007–08)', 5382 number of cases regarding tribal land alienation were registered before different courts in the state which involve an area of approximately 4,002 acres of land. The court has disposed a total number of 1,362 registered cases, among which 1,079 cases were settled in favour of the tribals.[17] Nevertheless, for the restoration of the alienated land, the poor tribals find it highly difficult in combating the legal battles. Therefore, it is extremely difficult in the part of the needy tribals to get their alienated land back from the clutches of the rich non-tribals. In some cases, it is found that lack of lawyers or lawyers not interested to pursue tribal land alienation cases which farther detained the legal process. As of March 2007, approximately, 5,500 tribal land alienation cases are pending in different courts of the state. The state government had allocated Rs 50 lakh for providing financial help to the tribals to fight the legal battle for their land alienation cases. But unfortunately, very less amount (approximately 10%) of the sanctioned budget has been expended for the last 6 years. Lawyers are not interested and are disinclined to take up tribal land alienation cases due to less assistance from the government. It is reported that, in Jharkhand, for the last six years, as part of government's legal assistance, the lawyers who are fighting cases on behalf of the tribals were compensated just Rs. 5,000 per case.[18]

[16]Government fails to stop grabbing of tribal land (2008). *The Sentinel,* 13 September. https://www.sentinelassam.com. Accessed 12 February 2019.

[17]Annual Report (2007–08), Government of India, Ministry of Rural Development, p. 276. https://rural.nic.in/sites/default/files/anualreport0708_eng.pdf. Accessed 12 November 2019.

[18]The Hindustan Times (Daily English Newspaper) (2007). 22 October, p. 8.

3.4.4 Karnataka

The tribals of Karnataka face the problems of land alienation and their inability to obtain land title deeds. The phenomenon of land alienation is referred to as the practice of purchasing or forcefully acquiring the agriculture land of the tribes by the mainland people. The mainland people give loans and advances to the tribes and give alcohol and good feasts to the tribes to influence them to sell their land at nominal prices. Due to the renewed industrial activity, and the formation of the contractual industries, land alienation in Karnataka took a different turn after 1960s. The pressure on land has increased due to raising industrial activity supported by foreign capital which forced the non-tribal industrialists and other rich persons from the mainland to look for alternate land in forest and tribal areas. The non-tribals have identified this substitute source for land in the tribal areas or tribal living forest land. This industrial process ensued the tribals dispossessing from their traditional land and have resulted in the displacement of the communities.

Tribal land alienation in Karnataka has continued and the state has failed to arrest tribal land alienation. It also remained unsuccessful to prevent further tribal land alienation in the state. As per the report of the Ministry of Rural Development, Government of India (annual report of 2007–08), in Karnataka, 42,582 cases of tribal land alienation (approximately 130,373 acres of land) have been registered in different courts. The court while providing judgement have settled 38,521 tribal land alienation cases where 21,834 tribal land alienation cases were decided favouring the tribals and 4,061 tribal land alienation cases are still pending in different courts of Karnataka.[19]

3.4.5 Madhya Pradesh

Tribal land alienation in Madhya Pradesh is a grave situation and the instances can be exposed from the census data where the number of Scheduled Tribes cultivators fell to 68.09% in 1991 in comparison to 76.45% in 1961. This indicates the rise of landless labourers among the tribals which is sheer case of tribal land alienation. Though landlessness as a condition is visible throughout different deprived groups and marginal communities, its effect on the tribals is more serious, because the tribals are totally dependent on land and are not suitable to carry out any other livelihoods due to lack of necessary skills and education. Therefore, for the tribals, loss of land means pushing them further towards extreme immiseration. In the state, the data of Planning Commission reveals that there are 47% of tribals who live below poverty line, where the number is 37% in case of SCs.

In the state, the study determined alienation of tribal land in large extent in Bankuri village due to heavy inflow of non-tribal outsider and privileged castes from mainland.

[19]Annual Report (2007–08), Government of India, Ministry of Rural Development, p. 276. https://rural.nic.in/sites/default/files/anualreport0708_eng.pdf. Accessed 12 November 2019.

These outsiders have occupied much of tribal land over time. It is reported that in Kanerkheda village, more than 36% tribal families were displaced from their land. It is 70% in case of Bankuri village. This is all happening despite the existing land alienation prevention laws. The administration and the revenue bureaucracy have no sympathy towards the tribals' plight and no interest in protecting tribal land rather it has conniving nexus with the land-grabbers and they unitedly have grabbed the tribal land. Owing to these circumstances, there are acclivitous tides of tribal land alienation in the state of Madhya Pradesh. The study also discloses the fact that in addition to the upper caste landlords, the Jat and Punjabi farmers are also grabbing tribal land through all means.

In the state, there is section 165(6) of the Madhya Pradesh Land Revenue Code (1959) which averts the transfer of tribal land in tribal majority areas. For any transfer of such tribal land, it requires the permission of the revenue officials with reasons mentioning in written document. In 1981, through a further amendment, sub-section 6-C was added that establishes the maxims to be conceived by the collector during providing permission for tribal land transfer or denying to grant permission. There is section 170-A of the said act which establishes for the restoration of alienated tribal land if coming into conflict with the above sections. There is also section 170-B that furnishes for the regression of tribal land or the land of the indigene tribes that was transferred illicitly. These are the important protections as far as tribal land in Madhya Pradesh is concerned.

Madhya Pradesh has also ordained laws to implement the PESA Act 1996 and to provide genuine power to *panchayats* and local communities regarding tribal land alienation. As per the study report, in spite of all these laws and provisions, tribals have not benefitted much and tribal land alienation is still going on as usual. In most of the cases, the enacted laws remained in paper and rigorous implementation remains a day dream.

As per the data of the Ministry of Rural Development, by 2007, after settlement of 29,596 land alienation cases, Madhya Pradesh is the only state which has not decided a single case of tribal land alienation in favour of the aboriginal tribals. Among the total of 53,806 tribal land alienation cases amounting 158,398 acres of land which were registered in different courts of Madhya Pradesh, 24,210 cases were still pending in the court.[20]

3.4.6 Maharashtra

The Maharashtra government has adopted a number of laws to prevent tribal land alienation. Among these laws, the Maharashtra Land Revenue Code (1966) forbids any transfer of tribal land without the District Collector's prior permission. The Maharashtra government has enacted another law, namely, 'Maharashtra Land Revenue

[20] Annual Report (2007–08), Government of India, Ministry of Rural Development, p. 276. https://rural.nic.in/sites/default/files/anualreport0708_eng.pdf. Accessed 12 November 2019.

Code and Tenancy Laws (Amendment) Act, 1974' due to the failure of 'Maharashtra Land Revenue Code, 1966'. The new law directs that by way of gift, sale, mortgage, exchange and lease; otherwise, no tribal can transfer his/her land to a non-tribal. The transfer needs the permission of the collector (a) in the case of lease or mortgage for a period of five years (b) with previous approval of government, in other cases with effect from 6 July, 1974.[21] The Maharashtra government accepted that permissions by the district Collectors appear to have been given as a matter of routine and the tribals were also induced to sell their land because of indebtedness and poverty.[22]

Further, to re-establish the alienated tribal land, the Maharashtra government ordained the 'Maharashtra Restoration of Land to Scheduled Tribes Act, 1974'. From 1 April 1957 to 6 July 1974, whatever tribal land were transferred to non-tribals, should be restore as per the above act.[23] But both the above tribal land protection laws have flunked to restore alienated land or to prevent further alienation. In the state, a total 45,634 land alienation cases were filled in different courts as per the annual report (2007–08) of the Ministry of Rural Development.[24] The court has settled 44,624 land alienation cases, where 19,943 cases having 99,486 acres of tribal land were settled in favour of the Scheduled Tribes and 1,010 land alienation cases were still pending in the court.[25]

In the state of Maharashtra, the Scheduled Tribes are not aware about the laws and are not organised to counter the land lobby of the affluent segment of the state. Due to lack of education and political awareness, they are deprived from the benefit of the laws like PESA and other land prevention laws. There is apathy in the part of the state administration and revenue officials and lack of political will to implement the existing laws to protect the tribal interest.

3.4.7 Rajasthan

In Rajasthan, of the two villages of Udaipur, the first one is Kodiyat-A village, which is more accessed to markets, has experienced substantial tribal land alienation, where Scheduled Tribes' land holding accounted only for 30% of the total village land.[26] In case of Kodiyat-B village that figure is still 80–90%. In case of Kodiyat-A village, tourism, is a significant push factor for land alienation, where tribal land is in demand with tourism lobby for building hotels and resorts.[27] The means of transfer of tribal land here is mostly illegal. There are nexus between the revenue

[21] http://rajbhavan-maharashtra.gov.in/rajbhavan/pdf/20_Act.pdf. Accessed 12 November 2019.

[22] ibid.

[23] ibid.

[24] Annual Report (2007–08), Government of India, Ministry of Rural Development, p. 276. https://rural.nic.in/sites/default/files/anualreport0708_eng.pdf. Accessed 12 November 2019.

[25] ibid.

[26] ibid.

[27] ibid.

officials and the brokers. Cheating and fraud means are prevalent to grab tribal land to construct hotels and resorts for tourism purposes and where these means do not work, pressure and force come in handy. *Benami* (illegal) transactions of tribal land to non-tribal outsiders are very common. As the tribals in this village are very poor and indebtedness among them is high, the pressure from outsiders for tribal land frequently works well. The land alienation processes that functioned and succeeded in Kodiyat-A village are applied and also acting unrelentingly in Kodiyat-B village. That means the outsider non-tribals and the brokers are making inroads in Kodiyat-B village too.

The state of Rajasthan has enacted the 'Rajasthan Tenancy Act, 1955' to preclude the sale of tribal land. As per this act, the sale or transfer of land to non-tribals is prevented, and the act does not allow for subletting or leasing out of tribal land. The act, through section 183 (B), empowers the revenue officers to resolve the issue if there is violation of law on tribal land and also directs to restore the alienated tribal land to the original tribal land owner. The state has also tried to implement PESA regulations and the 'Rajasthan *Panchayat* Act of 1999', which was formulated keeping in mind the PESA provisions. But unfortunately, the act was only passed in 2011. Despite the above laws and provisions to prevent tribal land alienation, the tide of tribal land alienation is still going on and the laws remain in paper only lacking stringent implementation. The reason of such poor implementation is the lack of political and bureaucratic will and the vested interests of the enforcers themselves.

To stop illegal transfers, in 1988, the government of Rajasthan has issued an order to affix photographs of both seller and buyer to the land documents, but the presence of both the buyer and seller in the land registrar's office is even not required. The *patwaris* are part of the nexus with the brokers and there is big business interest in tribal land transfer. The land officials and the revenue staffs have never visited the villages to check the land reality on ground and never tried to stop tribal land alienation process, rather the officials are a party to this as usual land business.

Therefore, the state government, despite all the preventive laws in hand, has failed to arrest tribal land alienation. The Ministry of Rural Development, Government of India (annual report 2007–08) has provided the data that a total number of 2,084 cases of tribal land alienation having 6,615 acres of land were registered in different courts of Rajasthan, however, 1,257 cases were settled by the court, where only 187 cases were settled in favour of Scheduled Tribes and 53 cases having 187 acres of tribal land were rejected by the court.[28]

3.4.8 *Odisha*

The annual report (2007–08), Ministry of Rural Development, Government of India brings out tribal land alienation situation in the state of Odisha. Land alienation in

[28] Annual Report (2007–08), Government of India, Ministry of Rural Development, p. 276. https://rural.nic.in/sites/default/files/anualreport0708_eng.pdf. Accessed 12 November 2019.

the state in general, and Koraput district, in particular, is rampant and widespread. In Narayanpatna and Beherguda village of Koraput district, it is reported that 25% households have lost their land due to NALCO and other projects. In the tribal areas of Koraput district, land alienation through encroachment and indebtedness is most frequent and very common method. Brokers and middleman are playing the vital role in tribal land alienation. These brokers and middleman are providing loan to tribals in exorbitant rate to maintain their basic day-to-day requirements and through these loans they entrap the tribals and get the tribals' land. Beside this, deceitful and fraudulent means and agreements were used by the lawyers, brokers and revenue officers where they all are party, against the desperate, illiterate and credulous tribals.

Tribal land alienation in the state of Odisha is established through the chronicle of inflow of the non-tribal outsiders to the tribal areas which also includes the entry of the *gauntias* (intermediaries between the tribals and the king) to tribal areas throughout the British period, and during the survey and settlement process in tribal areas. The colonial legacy of identifying and reserving tribal land as reserve forest was followed by the post-independence state which further aggravated the land alienation situation in tribal areas of the state. Development projects which require land acquisition add to this history of eviction of the tribals.

In 1963, in Koraput district, to start the Hindustan Aeronautics Limited factory, many tribal communities were displaced and large areas of tribal land were captured. In the above displacement cases, very small amount of compensation was provided and rehabilitation to all victims was not provided. Likewise, the National Aluminium Company (NALCO) has gained huge tribal land which has affected 53 tribal villages. Among these 53 villages, Beheraguda village was most affected due to NALCO project. Rehabilitation to all displaced families was not provided.

In Odisha, there are different laws which prevent alienation of tribal land. For non-Scheduled Areas, the chief legal instrument forbidding alienation of tribal land is the 'Orissa Land reform Act (OLRA) 1960'. For preventing tribal land in Scheduled Areas, there is the provision of 'Orissa Scheduled Areas Transfer of Immovable Property (OSATIP), 1956'. Apart from the permission of the authorities, in any circumstances, both the above laws disallow and forbid the transfer of tribal land to non-tribals. The OLR Act through section 23 and 23(A) directs for the restoration of tribal land, if legal procedure is not followed while transferring. There are other laws which prevent tribal land encroachment. The Orissa Prevention of Land Encroachment Act (OPLEA), 1972 and Orissa Government Land Settlement Act (OGLSA) are the important laws in the state as far as tribal land alienation is concerned. The state of Odisha has also accomplished laws with regard to PESA guidelines and rules.

In spite of various land protection laws, the performance of the state regarding prevention and restoration of alienated tribal land is very poor. There is problem within the law itself. PESA regulations do not cover municipalities in its ambit, and therefore tribal land alienation is rampant in different municipality areas. There is contravenes between OGLS and OSATIP. The OSATIP empowers the *gram sabha* for restoration of alienated tribal land while the OGLS treats the collector as the authority to do so. Other than this, there is nexus and collusion between the brokers and the revenue bureaucrats and the existing laws have not been implemented in its letter and spirit. Powerful vested interests are working there, which have dispossessed the tribals from their land and have denied their land rights.

Land alienation in tribal areas of Odisha is massive and rampant. As per the annual report (2007–08) of the rural Development Ministry, among the total number of 105,491 cases of tribal land alienation which were filled in different courts of Odisha, 104,644 cases were settled where 61,431 cases go in favour of the tribals contributing 56,854 acres of land which were restored to the landless tribals.[29] Due to this continuous tribal land alienation in Odisha, in general, and Koraput district, in particular, the district has witnessed various tribal movements among which the Narayanpatna movement (2009–14) is a unique one.

3.5 Understanding Tribal Land Alienation

The most important factor for land alienation of the tribals is the gradually shrinking economic base of the tribals. The tribals' non-monetised, simple, self-reliant economy collapsed and the tribals turned to cash transactions or barter system for their daily basic need. The tribals' common ownership of land has collapsed, and in that place the private property or the concept of *patta* land came which extinguished their free access to land and forest. The modern credit system, markets and settled agriculture render the tribal more vulnerable and dependant to outsider non-tribals. Non-availability of production and emerging food insecurity led the poor tribals in inveterate indebtedness. In this situation, the tribals became more dependent on non-tribal shylocks who ask exorbitant rates of interest which kept the tribals in an unceasing and perpetual debt trap. This continuous and chronic debt forces the tribals to mortgage their piece of land and ultimately loss of that land to the non-tribal moneylenders. Hence, indebtedness is the central factor of tribal land alienation.

The decrease of forestland and tribals' confined access to natural resources and common property impelled the tribals to depend on outside markets to get the items of daily requirement, i.e. food, livelihoods, materials for house construction like can, bamboo, etc. Indebtedness also occurs owing to social and religious responsibilities. Spending on medical treatment, litigation and alcoholism has farther accented the trouble of indebtedness leading to tribal land alienation. In addition to that, industrialisation and urbanisation have opened the tribal areas to outsider non-tribals who have grabbed the tribal land. In this regard, a report submits that all these factors with penetration of market forces in tribal areas were threatening to dispose the tribals off their land resources in large scale through land alienation and development-induced displacement.[30]

[29] Annual Report (2007–08), Government of India, Ministry of Rural Development, p. 276. https://rural.nic.in/sites/default/files/anualreport0708_eng.pdf. Accessed 12 November 2019.

[30] *Report of the High Level Committee on socio-economic, health and educational status of tribal communities of India* (May 2014). Ministry of Tribal Affairs Government

There are different reasons through which the tribals have lost their land. These include loss of land through mortgaging, loss of land through private transactions (with or without consent from the concerned authorities), tribal land loss due to *benami* (illegal) transactions, through adoption of non-tribals by tribals, land in the name of tribal spouses, long-term lease of land to non-tribals, land gifts by tribals to non-tribals, etc. Other factors of tribal land alienation include oral transfers of tribal land, especially occupancy of tribal land through impelling force. There is numbness, indifference and callous attitude of the revenue officers and administration in addressing tribal land problems. The tribals are also incognisant of the laws and legal procedures regarding land and are less organised. More than 85% of the tribals did not know that there were laws against transfer of tribal land.[31] For the resolution of this problem, the present study has proposed to plug the loopholes of the laws and advised for rigorous enforcement and continuous monitoring of the existing land protection laws. It further suggests to allow legal assistance to the victims and generating awareness among the tribals regarding tribal rights on land and the existing legal procedure to prevent tribal land alienation.

3.6 Conclusion

The above discussion on the nature and extent of tribal land alienation exposes the complex and composite matrices of laws, policies and local circumstances which compose the issue of tribal land alienation. In policy formulation, tribal land problems have been conceived by the plain lens of *patta* land alienation, but it depicts a partial picture. It is axiomatic that estrangement of *patta* land (legally own land by the tribals) by the outsider non-tribals through sale and mortgages is enormously severe. Throughout the history, *patta* land alienation has been the most vital way for the tribals where they have lost best quality of farming land. But, there are other modes of land alienation where the state through its developmental policies and forest reserve policies has displaced the tribals from their habitat making them landless. There are provisions of rigid laws that prohibit the tribal land transfer to non-tribals and provide for the recovery of the already illicitly transferred tribal land. The major intercession in this respect would be assuring proper effectuation of these already existing laws. The PESA act, which is a landmark in protecting tribal rights on land, must be expanded to municipality areas.

Due to faulty settlement and survey processes, and the declaration of forests by the government in tribal land, the tribals have been deprived from their traditional customary land and were treated as encroachers in their own land due to non-recognition of such land in the name of the tribals. In other cases, the customary and common ownership land of the tribals and land above 10 degree slopes in hilly

of India. http://www.indiaenvironmentportal.org.in/files/file/Tribal%20Committee%20Report,%20May-June%202014.pdf. Accessed 22 February 2019.

[31] ibid.

areas which are actually cultivated by the tribals have never been recognised in the name of the concerned tribals and these lands were diverted by the government for forest and plantation purposes. Though in some areas, the tribals are still farming these lands, but can't invest on such land and can't get formal credit against these lands owing to insecurity of tenure, non-recognition of rights and lack of *patta* (legal document). Now, different state governments are carrying plantation activities on such land. Due to lack of secure rights of the tribals on these customary lands, the state can displace the tribal from such land very easily at any time without providing any recompense. In the past, thousands of tribals have been forced out in this way owing to the making of industries, construction of dams, wildlife sanctuaries and other development projects. Displacement brings a desolating effect on tribals' life, on their psyche, as they are culturally attached to their land and clans. The tribals find it very difficult to adjust in a new environment and circumstances after displacement. It should be mentioned here that the resettlement and rehabilitation measures are disconsolate, and in most situation, tribals never get a piece of land against their displacement.

The tribal situation in our country is very precarious and was treated with utter disdain. The present plight and condition of the tribals remain due to various reasons. In India, the upper caste Hindu society which held the rein of power in the state has always treated the tribal communities with disrespect and scorn attitude. Evolutionism and negative stereotypes about tribal from the colonial era has merged with the Indian elite's ideas of 'assimilations' to produce a disdain for tribal culture that is almost universal among the non-tribals who live near tribals and have power over them. This disdain and contempt are manifested in dominant discussions regarding the tribals where shifting cultivation is treated as evil and pernicious, tribals are represented as culturally and socially backward, feebleminded, jungli, barbarous, etc. Any discussion with local officials or local non-tribal elite will bring out these biases that tribals are superstitious, dirty, backward, ignorant, loose morals, addicted to drinking, etc.[32] But in reality, these impeccant people are the best and honest, they are innocent, simple and straightforward people and they need to be saved and their unique and extinct culture needs to be conserved. Even when the culture of tribals is admitted to be special, it is sought to be captured in museums and monographs as show pieces.

Unfortunately, ameliorating the Scheduled Tribes' accession to the natural resources including the land is not a component of the discourse on development. Although, in the name of tribal development programme, the government is spending millions of rupees, there is lack of political and bureaucratic will for the actual development of the tribals and there is no empathy on the part of the rest of the society towards tribals' plight. This simple incertitude is concerning the very relevancy of the government's tribal development programmes.

---

[32]*Baseline Report on Restoration of Land to the Allottees of Ceiling Surplus and Government Wasteland* (November, 2006). Study undertaken by RCDC with support from NIRD, Hyderabad in Koraput District of Orissa.

References

Annual Report (2007–2008), *Government of India, Ministry of Rural Development*, pp. 1–291. https://rural.nic.in/sites/default/files/anualreport0708_eng.pdf. Accessed 12 November, 2019.

Baseline Report on Restoration of Land to the Allottees of Ceiling Surplus and Government Wasteland (November, 2006). Study undertaken by RCDC with support from NIRD, Hyderabad in Koraput district of Orissa.

Behura, N. K. (1982). Forest and tribal world view. *Journal of Social Research, XXV* (1), pp. 1–8.

Draft National Land Reform Policy (2013). Department of Land Resources, Ministry of Rural Development, Government of India, 24th July. https://www.slideshare.net/fundsforngos/draft-national-landreformspolicyjuly2013. Accessed 23 February, 2019.

Government fails to stop grabbing of tribal land (2008). *The Sentinel,* 13 September, p. 10. https://www.sentinelassam.com. Accessed 12 February, 2019.

http://rajbhavan-maharashtra.gov.in/rajbhavan/pdf/20_Act.pdf. Accessed 12 November, 2019.

Kumar, K. et al. (2005). *Scheduled tribes' land in Odisha: A socio-economic and legal study.* Bhubaneswar: Supported By World Bank, Washington. https://www.researchgate.net/publication/232062518_A_socioeconomic_and_legal_study_of_scheduled_tribes'_land_in_Orissa. Accessed 30 October, 2019.

Mohanty, B. B. (2001). Land distribution among scheduled castes and tribes. *Economic and Political Weekly, 36*(40), October 6–12, pp. 3857–3868.

Philip, Veigas. (1991). *Encroached and enslaved: Alienation of adivasi land and its dynamics.* New Delhi: Indian Social Institute.

Pradhan, G & Behera. S. (2007). *Position paper on land right issues in Orissa.*

Report of the Expert Group on Prevention of Alienation of Tribal Land and its Restoration (2006). Ministry of Rural Development.

Report of the High Level Committee on socio-economic, health and educational status of tribal communities of India, (May 2014). Ministry of Tribal Affairs Government of India. http://www.indiaenvironmentportal.org.in/files/file/Tribal%20Committee%20Report,%20May-June%202014.pdf. Accessed 22 February, 2019.

The Hindustan Times (Daily English Newspaper) (2007). 22 October, p. 8.

The State of India's Indigenous and Tribal People (2009). *Asian Indigenous & Tribal Peoples Network*, 31st March.

The Times of India (Daily English Newspaper, Hyderabad Edition) (2008). 3 September, p. 6.

Tribal land encroached by people of suspected nationalities (2008). *The Sentinel*, 6 May. http://www.indiaenvironmentportal.org.in/content/245398/tribal-land-encroached-by-people-of-suspected-nationalities/?page. Accessed 22 January, 2019.

Chapter 4
Land Alienation and the Politics of Tribal Exploitation in Odisha

4.1 Introduction

Land is the base for apprehending tribal people's identity, culture, religious ethos and personhood, because the peculiarity and uniqueness of tribal culture and tradition lies in the centrality of land to which the tribals are emotionally and culturally attached (Behura 1982: 1). They identified them as an inherent part of the land and not isolated from it. Tribals' religious activity revolves around land and land is comprehended as consecrated and like god. It is the land that owns people and gives them an identity and is the temple through which the tribal people become one with the Supreme Being, the spirits, their ancestors and other segments of the creation (ibid.: 2). Tribals' whole religious life are deeply rooted and centred on land. The tribal rituals, religious practices, festivals, ceremonies, dances are all associated with the concept of land. It is the soil, with which all patterns of tribal economic, social and religious activities are connected. Apprehending the concept of land in tribal situation allows an ethical basis of caring, sharing and a sense of responsibility. As per the tribal world view and perspective, land cannot be marketed or commercialised; instead it should be protected and preserved for the succeeding generations. It must be apportioned among all the denizens. According to tribal perspective, land should not be exploited, because it's the space that provides identity to the tribals. Beyond land, there is no separate identity and personhood of the tribal communities. The tribal land accommodates not only the village, clan and tribe as one, but it also unites them with the ancestors, spirits, Supreme Being and creation as one family (ibid.: 3). Therefore, land for the tribals is considered as mother. There are myths regarding most of the tribes that they are born from soil and earth or their descendants were originated from a big hole or stone of the earth. Hence, the tribals' sense of space, history and time revolves around the concept of land. When that land of the tribal is alienated or encroached; it seems to be loss of everything, i.e. their identity, culture, self, economy and freedom.

The tribal societies and its cultural and social existence are grounded on land, forest and mountains. The tribals inhabit in forested, mountainous regions of central

S. K. Malik, *Land Alienation and Politics of Tribal Exploitation in India*,
https://doi.org/10.1007/978-981-15-5382-0_4

India and forested upland of north-east India. The report of the expert group on prevention of alienation of tribal land, Ministry of Rural Development, Government of India has provided the following demographic data about the tribals.

> The Central Indian tribal homeland, located between 18 and 25° north of the equator across the Indian subcontinent, operationally cover nearly 100 districts in eight states of the country stretching from Banswara (Rajasthan) in the west to Purulia (West Bengal) in the east. These districts together accounts for about 55 million tribal people (roughly 70% of India's tribal population) spread over 68 million hectares of geographic area.[1]

The British has found the issue of alienation of tribal land as a significant administrative and political problem which leads to rebellion and unrest among tribal areas. Therefore to check tribal unrest and rebellion on the issue of alienation of land, the colonial government has enacted different laws and policies to protect tribal rights over land. Through Schedule V and Schedule VI of the Indian Constitution, protection of land rights of the tribal was guaranteed by the post-independence state. Despite of Constitutional protection, tribal land alienation in the country in different forms is happening. Legally, tribal land estrangement is understood as loss of private or *patta* land. Legally alienated tribal land is one among the various ways through which tribal land alienation occurs. This view doesn't accommodate and capture the collective and communal possession system traditionally practiced by many tribal groups. Other than alienation of private land, there is diversion of land by the state for various purposes which reduces tribal access to land are provided in the following paragraph.

> Except for north-east India, communal or corporate ownership of land was not formalised through the land and forest administration systems introduced by the British and further extended by the post-colonial Indian state. Loss of access to land and forests classified as state-owned and diverted for various purposes have rarely figured in the official discourse of tribal land alienation. However, review of literature dealing with poverty and livelihoods among tribal communities clearly bring out that apart from alienation of private land, diversion of land for different purposes by the state has also played an important role in reducing tribal access to land.[2]

The state facilitated diversions of tribal land include acquiring tribal land for developmental projects, encroachment, large scale plantation programmes, notification of forests, etc. Therefore, apprehending restraints on tribal accession to land too asks for taking into account the above process in addition to legal or *patta* land alienation.

At present, the threat has become more compounded than ever, due to the onslaught of industrialisation, urbanisation, commercialisation and infrastructural development. In the case of India's developmental model, displacement caused by large projects has actually resulted in a transfer of resources from the weaker sections of the

[1] *Report of the Expert Group on Prevention of Alienation of Tribal Land and its Restoration* (2006). Ministry of Rural Development. http://www.sakti.in/108-land-rights/tribal-alnd-rights/430-report-of-the-expert-group-on-prevention-of-alienation-of-tribal-land-and-its-restoration. Accessed 10 December, 2019.

[2] ibid.

society to more privileged ones (Pradhan and Behera 2007: 6). Due to these development projects, tribals are displaced from their natural habitats and are being sacrificed for the larger interest of the country. It can be said that, the tribals are compelled to accept the huge burden of development. The traditional mode of securing their livelihood is seriously threatened without any appropriate alternatives in sight. Regarding land question, tribals in the country in general, and Odisha in particular, are the biggest sufferers. Earlier, these tribal communities were not landless labourers and they have self-sufficient land in their hand. At present, the existence of landless category among the tribals is a clear gesture of land alienation. This process of tribal land dispossession has acquired impulse through various sources and patterns. As Viegas has mentioned, the dynamics of the process of dispossession involves an intricate of cultural, social, political and economic forces (Veigas 1991: 77).

With this background, the present chapter deals with the violation of land rights of the tribals and major issues related to loss of tribal access to land. The chapter examines different aspects and forms of tribal land alienation in Odisha. The chapter also discusses Odisha government's policy target on land and its critical appraisal. The final section of the chapter offers some policy suggestions as far as tribal land alienation and exploitation in the state of Odisha is concerned.

4.2 Violation of Land Rights

Tribal land alienation has a long history and is not due to the consequence of the present circumstances. Deprivation of tribals from their land has started with the colonial state's notification of reserve forests. The question of land is not just the result of the existing situation, its origin may be traced to the periods of deprivation of tribal land or to periods of the withdrawal of their rights to exploit forests. Owing to different alterations inside and outside the structure of the tribal systems, systematically and gradually the privileged sections of the society coerced the tribal communities to become landless labourers or to move back to nearby forests. Basically, traders, shylocks, rich peasants, feudal lords and the outsider non-tribals have oppressed and exploited the tribals. It can be safely said that tribal land has been alienated on a large scale, and in most of the cases, the land grabbers are invariably the non-tribals. This situation has farther been exacerbated with the egression of new forces of production. The National Commission on Backward-Area Development (1980) categorically stated that, many major irrigation projects were located in the tribal areas resulting in the submergence of extensive land belonging to the tribals.[3] Also, due to stripping of forests, the tribals are alienated from forests and woodland. The tribal land alienation process, owing to denudation of forests has farther broadened the

[3] *Report of the Expert Group on Prevention of Alienation of Tribal Land and its Restoration* (2006). Ministry of Rural Development. http://www.sakti.in/108-land-rights/tribal-alnd-rights/430-report-of-the-expert-group-on-prevention-of-alienation-of-tribal-land-and-its-restoration. Accessed 10 December, 2019.

breach between the landed non-tribal segments and the landless tribal communities. In 1969, the committee on plan projects (Planning Commission) remarking on the issues of tribal land alienation have submitted an account where the committee noted that,

> Tribal land in many areas passed into the hands of non-tribals, despite the legal prohibitions against such transfers. Sample studies in Andhra Pradesh, Odisha and some other states have shown that tribal land transfers have taken place on large scale without the permission of the collector or other competent authorities as required by law.[4]

The moneylenders and other privileged sections of the society have exploited the loopholes and ambiguities in the already existing laws and have circumvented the legal provisos by entering into clandestine and *benami* (illegal) transactions with the native tribals. The powerlessness and impotence of the legal provisions to check this developing menace and the lack of rigorous implementation of the already existing laws are the root cause for the alienation of tribal land.

4.3 Major Issues Related to Loss of Tribal Access to Land in the State of Odisha

Land and forest are necessary for tribals' livelihoods and survival. But tribals of Odisha have lost accession to forest and land through large number of processes. These processes are not only limited to alienation of *patta* land or legally owned land by sale or debt mortgaging, but also alienation of land by displacement, reservation of forests, non-recognition of customary and shifting cultivation land, faulty survey and settlement and unimplemented and unsuitable land laws etc. All these processes, over a period of time, have forced the marginal and impoverished tribal communities to loss of access or control over the sustenance support system which is vital for their existence. The entry of non-tribals to tribal areas, especially, in the last two centuries, has forced the tribals to the underneath of the power structure even in the areas where the tribals are in majority. The tribals' condition are more unhappy and execrable in the areas where they are in minorities. Alienation of tribal land and lack of ownership are the major factors and basic causes behind the current position of the tribals including tribal agitation.[5]

Throughout history, both the British and princely rulers favoured to ensconce tribal land with the outsider non-tribals. Earlier, the tribals were acted as the *gaontias* (intermediary tenure holders responsible for rent collection), but tardily, they were substituted by non-tribals in many tribal regions. For example, in the early 1800s, most *gaontias* in the Gangapur princely state of Odisha were tribals, but by 1890s, there was a greater penchant for non-tribal *gaontias* from *Teli* and *Agharis* castes.

---

[4] *The State of India's Indigenous and Tribal People* (2009). Asian Indigenous & Tribal Peoples Network, 31st March. http://www.aitpn.org/publications/the-state-of-indias-indigenous-and-tribal-peoples-2009/. Accessed 14 September 2019.

[5] ibid.

The British and the princely state rulers have actively facilitated and encouraged the inflow of non-tribal outsiders into tribal regions and resistance of the tribals to this inflow was subdued by force. The creation of non-tribal intermediary tenure holders or *gaontias* who had effective control over the administration in that area has accelerated the process of tribal land alienation. These *gaontias* have acquired large amount of tribal land through various illegal means due to their proximity to the revenue officials and administration. At the same time, the raising value of forest based revenues led the princely state and the British rulers to notify or reserve more and more areas as forests under various forest rules and laws, enforcing confinements on the tribals to use the forests and forest based resources.

Confinements on shifting cultivation (slash and burn cultivation) by the tribals on areas notified as forests were the major strategy of the colonial and post-colonial state for enhancing the market value of these tribal lands. The state has never recognised these customary lands in the name of the tribals and was declared and notified as reserve forests restricting the tribals' entry and use of such land. Many tribals had practiced the clan and lineage territory system since generations. But, lineage and clan-based territories were not settled with the tribals during the survey and settlement process. Without proper survey and settlement, frequently, forest notifications were carried out in tribal areas and permanent cultivation land of the tribals was declared as reserve forest land. Earlier, the tribals were carrying out cultivation in hill land above 10° slope. But, in the survey and settlement operations, land above 10° slope was not surveyed and was not settled with the tribals. Hence, the tribal communities have lost huge amount of land mainly in two ways. Firstly, in the colonial period, the paddy land and the lowland which were under the private ownership of the tribals were lost owing to the inflow of non-tribals and *gaontias* in tribal areas. Secondly, the tribals became dispossession of their swidden land on account of the forest notification or notification as government land. These processes were aided by the expansion of state and markets into the tribal areas and these trends have continued even after independence.[6]

4.4 Forms of Tribal Land Alienation

There are various forms of land alienation occur in tribal areas of Odisha. Different types of tribal land alienation are provided in the following points.

- Manipulation of land records is the first kind of tribal land alienation. The problem of tribal land alienation happens owing to inadequate state of land records. Land which was traditionally cultivated by the tribals was never legally settled and recognised with their names.

[6]*The State of India's Indigenous and Tribal People* (2009). Asian Indigenous & Tribal Peoples Network, 31st March. http://www.aitpn.org/publications/the-state-of-indias-indigenous-and-tribal-peoples-2009/. Accessed 14 September 2019.

- *Benami* or illegal transfers of tribal land is considered as the second type of land alienation in tribal areas. The Union Home Ministry in its study report (May 1975) indicated that, large scale tribal land were handed over to non-tribals by conniving civil proceedings, *benami* and illegal transfers in which land remains in the name of the original owners who are reduced to the level of sharecropper.[7]
- Mortgaging and leasing of tribal land is some other type of land alienation. To meet the basic needs and daily requirements, the tribals have to mortgage or lease their fertile land to the rich farmers and to the moneylenders.
- Intrusion or encroachment is another way of alienating the tribal land. Where there is lack of proper records, the new entrants (non-tribal outsiders) find it an opportunity to grab the tribal land. In these cases, the non-tribals provide bribe to the local *patwaris* for fudging the date of settlement of land disputes and manipulating land records.
- Material alliance with tribal or concubinage of tribal woman is the other way to outfox the tribals and to seize tribal land without any price.
- Sometimes, the tribal families also adopt the non-tribals, which easily transfers tribal land to the hands of non-tribals.
- Lethargy and slackness in the effectuation of the already existing preventive laws to protect tribal land urge the outsider non-tribals to invade the tribal land.
- Other than these *patta* or private land alienation, the state in various ways has also facilitated tribal land alienation through its forest reservation policy, developmental projects, building dams, national parks and sanctuaries.

This increasing and alarming trend of land alienation has threatened the life and livelihood of the tribals. In this connection, without understanding the class connection and state's involvement, it is being unfortunate to interpret and remark that the problem is due to the traders, moneylenders, landlords, etc. The post-independence state has more or less followed the colonial legacy where the irregular land records of the colonial periods were adopted by the present state. Though laws were enacted by the post-independence state to protect tribal land, but these laws remained full of loopholes and ambiguities and the outsider non-tribals have used these for their benefits. This equivocal and ambiguous character of the state and its land policy remained as one aspect of these contradictions which indirectly have encouraged tribal land alienation.

There is a long history of non-tribals' move into tribal areas and it is not simply the intrusion of the non-tribals, instead, the state has backed the outsider non-tribals to ensconce in the tribal land. Due to the outsiders' encroachment in tribal land, the tribals are now deprived from the natural resources and land to which they were owners earlier. From their earlier self-reliant status, the tribals were relegated and reduced to the level of sharecroppers and dependent one. The state legislations also turned out damaging for the tribal interest. Hence, to realise the root causes of

[7] *The State of India's Indigenous and Tribal People* (2009). Asian Indigenous & Tribal Peoples Network, 31st March. http://www.aitpn.org/publications/the-state-of-indias-indigenous-and-tribal-peoples-2009/. Accessed 14 September 2019.

tribal land estrangement, its interrelations with the altering conditions and the social-economic construction should be properly understood. There are different forms of land alienation which happen in tribal areas. The types and nature of tribal land alienation in different tribal areas of Odisha were discussed below.

4.4.1 Patta *Land Alienation*

In the tribal districts of the state, 3/4th of the land is owned by the state and the rest 25% of land settled with the landholders within which 64% of the land belongs to tribals.[8] The average land holding of tribal households in the tribal districts is only 1.06 standard acres, with approximately 20% of households being landless and 65% being small and marginal farmers.[9] Through different processes of land alienation, even this small piece of land is being lost. Landlessness in tribal areas is broadly of three types: (i) Loss of land through survey and settlements; (ii) Loss of land through private transactions and (ii) Land alienation through displacement. In more specific way, the process can be separated under the following headings:

- Mortgaging of private or *patta* land by the tribals.
- Sale of tribal land after permission from the concerned authority.
- Sale of tribal land through *benami* (illegal) transactions.
- Tribal land alienation by outsider non-tribals through encroachment.
- Alienation of tribal land before survey and settlements.
- Loss of tribal land due to unsurveyed areas.
- Encroachment land eligible for regularising but not regularised.
- Forest land, where exhaustive survey and settlement have not taken place.
- Shifting cultivation (burn and slash cultivation) land of the tribal notified and categorised as reserve forests.
- Private and *patta* land alienation by way of land acquisition.

4.4.2 Policies Considering Shifting Cultivation on Revenue Land

As per Behuria's report, the tribals of Koraput, who were practicing shifting cultivations for less than continuous 12 years are not recognised as '*ryot*' (landholders under the *ryotwari* system). The report was provided in the following paragraph.

> In undivided Koraput, during the first survey and settlements (1938–1964), the board of revenue ruled that since shifting cultivators are not in continuous possession of land for

---

[8] *The State of India's Indigenous and Tribal People* (2009). Asian Indigenous & Tribal Peoples Network, 31st March. http://www.aitpn.org/publications/the-state-of-indias-indigenous-and-tribal-peoples-2009/. Accessed 14 September 2019.

[9] ibid.

12 years, they can't be treated as *ryots* as per Madras Estate Land Act, 1908, and therefore these land were not to be settled in their names (Behuria 1965).

As per the board of revenue rule, the earlier shifting cultivation land of the tribals was passed to the exclusive ownership of forest department or revenue department. Thus, the approach was to convert shifting cultivation land to state land wherever possible by using the pre-independence land tenure system. The manoeuvres and tactics of considering the shifting cultivation land of the tribals as 'non-continuous cultivation' were applied to deprive the tribal under the prevailing laws such as 'Madras Estate Land Act' (MELA), 1908 (as in Koraput district) which provided *ryoti* rights only to continuous possession of land for twelve years. This decision denied the rights over land that the tribals had cultivated for generations which have had far-reaching impact on tribal economy and welfare. The tribal communities like *Kutia Kondhs* and the *Juangs,* who were practicing communal tenure land ownership system on their swidden land were settled as government land. With this decision and settlement, the Primitive Tribal Groups (PTGs) were mostly suffered which leads towards displacement from their land. In the similar manner, none of the shifting cultivation areas were settled with the *Kondhs*, and in the records of rights, all these lands were demarcated as *Abad Ajogya Anabadi (*AAA) or state-owned wasteland.

Traditionally, in hilly areas, the tribals have cultivated land above 30° slope, however, none of the land on the higher slopes (land above 10° slope) was settled with them where the villagers continued to cultivate them. The government converted acres of terraced land into plantation land under various government programmes. Land claim customarily by the tribals has been converted to cashew plantations leased out to a government corporation. In consequences, on this plantations or land, the tribals have no rights. Plantations were also carried out in the forest areas and shifting cultivation land of the tribals under the forest department.

The approach of the state is to refuse tribals' rights over shifting cultivation land, so that, the practice dies out on its own. Shifting cultivation on revenue land was treated as an encroachment, and cases were filed against the tribal cultivators. In most of the cases, the tribals are treated as encroachers because most of the tribals cultivate the land demarcated as 'objectionable land' (land not entitled for issue of *ryoti* or peasant right as per law) and these land were not settled under the provisos either OLR, 1960, OGSL, 1962 or OPLE, 1972.[10] To wean away the tribals from their shifting cultivation land, different measures and steps were taken up. These measures include allotment of agricultural land, providing land for settled cultivation, establishment of tribal colonies, etc. But these positive steps and measures could not alter the tribals' condition in a significant way.

In the state of Odisha, during the 1960s and 1970s, large areas of shifting cultivation were planted with cashew and sisal. Most of these cashew plantations on revenue land to the extent of 36,000 ha were leased out to Cashew Development

[10] *Baseline Report on Restoration of Land to the Allottees of Ceiling Surplus and Government Wasteland* (November, 2006). Study undertaken in Koraput district of Odisha by RCDC with support from NIRD, Hyderabad.

Corporation ltd. on an annual basis (Kumar et al. 2005: 50). In 1980, the Government of Odisha (GOO) initiated the programme of Economic Rehabilitation of Rural Poor (ERRP), which provided for 'use rights' to rural poor on plantations on state-owned land (ibid.). Hill land with shrub and generally the shifting cultivation areas beneath fallow cycle was adopted for plantations, mostly horticulture, through ERRP programme. The Tahasildar could confer *usufructuary* rights to the eligible beneficiaries in respect of plantations of various categories (ibid.). But, only collection of deadwood was allowed to the beneficiaries and the beneficiaries are not allowed to cut any tree where the right over the land was to rest with the state. With the permission from the Tahasildar, the *usufruct* right which is heritable can be transferred in favour of similar beneficiaries. Another initiative taken by the Government of Odisha for shifting cultivation areas was the allotment for plantation to *podu* (burn and slash) *c*ultivators in the *podu*-affected government land, vide circular No. GE (GL)-S-69/79-3755/Rev, Revenue Department, Government of Odisha, dated 18 January 1980.[11] The scheme envisaged plantation of commercial fruits like tamarind, mango, orange, guava, jackfruit, etc. by the *podu* cultivator with a bulk of investment on plantations. The scheme was implemented by horticulture department with finance from department of tribal welfare (Kumar et al. 2005: 50).

Under this approach, separate schemes by the government of Odisha under circular No. GE (GL)-S-/81-37565/REV came out. This notification laid down the provision of usufructuary rights on plantations taken up under the programme on government land (except reserved forests).[12] Under the scheme, usufructuary rights were being given to each beneficiary, for different plantation crops like sisal, cashew, coffee, mulberry and tussar. Usufructuary rights on plantations are conferred at the rate of three acres, two acres and one acres, half acres, respectively, only when they yield reasonable income after proper development by the concerned department. Measures against shifting cultivation for *podu*-affected government land were given by conferring of *usufruct* rights on temporary basis as per Government of Odisha, Revenue Department Letter No. GE (GL)-S-69/79-3755/Rev, dated 18 January 1980 as prepared for *podu* cultivators of each village or a group of village.[13] In the last year or last two years of *podu* cycle, only *podu*-affected government land in actual occupation of the *podu* cultivators was selected. The cultivators were to be given usufructuary rights of trees and intercrops raised only. These rights are heritable, but not alienable by the right holder. The same cultivator was authorised to take up plantation from year to year over a different piece of land which are in last year or last two years of *podu* cycle subject to a condition that the total area under these plantations along with any other land he/she may be having shall not exceed the ceiling limit permissible for him/her under Odisha Land Reforms Act, 1960.[14]

---

[11]*Baseline Report on Restoration of Land to the Allottees of Ceiling Surplus and Government Wasteland* (November, 2006). Study undertaken in Koraput district of Odisha by RCDC with support from NIRD, Hyderabad.

[12]ibid.

[13]ibid.

[14]ibid.

The Odisha government for the first time has accepted that there is a need to fix and settle upland and hill slopes with the tribals and has issued a decree that accorded for settlement of hill land up to 10° slope with the tribals and decided to provide *usufructuary* or user rights beyond 10° slope. Sometimes, there was contravenes over the ownership of this land, because, often the land traditionally belong to one household and settled with another household. The Kashipur order was extended to all tribal areas of the state vide Government of Odisha letter No. 14643-R-S-60/2000 dated 23 March 2000 which has allowed for settlement of land up to 30° slope with tribal shifting cultivators (Kumar et al. 2005: 51). This is a new strategy and a major policy initiative which has the potentiality to change tribal landownership system in shifting cultivation land in hilly areas.

> The International Fund for Agriculture Development (IFAD) sponsored the 'Odisha Tribal Development Project (1988–97)' which funded for 4,000 local non-tribal households and 12,500 tribal families of Kashipur block in Rayagda district. During the project, record of rights for *dongar* (hill land under burn & slash cultivation) or shifting cultivation were issued in 236 villages covering a total area of 17,175 acres where tribal households were benefitted (Kumar et al. 2005: 51).

However, the actual implementation of this circular has been very tardy, mainly due to lack of political and administrative will and the problems in surveying the hill slope. The Odisha Tribal Empowerment and Livelihood Project (OTELP) funded by International Fund for Agriculture Development (IFAD) and Department for International Development (DFID), have been initiated in 30 tribal blocks of Odisha and implemented on watershed basis (Kumar et al. 2005: 51). As per the above circular, the main element of this project is to facilitate settling of land with the tribals. However, till date, these processes have not been fully operationalised in the project (ibid.).

4.4.3 Unsurvey Areas of Tribal Land

As per the Board of Revenue (BOR) estimate,

> Approximately 640,702 acres of land in Odisha have not been covered by survey and settlement process and most of these are remote hilly areas inhabited by tribals, including Primitive Tribe Groups (PTGs). Thus, there has been no settlement of rights in these areas at all (Kumar et al. 2005: 51).

In undivided Koraput district, the survey and settlement process left out vast stretches of land which includes land above 10° slope, the protected and reserve land. The areas in Koraput which were left unsurveyed and unsettled during the survey and settlement period of 1938–1964, actually works out to almost half of the total area of the undivided Koraput district (ibid.: 52). Later, surveys were taken up in some areas, but due to lack of settlement of rights, legal rights were denied. The areas in Koraput which were left unsurveyed and unsettled are especially categorised as forests, identified as government land which has not been surveyed and rights were not been settled in favour of the tribal communal cultivators.

4.4.4 Land Under Permanent Cultivation Was not Settled with the Tribals

It was found that even permanent land cultivated by the tribals was not settled with their name in many tribal areas, owing to various reasons. Often this occurred, because the land is categorised as forests. In other cases, even land on lower slopes was settled as government land. In distant and remote areas, it is found that tribals have lost their land because many of them were frightened and did not approach the settlement and survey persons as they thought that the revenue on their cultivated land would be high (Kumar et al. 2005: 52). In between 1938–1964, the survey and settlement in Koraput district were carried out. In undivided Koraput district, out of a total area of 25320.96 km^2, the survey and settlement covered 17254.40 km^2, and the areas which were excluded on different grounds were provided below.

(i) All reserved and protected land (ii) Forests proposed for reservation in 239 villages of Mathili and Malkangiri (iii) Police station areas of Malkangiri subdivision (iv) Thickly forested tracks in 1763 villages in Gunupur tahasils with Narayanpatna, Pattangi, Padwa, Laxmipur, Gumma, Kakirigumma and Dasamanthpur areas. (v) Bonda Hills and Kondakamberu areas (vi) All land above 10° slope (Behuria 1965).

So, a total area of 5289.40 km^2 was left unsurveyed and identified as 'uncultivable wasteland' (called *Abad Ajogya Anabadi*, in Odia language), most of which were used for shifting cultivation by the tribals of Koraput (Behuria 1965). It also identified that many of these plots were settled as government land at the time of settlement, because these land had bushy growth on them. Often, permanently cultivated land was identified as government land and was not regularised in the name of the tribals during the survey and settlement process. Tribal also makes allegations that settlement officers ask for bribes for settling such land in their names. However, from that period, the protected and reserved land have never experienced any exhaustive survey and settlement by the administration in the district.

4.4.5 Debt Mortgages: The Prime Factor For Tribal Land Alienation

In Odisha, most of the literature concerning tribal land alienation focalise on loss of private or *patta* land by way of sale, lease or mortgage. In tribal areas, the most significant way of alienation of tribal land is mortgaging. The main condition of land mortgaging is that the persons who lend the money cultivate the land till the money is returned. In all the cases, legally and privately owned land was preferred for mortgages. Even within *patta* land, paddy land (valley bottom land irrigated by stream flow) mortgaged most often, consisting of 57% of mortgage transactions respectively. Viegas' study in four district of Orissa found that Scheduled Tribes had lost almost 56% of their private land, out of which 40% was lost through debts and mortgages and rest 16% through personal sales (Viegas 1991). S.N. Dash in his study on Koraput district (18 villages) found that, in these villages, the tribals have lost 13.72% of land during the period of 1990–94, where out of these lost land, 51% was lost through sale after permission from the competent authorites, 26% through mortgages and 15% byoral transfer (Dash 2001).

Money lending to the Scheduled Tribes is regulated under Odisha (Scheduled Areas) Money Lenders' Regulation Act 1967. The regulation was amended in 2001. As per the amended regulations, prior recommendation by the *gram panchayat* in consultation with the *gram sabha* (general body of the *gram panchayat*) is mandatory before a Scheduled Tribe can be advanced for taking loans by mortgaging land with any moneylender within Scheduled Area.[15] Without prior permission from the *gram panchayat,* the borrower is not liable to return the money or interests on it. However, money lending is mostly an informal activity in tribal areas, and oral transactions are common. In such a situation, the above amendment is unable to achieve much and remains on paper. Mortgaging of Scheduled Tribe's land was also prevented by "Orissa Scheduled Areas Transfer of Immovable Property (OSATIP) Regulation, 1956". As evident from existing literature, informal mortgaging where lender cultivates the land is common. At the same time, it is very difficult for the Scheduled Tribes to receive loans from banks, since they can't mortgage their land to the bank. Now, a committee constituted by the Government of Odisha has suggested that the OSATIP Regulation, 1956, be amended to allow mortgaging of land to banks and other financial institutions for loans.[16]

Improving access to resources and generating income among the tribals should be given priority as an alternative solution to mortgaging land for loan. This needs to be supplemented by monitoring of land mortgaging at local level, and prompt legal action under the law when such mortgages are detected. The thrust on Self Help Groups (SHGs) under various government and non-government programmes has been an important step forward towards improving credit access to tribals. The SHGs through local development programmes have generated wage incomes for tribals and have checked the debt mortgage of tribal land. So, it needs further research, in order to understand the positive and increasing role of SHGs on tribal land alienation process.

4.4.6 Loss of Tribal Land in Scheduled Areas Before 1956

In the Scheduled Areas of the state, the 'Odisha Scheduled Areas Transfer of Immovable Property' (OSATIP) was implemented in 1956, and in the non-Scheduled Areas, the 'Odisha Land Reforms Act' (OLRA), 1960 came into force in 1965.[17] Prior to these laws, there were different laws existed in different parts of the state to protect

[15] *Ama Jami* (my land), *Society for Promoting Rural Education and Development* (SPREAD) Report, Koraput. https://spread.org.in. Accessed 22 November 2019.

[16] ibid.

[17] *Ama Jami* (my land), *Society for Promoting Rural Education and Development* (SPREAD) Report, Koraput. https://spread.org.in. Accessed 22 November 2019.

the tribal land. These already existing laws were almost full of ambiguities and failed to check the transfer of tribal land. This was also observed mostly in breach, as there was little administrative infrastructure and lack of political will to regulate such transfers. It is found that, the non-tribals intermediary tenure holders (*gaontias)* are controlling and administering the land system. During the settlement and survey in Koraput district, it was identified that these *gaontias* have settled the land of the tribals in their own name or in the name of their relatives in 164 cases.[18] Behuria has depicted the instances of tribal land alienation in the Koraput district of Odisha in the following paragraph.

> It was identified that in 604 cases of land alienation from Scheduled Tribes to non-tribals covering an area of 1790 acres were transferred during the survey and settlement operation in the Koraput district of Odisha. The above figure seems to be underestimates, given the fact that the records were not maintained properly by the intermediary tenure holders and that castes like *Goudas* (milkmen, OBC), *Dombas* (SC) and *Malis* (gardener, OBC) were included in the category of hill tribes to grab tribal land (Behuria 1965).

The period between 1948 and 1956 is very crucial for tribal land alienation because there were no laws applicable for the protection of tribal land in many areas of the state at that period. There were restrictions on land transfer from tribals to non-tribals in all the ex-princely states having tribal populations. However, with the amalgamation of princely states with Odisha, such protection was automatically repealed and was replaced by the Merged Estate (Laws) Act, 1950, which provided protection against land alienation of aboriginal tribes. But, this provision remained ineffective as the state government did not define 'aboriginal tribes' till 1962. There were non-existent of laws to protect tribal land in ex-princely state areas, especially from 1948 to 1956 in Scheduled Areas and from 1948 to 1962 in non-Scheduled Areas. Therefore, till the effectuation of OSATIP, 1956 and OLR Act, 1960, tribal land laws were more or less ineffective (Kumar et al. 2005: 44).

Before this period, through sales or mortgages, much of the tribal land was transferred to non-tribals. For example, the *Malis,* (gardener and categorised as Other Backward Class) and *Dombas* (Scheduled Caste) have entered in the tribal areas and requested the aboriginal *Paraja* tribe to provide some land to cultivate. The *Parajas* lost much of their land to *Malis* and *Dombas* through debt mortgaging and sale. At the time of the settlement, it is found that, *Parajas* owned only 19.7% of the land in Sorisiapada revenue village where almost 35% of the *patta* land belonged to the *Malis* (Kumar et al. 2005: 45). There seem to be little scope of undoing the tribal land transfer before 1956 in Scheduled Areas and before 1965 in non-Scheduled Areas (ibid.). For the state, in these cases, the only viable solution is to purchase or acquire land from non-tribals to distribute among the landless tribals. This step, among others could specifically be taken up in areas inhabited by PTGs, on individual or communal basis as per their social and cultural practices (ibid.).

The report by Kundan Kumar and others work regarding the loss of tribal land to non-tribals in the Scheduled Areas of Odisha was highlighted in the following paragraph.

---

[18]ibid.

> In many of the tribal areas, the survey and settlement process didn't formalise the ownership of the land occupied by the tribals for agriculture. Clan and lineage based territories practiced by tribes were not recognised in the settlement process. The communal nature of ownership of land, especially swidden land amongst tribal like the *Juangs*, the *Kutia Kondhs* etc. in Odisha were totally ignored, and such areas were classified as government land. Even in tribal areas where customary individual ownership over hillsides were recognised, the cultivated hill slopes (above 10°) were settled as government land. The most important factor in loss of land by Scheduled Tribes in Odisha has been the non-recognition of rights on shifting cultivation land. All these tribal land were lost through survey and settlement and forest reservations (Kumar et al. 2005: 45).

4.4.7 Sale of Tribal Land After Permission

Land transfer from tribals to non-tribals in non-Scheduled areas is regulated under section 22 of OLR Act, 1960 and in case of Scheduled V areas, it is regulated by section 3 of OSATIP Regulation, 1956. Both laws provided for sale of land after obtaining permission from the competent authorities (Kumar et al. 2005: 42). Panigrahi has provided an account regarding the amount of land transferred after permission in the following paragraph.

> Approximately 8,550 acres of land has been sold through permission during the period 1957–1997 in Odisha on the basis of U/S 3(1) of the Regulation 2 of 1956 Act. Out of this, almost half was transferred in the four districts of Malkangiri, Rayagda, Nawrangpur and Koraput (earlier, these four districts were under 'undivided Koraput' district) (Panigrahi 2001).

But, in 1989, a correction in the OSATIP Regulation, 1956 has prevented sale of land from tribals to non-tribals, if the total land holding after sale was less than five unirrigated acre or two irrigated acres. Since, 2002, in Scheduled Areas, sale of land by tribals to non-tribals is totally prohibited after the excision of the U/S 3(1) provision from the regulation 2 of 1956. But, almost 80% of these purchases have been carried out before the provision came into force and these land include valuable paddy land.

4.4.8 Land Alienation in Tribal Areas Through Mining, Conservation and Development Projects

Most of the tribal districts of Odisha are enormously rich in minerals. These tribal districts with its availability of water and hilly terrain attract the projects for dams and reservoirs. The major dams like Machkund, Indrawati, Balimela, Salandi, Mandira and Upper Kolab are being constructed in the Scheduled Areas of Odisha. NALCO's Alumina refinery at Damanjodi, Hindustan Aeronautics Limited (HAL) at Sunabeda, and the Raurkela steel plant are the major industrial projects which were taken up in Scheduled Areas of the state (Panigrahi 1986: 32). Wildlife sanctuaries and national parks were also taken up in these Scheduled Areas due to the richness of the flora and fauna of these areas. These projects in the tribal areas (Scheduled Areas) created lot of problems for the denizens as these affect their life, livelihoods and on certain occasion lead towards deracination. Kumar and others have mentioned the consequences of these development projects taken up in Scheduled Areas which were quoted below.

> An estimate of 1.5 million people being displaced by development projects between 1951 and 1995, of which 42% were tribals. After displacement, landlessness increased to 85.25%, the average legal landholding declined to 0.62 acres and the average government land cultivated came down to only 0.2 acres in tribal areas of Odisha (Kumar et al. 2011: 40–41).

The other forms of displacement in the tribal areas are the industrial projects and mining activities. The iron ore and manganese in Keonjhar and Sundargarh districts, bauxite in Kalahandi district, coal in Rayagda, Koraput and Sundargarh district are the most important mining zones within the tribal areas (Panigrahi 1986: 32). Apart from displacement, due to industries and mining activities, non-tribals inflow to tribal areas happened, which frequently lead to political and social marginalisation of the tribals along with tribal land alienation. Displacement through development projects, especially dams, mining and industrial projects have been an important reason for land loss of tribals. Almost all the dam projects are in hilly tracts which have higher proportion of tribal population. In many cases, the official displacement figures are underestimates, and many of the major projects like Hirakud provide no figures about the displaced tribal households. In his article, Kundan Kumar has mentioned the degree of dispossessions in the tribal districts of Odisha which were provided in the following paragraph.

> It is estimated that, till 2000, about 2 million people in Odisha have been directly affected by development projects in varying degrees out of which about 0.5 million have been physically displaced losing their home & hearth from original habitat. The estimate figures further suggest that irrigation projects/dams have displaced 0.35 million people (70% of the total displaced persons), the projects on industry purpose have displaced near about 60,000 persons (12% of the total displaced) and the urban development projects, thermal projects, mining projects, & wild life sanctuaries have displaced 3.37%, 12.86%, 2.60% and 0.5% respectively of the total displaced people in the state of Odisha. The undivided Koraput district alone has lost 7.42% of its total land area to 18 development projects (Kumar et al. 2005: 62).

This has meant that Scheduled Tribes have not provided legal rights over their ancestral land. Large areas of such land cultivated by tribals were not legally settled in their names and therefore, no compensation was provided on the land which is being taken for the development projects. Thirty-two tribal households have lost 20 hectare of cultivating land in Mangara village of Koraput district, as these land submerged by the Telengiri medium irrigation projects (cited in Kumar et al. 2005: 63). The Government of Odisha is planning to amend the OSATIP Regulation, 1956, by introducing a clause, to lease out land to any corporate body or to provide land for the purpose of development. Such an amendment will remove all protection for tribal land alienation, where any non-tribal could bribe the local administration to arrange a donation of land by the tribals for his or her company.

4.4.9 Tribal Land Alienation Owing to Plantations

Since 1950s, plantations were used as a way to reinstate the shifting cultivation land both on revenue department land and on forest land by the government. This has created conflict between the plantation agencies and the tribals who were the real owner of these shifting cultivation land taken out for plantation purpose. This has led to loss of tribal access to vast areas of shifting cultivation land. The government of Odisha, in 1980, has started the policy for allowing usufructuary rights on plantations taken up on revenue land. However, in many cases, such allocation of usufructuary rights have conflicted with the pre-existing customary ownership, creating conflicts (Kumar et al. 2005: 68). No usufructuary rights are provided on plantations on forest land. Since last few years, usufructuary rights on plantations carried out on revenue land under various development programmes. However, the allocation of usufructuary rights is not priority and is often done in a slipshod manner, creating conflicts and confusion.

> In the last four years, most of the slopes in Dekapar village (under Semiligula tahasil of Koraput district) have been planted under various schemes such as coffee plantation, cashew plantation by soil conservation department and the watershed projects. The villagers haven't destroyed these plantations as they have been promised rights over them, however, no action has been taken regarding issuing of usufructuary rights. Due to the plantation, the villagers of Dekapar have lost near about 142 acres of cultivable land and 23 households have migrated, because they had no *patta* land, and on their customary owned land, plantations were carried out. These families have migrated to neighbouring Nabarangpur district and to Andhra Pradesh. Little is known about their current situation (Kumar et al. 2005: 69).

4.4.10 Compensatory Forestation Leads to Displacement of Tribal Land

Juangs, a Primitive Tribal Group (PTG) of Odisha, lives in forested areas and have displaced from their customary swidden land which was not recorded in their names due to the afforestation project. Under the Forest Conservation Act, 1980, the compensatory afforestation is taken up. The afforested land has to be re-categorised as forest land under the regulations of the Forest Conservation Act. For the helpless *Juang* tribes, the series of plantations on their customary land have been a double tragedy for them. The Forest Department converted the communal land of the *Juangs* into plantations which deprived them of the access to their land. Apart from its ethical and social justice implications, this process of converting tribal land into forest land has violated many laws. Importantly, it violates the provisions of the Indian Constitution under Schedule V which directs the state to defend the Scheduled Tribe's land in the Scheduled Areas. The section 3(iii) of the OSATIP Regulations 1956 is also violated that directs a minimum benchmark of five acres of unirrigated land or 2 acres of irrigated land for ownership by Scheduled Tribes before any land of their possession can be transferred.

4.4.11 Lack of Implementation of Land Reform Legislations

The prime objective of land reforms in the country was to bring about increased productivity in the agricultural sector while bringing equality and social justice to the marginal groups of the Indian society (Ambagudia 2010: 60). The principle of land reforms was guided by the value of social justice which sought to ensure equitable and minimum entitlement to land and prevent concentration of land ownership. In addition, it was also treated as part of uplifting large number of backward communities from oppression and dispossession, as land was central to the issue of social relations, social interaction and determination of categories at the grassroots level. But how far have these steps been effective in bringing about a just pattern of land ownership? Have these measures succeeded in empowering the landless, especially the tribals politically, economically and socially? As far as the tribals land questions are concerned, these are important questions that remain unreciprocated. Regarding the continuous suffering of tribals of Odisha, Ambagudia in his article has depicted the picture in the following manner.

> Tribals in Odisha continue to suffer land deprivation and dispossessions of different kinds despite special enabling provisions in the Constitution, a legal framework for their implementation and several targeted public policy initiatives taken by the state government. The erosion of the *adivasi* way of life, landownership system, land alienation and imposition of the values and dominance of outsiders in collaboration with the government has ensured that the *adivasis* in Odisha continue to be impoverished and dispossessed (Ambagudia 2010: 60).

The issue of land rights is nowhere as central with respect to the marginalised sections of the society, as with the tribal. The problem of land alienation among tribals is seen in the circumstances of the problem of tribal struggle for survival in the absence of viable alternatives. The major cause of concern regarding the present tribal problem is the loss of private holdings, where the existing laws passed by both the pre-colonial as well as post-colonial state remain failed to counter land estrangement.

The ongoing land conflict in some district of south Odisha, especially in Malkangiri, Koraput and Nabarangpur add new dimensions to the relationship between the land laws and the tribal rights (Ambagudia 2010: 60). Land has always been associated with social status in India, and has historically remained in the control of certain social groups. Some groups are not included under this banner, especially the 'tribals and *dalits*' with limited access to productive resources. So, the history of the tribals has been one of the deprivations, dispossessions and marginalisations. It is in the broader context of the land disparities that exist in Indian society, that the land problem in the tribal areas assumes much importance. The government has been concerned about these aspects and it has taken certain legislative and executive steps. Within this framework, land reform was one of the significant possible alternatives to address the social inequality and to provide autonomy to different categories in the matters of production, sale and distribution. It, however, argues that, despite the existence of legislative protection in Odisha, there is an apparent visibility of widespread process of land alienation in different tribal tracts. The poor access to land is not only the outcome of the forest policies adopted by the state but also due to tribal land alienation and encroachment by the outsiders.

In order to improve the marginalised section, especially the STs' and SCs' access to land, Odisha has enacted a number of legislative initiatives and reform measures. In this direction, the OLR Act, 1960 was considered a landmark in providing land rights to the landless tenants. With the intention of bringing social justice and economic upliftment among the marginalised sections, the Land Ceiling Act was implemented in 1974. The prime objective of the act was to acquire surplus land and redistribute among the landless. As per the ceiling surplus rule, each landless person should be accorded 0.7 standard acres for agriculture.

The Government of India (GOI) enacted the *Panchyat* (Extension to the Scheduled Areas) (PESA) Act, 1996.[19] The Fifth Scheduled Areas of Odisha come under the purview of this act and made applicable. It recognised the traditional rights of tribals over community resources. It empowers the '*gram sabhas*' to preserve the community resources of the tribals, cultural identity of the tribals, and the right to approve government programmes and projects within their jurisdiction. The act also mandates the provision that the *panchyats* or the *gram sabhas* have to be consulted before the land acquisition for development projects in the Scheduled Areas.

4.4.12 Poor Implementation of the Land Laws and Policies

There were many disadvantages in the policies and laws addressing the land rights of the tribals which have resulted insecure rights of the tribal over their land. These include lack of rigorous implementation of the acts like OSATIP Act 1956, OGLS Act 1962, OPLE Act 1972 and the OLR Act 1960. How the provisions of the laws were avoided while implementing land laws were provided in the following paragraph.

> The provisions of the OGLS Act, 1962 was not followed which directs for the settlement of land with the SCs, and STs. Section 7(2a), of the OPLE Act, 1972 which provides for the regularisation of encroachment land up to one standard acres have not been followed strictly (Kumar et al. 2005: 71).

Due to various reasons, the Land Ceiling Act failed to operate. The reasons include poor land quality, inaccessibility of land record and records of rights, lack of physical possession or genuine ownership by the beneficiary and trouble in recognising and identifying such land. It is observed in some cases that, the previous owner has still occupied the allotted land though the beneficiaries have *pattas*. Additionally, in the state of Odisha, land that has been received in donation under *bhoodan,* remains either undistributed or has been reoccupied by the previous owner.

Due to lack of rigorous implementation of the above laws and policies in the Scheduled Areas of Odisha, almost 50% of the tribal cultivators became marginal

---

[19]Report of the *Panchayat* Extension to Scheduled Areas Act 1996 (PESA). Enquiry Committee, Ministry of Panchayat, GOI (2006). https://www.undp.org/content/dam/india/docs/UNDP-Policy-Brief-on-PESA.pdf. Accessed 12 October 2019.

and landless, having 0.45 standard acres in an average only (Pradhan and Behera 2007: 6). According to the government of Odisha report, there are 150,000 landless tribal families in the state, having 11,672 families in the Koraput district alone. The state government also claims to have distributed 377,000 acres of land to 224,000 Scheduled Tribe families since 1975 (Kumar et al. 2005: 71). The need of the hour is to hasten the land distribution programme in the tribal areas where adequate revenue land is available. In Odisha, districts like Rayagda, Gajapati, Koraput, Kandhamal, Malkangiri, the Scheduled Areas in Keonjhar and some parts of Kalahandi should be given priority in the land distribution programme due to the acute landlessness in these tribal areas. The 'ceiling surplus land' and the '*bhoodan* land' that are lying with the Department of Revenue, Government of Odisha and has not been distributed to landless STs and SCs, should be allotted immediately and efficiently.

Exploring the deficiency of the existing land legislations, government of Odisha has made necessary rectifications at different times on the OSATIP Regulation 2 of 1956 which makes the law more stringent in protecting the tribal land and ensuring that land could not be transferred to non-tribals in Scheduled Areas. The government led by *Biju Janata Dal* (BJD) amended the law in 2002 which made it effective and completely banned the transfer of *patta* land to non-tribals (Ambagudia 2010: 64). The amendment made mandatory for all the non-tribals owning tribal land that they are bound to submit the manifest within one year to prove that they had possessed the land by fair means. Failing to the above provisions, the illegal land grabber would be imprisoned and such land would retrovert to the original tribal owner.

Though the government of Odisha at different times has initiated number of progressive legislations and has also adopted the central government's policy, but was not implemented properly which remain major concern. Due to large number of appeals from both the civil society organisations and tribal organisations, the government responded with a new policy campaign in 2007 named '*mo jami mo diha*' (in odia language it is translated as 'my land and my homestead land') that assure possession and ownership in a specific time period. But this new policy facing the same problem of rigorous implementation due to lack of political will, bureaucratic apathy and rampant corruption.

The present BJD government is paying special attention to implement the existing provisions rigorously. For instance, with the emergence of the recent tribal movement in Narayanpatna block of Koraput district, the government has issued instructions to all the concerned authorities of the four districts, such as Koraput, Malkangiri, Nabarangpur and Rayagda, to check the detailed procedure of land transfer from tribals to non-tribals since 1956 (Ambagudia 2010: 64). But the government has not issued such instruction to other districts of Odisha. The revenue minister announced that if the transfer of tribal land has not been supported by the declaration, the land will revert back to the original tribal owner. But, he did not mention anything about the land acquired by the private companies (ibid.). The recent amendment outrightly banned any transfer of tribal land to non-tribals but with certain relaxation with certain cases; the mortgage in favour of any financial institution, case of a gift or exchange for public purpose, construction of residential houses, for securing loans for agriculture, self-employment business and higher studies of children with the prior permission of the sub-collector in writing.

4.4.13 Tribal Land and the Forest Rights Act

The Scheduled Tribes and Other Traditional Forest Dwellers (Recognition of Forest Rights) Act, 2006 or simply the forest rights act came into effect in Odisha in 2008, which recognised rights of the forest dwellers over the forestland that have been occupied by them for generations but their rights over the forest could never be recognised earlier.[20] On 15 February 2008, the Scheduled Caste and Scheduled Tribe Development Department, Government of Odisha, issued a letter to all the collectors regarding the implementation of the said act.[21] It recognised the forest rights of the Scheduled Tribes who had in occupancy of the forestland before 13 December 2005. It also acknowledged the rights of other traditional forest dwellers who are in occupancy of forestland up to a maximum of four hectares for at least 75 years or almost three generations.[22] For both the Scheduled Tribes and other traditional forest-dwelling communities, the act recognised 13 sets of rights which include rights over community forest resources and rights over the land under individual and community control, etc.[23] Section 4 (4), FRA-2006, has mentioned that the rights provided under the act are not alienable or transferable but heritable. The act {section 3(1) (a)} specifies that 'forest rights' include: the right to hold land and live on it under common or individual occupation for self-cultivation, livelihood and habitation.[24]

Under FRA, about three hundred thousand households have been distributed individual forestland *patta* in Odisha as reported by the United Nations Development Programme (UNDP).[25] Though in comparison to other states, Odisha has done reasonably well in the implementation of Forest Rights Act, it still faces a number of challenges. Prominent among them are (i) quantum of forest land recognised is

---

[20]The Scheduled Tribes and Other Traditional Forest Dwellers (Recognition of Forest Rights) Act (2006). Ministry of Tribal affairs, Government of India, p. 3. https://tribal.nic.in › FRA › data › FRARulesBook. Accessed 21 November 2019.

[21]*Land Rights and Ownership in Orissa* (August 2008). Status Report, United Nations Development Programme. https://www.undp.org/content/dam/india/docs/land_rights_ownership_in_orissa.pdf. Accessed 22 October 2019.

[22]The Scheduled Tribes and Other Traditional Forest Dwellers (Recognition of Forest Rights) Act (2006). Ministry of Tribal affairs, Government of India, p. 3. https://tribal.nic.in › FRA› data › FRRulesBook. Accessed 21 November 2019.

[23]ibid, p. 4.

[24]ibid.

[25]*Land Rights and Ownership in Orissa* (August 2008). Status Report, United Nations Development Programme. https://www.undp.org/content/dam/india/docs/land_rights_ownership_in_orissa.pdf. Accessed 22 October 2019.

less than claims; (ii) there have been few community claims and (iii) a good number of forest-land occupants are still not aware and have not applied for land.

4.5 Odisha Government's Policy Targets on Land

Besides the above-discussed land legislations, the government of Odisha has also launched a number of projects related to land rights of the landless, especially for the tribal of the state.

4.5.1 The Vasundhara *Project—2006*

In 2006, the Government of Odisha launched the '*Vasundhara* project' with the aim of providing house sites to homesteadless families. The details of the house provided under the '*Vasundhara* project' were provided below.

> Under this project, 98,774 homesteadless families have been provided house sites in 2006–07, which included 46,196 tribal families, 25,721 Scheduled Caste families and 26,857 other families. During 2007–08, house sites are also provided to 58,516 homesteadless families out of which 22,584 were tribal families; 15,118 were Scheduled Caste families and 6,067 other category families have been benefited. A total of 19,314 families which included 9,614 ST families, 3,633 SC families and 6,067 other category families have been covered under this project during 2008–09 (cited in Ambagudia 2010: 65).

In addition to the '*Vasundhara* Project', in 2007, the state government launched the '*mo jami mo diha*' (in odia language, it is translated as 'my land and my homestead land') campaign to secure and protect the land rights of the marginalised, particularly the STs and SCs. The project aims to enquiry the homesteadless cases, actual possession of ceiling surplus land, waste land distribution for agricultural purposes, and the restored cases under section 23 of the OLR Act, 1960 and Regulation 2 of OSATIP Act, 1956.

4.5.2 Odisha Land Pass Book Rules, 2006 (OLPBR)

The Status report by UNDP (2008) has mentioned about the Odisha Land Pass Book Rules. The report stated that,

> The state government has also started issuing land pass book to individual land holding families under 'The Odisha Land Pass Book Rules, 2006'. This pass book will enable families to use it as an authorised document for; (i) caste certificate, (ii) socially and economically backward class certificate for educational purposes, (iii) legal heir certificate for limited purposes,

(iv) income certificate, (v) residential certificate, (vi) identification of bellow poverty line families, and (vii) farmer's identity card.[26]

4.5.3 Odisha Tribal Empowerment and Livelihoods Programme (OTELP)

The state government with the help of the central government and other agencies have started the 'Odisha Tribal Empowerment and Livelihoods Programme' (OTELP). It's a joint venture and the scheme is supported by 'International Fund for Agricultural Development' (IFAD), 'Department for International Development' (DFID), World Food Programme (WFP), the state government and the central government. The programme ensures the livelihood and food security of poor tribal households and tries to improve the conditions of the tribals by promoting a more equitable, self-managed, efficient and judicious consumption of resources through non-farm/off-farm enterprise evolution. The nodal agency to implement such programme is the Scheduled Tribe and Scheduled Caste development department under the state government. The programme is functioning in 30 blocks of 7 districts in the state.[27]

4.5.4 Rural Development Institute (RDI)

The Rural Development Institute (RDI) is a non-profit organisation working globally to secure land rights to the poorest. RDI strongly believe that secure land right would provide the poor with a foundation for economic and social betterment. The RDI, in its endeavour to secure land rights, has interventions in four states, namely, Karnataka, Andhra Pradesh, West Bengal and Odisha addressing on micro-land ownership to poor agricultural families especially to poor agricultural women. The RDI, in Odisha, is trying to workout effective livelihood models focusing on the line of the homestead land distributed under the '*Vasundhra* scheme' being implemented by the government of Odisha.[28] In post-independence India, numerous efforts have been made to bridge the gap between the rich landed peasantry and the poor landless with the promulgation of a number of land reform legislations and land distribution programmes. So, the government of Odisha had adopted legislation like the OLRA, 1960 and Odisha Land Ceiling Act (OLCA) 1974, etc. But in spite of all these efforts, the poor access to land persists a major area of concern for the state, where the people either have *pattas* (title)

---

[26]*Land Rights and Ownership in Orissa* (August 2008). Status Report, United Nations Development Programme, p. 22. https://www.undp.org/content/dam/india/docs/land_rights_ownership_in_orissa.pdf. Accessed 22 October 2019.

[27]ibid.

[28]*Land Rights and Ownership in Orissa* (August 2008). Status Report, United Nations Development Programme. https://www.undp.org/content/dam/india/docs/land_rights_ownership_in_orissa.pdf. Accessed 22 October, 2019.

without possessing of the land or possession without *patta*.[29] Government of Odisha in 2005–06, made an excellent innovation to creatively use existing revenue laws like the 'Odisha Prevention of Land Encroachment Act' and the 'Odisha Government Land Settlement Act' to provide homestead land up to 10 decimals to the rural homestead less people.[30]

But still, a substantial chunk of people still remain homesteadless; they either not been included in the schemes as homesteadless or haven't seen the land they have been allocated. Assessments revealed that implementation was crippled by a severe shortage of revenue staff at the field level to carry out enumeration of homesteadless families and process their claims. Though the government responded to *patta* and possession challenges by promulgating the *mo jami mo diha* (my land and my homestead land) campaign in 2007, the situation didn't improved substantially due to operational bottlenecks. To address the problem mentioned above, active steps have been carried out by the OTELP and RDI primarily in 1000 villages in the seven project districts in the state. The programme has the objectives to ensure land (both homestead and agricultural) within two years time bound but remain unsuccessful.

4.6 Critical Appraisal of Odisha Government's Policy on Land

The various legislation described above is based within the same matrix of colonial legal framework (Viegas 1991: 34). After the adoption, the tribal situation has not been systematically reviewed to ascertain whether these laws and institutions need any adaptation or changes before they are extended to and established in these areas. So, the continuation of the British pattern policies stands today as an obstacle to social justice (Ambagudia 2010: 65). This is quite contradictory to the commitment of the state government that planned development has to be based on the double principle of maximising the productivity of the natural and other resources, combined with social justice to all. Whether under colonial or post-colonial period, the role of the state is based on the principle of 'Eminent Domain' which has stricken the root of the customary rights of the tribal people. To put it differently, the state of Odisha does not respect the material context of the survival strategy of tribals. The land reforms and other laws are based on the formal system whose framework is in contradiction with the society and economy that the tribals are accustomed to (ibid.: 66). That became the basis of their alienation from land and other natural resources. It has also observed that the tribals become bonded or semi-bonded labourers on their own land. In Odisha, there have also been many cases where the land is in the name of the tribals, but, non-tribals who have loaned money to tribals cultivate it. All the above

[29] ibid.

[30] ibid.

protective laws discussed over are meant for record and for paperwork only, and the actual implementation remains a challenge with multiple complex issues related to it.

The progressive erosion of the tribal ways of life, imposition of the values and dominance of outsiders, the break-up of their land system, land alienation and encroachment, and the nexus between the dominant groups and the government has ensured that the tribals remain impoverished and disposed.

> Despite the enactment of several legislations by the government of Odisha to render social and economic justice to the tribals, the ground reality in Odisha, however, appears to suggest a different scenario. Similarly, there is no legislation relating to the allotment of government wasteland to SCs and STs in Odisha. The government of Odisha has, however, issued a set of instructions for the settlement and lease of waste and encroached land in which the SCs and STs have been given the first and second priority (Ambagudia 2010: 66).

In Karnataka, under the Mysore Land Grant Rules, 1959, 50% of the available land for allotment is reserved for SCs and STs and if the land is less than 10 acres, the entire land is reserved for SCs and STs.[31] But in Odisha, the landless persons are required to file an application before the local *Tahsildar* for the allotment of waste and encroached land.[32] Sometimes, this process also claims some amount of money. The tribals often complained that *pattas* (document showing ownership) of land are not issued to them even after several years of allotment of land. Meanwhile, in the absence of ownership rights, they are not able to access the government facility of loan, which compels them to go to the moneylenders for taking loans which ultimately transfer of land to non-tribals. The terms and conditions are dictated by the moneylender and this is facilitated by the inability of the tribals to read and write. Therefore, inadequate legislation, poor implementation, the ignorance of tribals and bureaucratic apathy are the main causes of land alienation in Odisha.

There are legislation protecting tribal land rights, but actually, that laws and regulations are often circumvented by the vested interests in convenience with the officials. The land redistribution measures followed by the government lay down various conditions whereby the land cannot be alienated. However, these are not strictly observed. In short, despite the overwhelming legislative and executive measures adopted by the government of Odisha for the protection of tribal land, the ground reality remain disturbing. So, the biggest challenge for the state government is to implement the existing legislations more effectively and meaningfully in all parts of the state and to reframe the legislations in accordance with the needs of the tribal society. The recent Narayanpatna land conflict between tribals and non-tribals which leads to the Narayanpatna movement may be attributed to the negligence of the state administration in implementing the land legislations. In this context, I here quote, the very word of Jaipal Singh in the Constituent Assembly, when he argued

---

[31] *Land Rights and Ownership in Orissa* (August 2008). Status Report, United Nations Development Programme. https://www.undp.org/content/dam/india/docs/land_rights_ownership_in_orissa.pdf. Accessed 22 October 2019.

[32] ibid.

> Land is the bulwark of aboriginal life. Whenever we have been (in tribal areas), it has been argued upon us that for several years to come, the aboriginal land must be inalienable. We have been talking about equality. Equality sounds well, but I do demand discrimination when it comes to the holding of aboriginal life (CAD, Vol. III: 462–63).

4.7 Some Suggestions

The following points are some of the suggestions as far as tribal land alienation in Odisha is concerned. If the suggestions will implement properly, then the problem of tribal land alienation in Odisha will partly solve.

4.7.1 Adoption of Rights Over Swidden and Shifting Cultivation Land

The state has done a greater injustice against the tribals by denying their rights over their shifting cultivation land and customary swidden land. The sad thing is that most of these customary land of the tribals were grabbed after independence. This single factor has largely contributed towards tribal land alienation and remained the most important source of loss of land for the tribals who practice this kind of cultivation earlier. Shifting or swidden cultivation has been demonised without much scientific proof, and the state has forcefully converted all these lands as forestland or revenue wasteland after denying tribal rights over these lands. This has created a condition where the tribals are still continuing cultivation on these customary land without tenure security and therefore treated as encroachers in their own land.

The tribal communities which practice individual ownership on swidden land, often exercise customary communal ownership over forests, common land, etc. The individual ownership is often embedded in the larger context of communal or clan control. Such customary or common control land should be recognised. At present, the revenue department is controlling such land in case of revenue land, and in case of forestland, it is the forest department. These two categories of land controlled by the revenue and forest department comprise 75% of the total land in scheduled districts of the state. The local tribals have no control or say over these lands, though, for livelihoods, the tribals are even using these lands. The control over such land must be handed to the local tribal communities and this was precisely the premise of the Bhuria Committee Report.[33] *Panchayat* Extension to Scheduled Areas (PESA) Act, 1996 as well as Odisha *Panchayati Raj* Act, 1964 were never operationalised in their letter and spirit. The Odisha *Panchayati Raj* Act, 1964, clearly mentions in section 71(4), that,

---

[33] *Report of the Scheduled Areas and Scheduled Tribes Commission*. Government of India, Volume I (2002–2004). http://www.tribal.nic.in/writereaddata/AnnualReport/BhuriaReportFinal.pdf. Accessed 10 October 2019.

> Properties vested in the *gram sasan* and under its management, direction and control include wasteland and protected forests within the meaning of Indian Forest Act, 1927 and unreserved forests within the meaning of Madras Forest Act, 1882, in respect of management, protection and maintenance for timber, fuel, and fodder purposes.[34]

4.7.2 Government of Odisha Should Implement the Maxims of Samata Judgement

In Odisha, as far as tribal loss of livelihoods and land is concerned, development projects or development induced displacement remained a major source. By various means, the state administration has circumvented the protection in land provided to Scheduled Tribes in the Indian Constitution. The increasing industrialisation and extractive mining in Odisha is concentrated primarily in Scheduled Areas. Such activities not only lead to displacement of Scheduled Tribes, but also disrupt their social-cultural milieu through invasion of outsiders. It is, with such a position, that the Supreme Court's 'Samata Judgement' was passed, which enjoined upon all states to pass laws similar to that of Andhra Pradesh to protect tribal interest in land.[35] The government of Odisha has ignored the judgement in the case of Vedanta and Kadalibadi, as well as in Keshipur case (Kumar et al. 2005: 77). It is most required that transfer of land to non-tribals in Scheduled Areas should be banned completely, as it is in Andhra Pradesh at present and as directed by the Supreme Court in its Samata Judgement.

4.7.3 Government Should Strictly Enforce the OSATIP, 1956

In case of tribal land transfer, the minimum land ownership principle is defined by the existing laws. It is defined that a person or a tribal is to be regarded as landless if the family owns less than one acre of land. The OSATIP, 1956 indicates that if there are less than 2 acres of irrigated land or 5 acres of unirrigated land for a tribal household, than no land can be transferred from him/her (Kumar et al. 2005: 77). To maintain his/her family, it is sufficient for a tribal to possess 5 unirrigated acres of land or 2 irrigated acres of land as per the law. However, the average land holdings of a marginal Scheduled Tribe farmer in Scheduled Areas of the state is only 0.44 standard acres (ibid.). This implies that, there is acute land shortage for most of the tribal households, even though there are large extents of state-owned land available in

[34]Orissa Panchayati Raj Act (1964). http://odishapanchayat.gov.in/English/download/ORISSA%20GP%20ACT%201964.pdf. Accessed 22 December 2019.

[35]Samata vs. State of Andhra Pradesh (1997). http://www.samataindia.org.in/documents/SAMATA_EDIT1.PDF. Accessed 12 June 2019.

the tribal districts. These lands should be redistributed among the landless tribals on the basis of minimum land ownership principle as per OSATIP, 1956.

4.7.4 PTGs Homelands Should be Protected

The Kadalibadi case of *Juangs,* the Vedanta controversy and the plight of *Chuktia Bhunjias* in Sunabeda sanctuary have exemplified the miserable condition of the PTGs while facing the forest and land laws of the government (Kumar et al. 2005: 77). The insensitivity attitude of the local revenue and administrative officials towards their situation and their customary rights over land have made these PTGs more miserable. Development projects including mining and afforestation and in other cases conservation itself, have posed threats to these primitive tribes. For example, *Chuktia Bhunjias* in Sunabeda Sanctuary, *Kutia Khonds* in Kotagarh sanctuaries, *Lanija Saoras* in Lakhiri sanctuary, and *Mankadias* in Simlipal sanctuary are affected by these development projects including mining and afforestation (ibid.). Also, *Bhuiyans* and *Juangs* were affected by iron ore mining, *Donghria Khonds* were affected by bauxite mining. So, the government should declare the habitat areas and homeland of these aboriginal primitive tribes as prohibited land and all mega development projects in these primitive tribal areas should be stopped immediately. Environment conservation in their ancestral areas should be focused on the PTGs and the biodiversity. Functioning of the existing laws, such as Wild Life Protection Act (WLPA), 1972, and Forest Conservation Act (FCA), 1980 should be drawn back through exceptional powers of the Governor in Scheduled Areas. New laws should be framed to prohibit the non-PTGs possession of land in these primitive tribal areas and allowing communal rights to PTGs in such forestland.

4.7.5 Simplification and Transparency in Land Administration Should be Maintained

In tribal areas, the most imperative principle that should be followed is the simplification and transparency in land administration. The tribals are mostly illiterate and do not understand the complexity of land administration or the complex legal processes related to land. At present, it is extremely difficult for a layperson as well as for a researcher to be able to access land records. The forest and revenue officers are not cooperative or accountable to the tribal people. Lack of transparency and accountability gives tremendous powers to the local officials over landholders, especially over illiterate tribals. Nowadays, computerisation of land records has increased transparency, but, in absence of proper record maintenance, it has been only partially useful (Kumar et al. 2005: 77).

4.7.6 There should be Synergy between Tribal Development and Land Administration

In the name of poverty alleviation and tribal development, huge quantities of funds are being flowed into tribal areas. These include watershed development, plantation of horticulture species among other initiatives. Many of these initiatives, especially land-based ones, tend to be found unsuccessful because of land tenure related issues. Without proper access to land and land-based resources, it is impossible to eradicate poverty and underdevelopment in tribal areas. Unfortunately, there seems to have been little synergy between land administration and development administration, and land reforms haven't been integrated till now into development strategy. Given the situation as described, within the development strategy for tribal areas, land administration reforms should be focused as the core strategy. Other development strategies should be reinforced around the problem of land rights and land access to the tribals. Without providing land rights and access to tribals, all the development measures initiated for tribal development in tribal areas would be unsuccessful and unproductive.

4.7.7 Land Records Including Customary and Swidden land Should be Maintained Properly

At present due to digitalisation and computerisation of land records, it has become easier to monitor the land transaction in a village. But, all land records including customary and swidden land of the tribals and lands above 10°–30° slope should be recorded properly. It is advised that to carry a detail review of land ownership in the villages of tribal areas on a random sample basis, a third party should be employed. The third party will verify the ground reality vis-à-vis the records. There should be a mechanism to identify cases relating to land alienation in tribal areas through oral mortgages or *benami* (illegal) transactions. The agency or the government will take action to get the alienated land restored to its previous owner.

4.7.8 Land Ownership Analysis Should Be Compulsory for Any Schemes

Any area-based scheme to be taken up in tribal village, including programmes like watershed development, irrigation projects, etc., land ownership survey and analysis should be made mandatory. This survey will examine the legal status of such land, the actual ownership of land for every tribal household in a particular village or area, and amount of land mortgaged out by Scheduled Tribes and others. These survey reports and the investigation reports on land will be applied to validate possession over the land owned by the state, recovery of mortgaged land and the land entitled for regularisation. In tribal areas, for rural development projects having any participatory planning or micro-planning, such a survey and analysis report having projected action plan should be mandatory.

4.7.9 Apportioning Ceiling Surplus Land to the Landless Tribals

In the state of Odisha in general, and Koraput district in particular, ceiling surplus land has not been allocated to the landless STs and SCs, even though section 51 of the OLR Act, 1960 clearly specifies that at least 70% of the ceiling surplus land should be settled with Scheduled Caste and Scheduled Tribes in proportion to their respective population in the village where the ceiling surplus land is situated.[36] A review of all ceiling surplus land in tribal districts must be carried out.

4.7.10 Government Should Take Initiative for Tribal Land Bank

In such a situation where the tribals can't transfer or sell the land to non-tribals, the land market is depressed for the tribal-owned land. These circumstances facilitate the informal mortgages or *benami* (illegal) transactions of land among the tribals at very low rate which contribute for effectual tribal land alienation. To avoid this, the state government may think of setting up a 'tribal land bank' in Scheduled Areas, which could offer loans to tribals in lieu of land mortgage or may buy land from the tribals when they are in emergency and do not find a fair market price for their land (Kumar et al. 2005: 78–79). Land that the tribals have transferred or mortgaged and could not redeem and returned back, should be apportioned among the landless tribals of that village.

4.7.11 Restoring Alienated Tribal Land as per OSATIP, 1956

The OSATIP 1956, section 3(b) directs to each and every person who is in possession of tribal land as on 4 September, 2002, to provide before the sub-collector all the documents regarding how that person came to possess tribal land between 1956 and 2002, within two years of time bound, failing which the land will be reverted to

[36]The Orissa Land Reform Act (1960). http://revenueodisha.gov.in/sites/default/files/Acts_Rules/Acts/OLR_Act.pdf. Accessed 22 November 2019.

the original tribal owner.[37] Initially, September 2004 was announced as the deadline for the submission of the details, and it further extended up to September 2005, but nothing remarkable has done so ever in this regard. Government should strictly deal with those persons who illegally possess tribal land, and after the deadline, the administration should rigorously implement the regulation.

4.7.12 Purchase of Land from Non-tribals for Allocation to Tribals

Keeping in mind the regions where there are no other sources of land, but tribal landlessness is acute, the government for the purpose of allocations of land to landless tribals should purchase land from the non-tribals. Especially, in the areas where Primitive Tribal Groups reside, this provision seems to be applicable.

4.7.13 Local Credit Systems Should Be Ensured

Due to chronic poverty, the scheduled Tribes faced lot of problems to maintain the daily requirements and expenses. Owing to hospital and marriage expenses, the situation of the tribals become more miserable. As per law, the tribals can't sell their land to non-tribals. In such circumstances, it is significant to encourage local community-based credit systems or thrift system which will provide money to the tribals during exigency. The spreading network of Shelf Help Groups (SHGs) and *grameen* banks in the tribal areas is extremely significant in this regard (Kumar et al. 2005: 79). Further support can be provided through these *grameen* banks and Shelf Help Groups to assure that without selling the land or mortgaging the land, the tribals can get credit within community.

4.7.14 There Should Be Record of Rights Through Survey and Settlements

Among most of the tribes, the shifting cultivation area of a clan or settlement is much demarcated. For example, tribes such as *Khonds* and *Saoras* have their own traditionally boundary, the individual lineages tend to have well-defined areas where households return after every fallow cycle. This, in effect, is individual ownership of

[37] The Orissa Scheduled Areas Transfer of Immovable Property (By Scheduled Tribes) Regulation (1956). http://revenueodisha.gov.in/sites/default/files/Acts_Rules/Acts/regulation2.pdf. Accessed 24 October 2019.

swidden land, and nowadays, in most of the areas, it is considered as short fallows, because the cycle has become short enough. However, during the survey and settlements, these land areas were intentionally categorised as non-continuous cultivation area and hence were not eligible for *ryoti* (peasant) rights. In spite of all attempts to curtail shifting cultivation, the practice continues due to its vital economic and cultural importance for the swiddening tribes (Kumar et al. 2005: 79). Such land should be expressly settled with the tribal households who cultivate them. How much land of this kind could be settled with each tribal family should be imposed on the basis of a ceiling provision. Therefore, a fair ceiling could be enforced while deciding *ryoti* (peasant) rights of this category of shifting cultivation or swidden land.

4.7.15 Withdrawing 10° Slope Criteria in Tribal Areas

In tribal hilly areas and upland areas, it is not necessary to fix the 10° slope criteria as many tribals cultivate land above 10° slope in hilly areas. These areas were demarcated as forestland and has provided under the management and ownership of the state government. But there is little evidence that, state ownership and management will lead to better and more sustainable management of these land. However, there is sufficient evidence that in different places of Korapt district, tribals are managing these land in a better manner by horticulture, agro forestry and through terracing. Such land should also be settled with the tribals.

4.7.16 Forest Rights Act Needs to Be Implemented Rigorously

The Forest Rights Act which resolves a number of problems that have become urgent in the tribal districts. It provides for rights to pre-1980s cultivation by the Scheduled Tribes in Scheduled Areas to the extent of 2.5 hectare of land per household and also rights on forests and forests product in Scheduled Areas.[38] A coordinated effort is required from the civil society, including NGOs and tribal organisations, to ensure that the law is implemented properly. However, the act is strongly contested by a strong conservation lobby. In this situation, immediate action should be taken to produce data bases on the extent of forest land under cultivation by tribals, the legal situation of such cultivation, and how these land can be regularised with the cultivators (Kumar et al. 2005: 81).

[38]The Scheduled Tribes and Other Traditional Forest Dwellers (Recognition of Forest Rights) Amendment Rules (2012). https://www.fra.org.in/document/FRA%20Rule_2012_complied%20version.pdf. Accessed 21 November 2019.

4.8 Conclusion and Suggestions

The economic and social wellbeing of the people in the tribal areas is directly related with the ownership and control over land. This also forms the basis of social status and political power. Although the state government has enacted different laws to prevent alienation of tribal land and to restore the already unlawfully alienated lands, but regrettably these laws were largely remained on paper and persisted unsuccessful to check tribal land alienation. Tribal land alienation is still going on through industrialisation, mining, development projects, lease of forestland to corporate bodies, etc. where the life, security, livelihood and freedom of the indigenous tribals are in great danger. Keeping the above issues in mind, the chapter suggests the following points as far as tribal land alienation in Odisha is concerned.

- The State of Odisha should bring a new law in place of the existing legislations which have loopholes to prevent tribal land alienation.
- The state may consider bringing the new law following the "Andhra Pradesh Scheduled Areas Land Transfer Regulation 1959", and the regulation amended in 1970. It will integrate a probable clause to assure complete protection of tribal land.
- The state may bring requisite corrections in the existing laws to make the consent of the *gram sabha* as compulsory requirement while dealing with tribal land for any purposes.
- Minimum land ownership principle (2 irrigated acres or 5 unirrigated acres) should be implemented rigorously when the tribal desires to sell his/her land to others.
- *Benami* (illegal) transfer of tribal land should be totally banned and if such cases found in any manner, it should be the duty of the concerned authority to restore the same within a specified period.
- There should be a provision in the law for the speedy disposal of tribal land alienation and restoration cases within a limited time.
- Tribal land bank should be open in tribal areas by the state government, so that the tribal can get loan by mortgaging the land.
- The tribal should get *patta* (deed) on the land cultivating for more than 10 years.
- Without the consent of the *gram sabha,* no developmental projects or industry can be allowed in tribal or Scheduled Areas.

References

Ama Jami (my land). (2005). Society for Promoting Rural Education and Development (SPREAD) Report, Koraput. https://spread.org.in. Accessed 22 November, 2019.

Ambagudia, J. (2010). Tribal rights, dispossession and the state in Odisha. *Economic & Political Weekly*, *XLV*(33), 14 August, 2010.

Baseline Report on Restoration of Land to the Allottees of Ceiling Surplus and Government Wasteland (November, 2006). Study undertaken by RCDC with support from NIRD, Hyderabad in Koraput district of Orissa.

Behura, N. K. (1982). Forest and tribal world view. *Journal of Social Research, XXV*(1).

Behuria, N. C. (1965). *Final report on the major settlement operation in Koraput District* (1938–64), Cuttack: Orissa Govt. Press.

CAD, Vol. III. https://www.constitutionofindia.net/constitution_assembly_debates/volume/3. Accessed 28 May, 2020.

Dash S. N. (2001). A study of the problem of land alienation in tribal areas with special reference to the district of Koraput. Bhubaneswar: Utkal University.

Kumar, K., et al. (2005). *Scheduled Tribes' Land in Odisha: A Socio-Economic and Legal Study.* Bhubaneswar: Supported By World Bank, Washington. http://citeseerx.ist.psu.edu/viewdoc/download?doi=10.1.1.631.7926&rep=rep1&type=pdf. Accessed 30 October, 2019.

Kumar, K. et al. (2011). *A Status of Adivasis/Indigenous Peoples Land Series–2.* New Delhi: Aakar Books. http://theothermedia.in/downloadables/SAIP_Reports/SAIP_Land_Series_2_Orissa.pdf. Accessed 8 June, 2014.

Land Rights and Ownership in Orissa (August 2008). Status Report, United Nations Development Programme. https://www.undp.org/content/dam/india/docs/land_rights_ownership_in_orissa.pdf. Accessed 22 October, 2019.

Orissa Panchayati Raj Act. (1964). http://odishapanchayat.gov.in/English/download/ORISSA%GP%20ACT%201964.pdf. Accessed 22 December, 2019.

Panigrahi, N. (1986). *Men and mining in western Orissa.* Study Report Submitted to Participatory Research in Asia (PRIA), New Delhi.

Panigrahi, N. (2001). Impact of state policies on management of land resources in Tribal areas of Orissa. *Man & Development*, Vol. XXIII, No. 1.

Pradhan, G., & Behera, S. (2007). *Position Paper on Land Right Issues in Orissa.*

Report of the Expert Group on Prevention of Alienation of Tribal Land and its Restoration. (2006). Ministry of Rural Development. http://www.sakti.in/108-land-rights/tribal-alnd-rights/430-report-of-the-expert-group-on-prevention-of-alienation-of-tribal-land-and-its-restoration. Accessed 10 December, 2019.

Report of the *Panchayat* Extension to Scheduled Areas Act 1996 (PESA). Enquiry Committee, Ministry of Panchayat, GOI (2006). https://www.undp.org/content/dam/india/docs/UNDP-Policy-Brief-on-PESA.pdf. Accessed 12 October, 2019.

Report of the Scheduled Areas and Scheduled Tribes Commission, Government of India, Volume I (2002–2004). http://www.tribal.nic.in/writereaddata/AnnualReport/BhuriaReportFinal.pdf. Accessed 10 October, 2019.

Samatha vs. State of Andhra Pradesh. (1997). 8 SCC. www.samataindia.org.in/documents/SAMATA_EDIT1.PDF. Accessed 12 June, 2019.

The Orissa Land Reform Act. (1960). http://revenueodisha.gov.in/sites/default/files/Acts_Rules/Acts/OLR_Act.pdf. Accessed 22 November, 2019.

The Orissa Scheduled Areas Transfer of Immovable Property (By Scheduled Tribes) Regulation. (1956). http://revenueodisha.gov.in/sites/default/files/Acts_Rules/Acts/regulation2.pdf. Accessed 24 October, 2019.

The Scheduled Tribes and Other Traditional Forest Dwellers (Recognition of Forest Rights) Act. (2006). Ministry of Tribal affairs and Forestry, Government of India. http://tribal.nic.in/FRA/data/FRARulesBook.pdf. Accessed 21 November, 2019.

The Scheduled Tribes and Other Traditional Forest Dwellers (Recognition of Forest Rights) Amendment Rules. (2012). https://www.fra.org.in/document/FRA%20Rule_2012_complied%20version.pdf. Accessed 21 November, 2019.

The State of India's Indigenous and Tribal People. (2009). *Asian Indigenous & Tribal Peoples Network*, 31st March. http://www.aitpn.org/publications/the-state-of-indias-indigenous-and-tribal-peoples-2009/. Accessed 14 September, 2019.

Veigas, P. (1991). *Encroached and enslaved: Alienation of Adivasi Land and its dynamics*. New Delhi: Indian Social Institute.

Chapter 5
Narayanpatna Movement in the Koraput District of Odisha

> The desire to humanise the demonised and to get to know the tribal problems at first hand, i.e., not simply through books, conversations, and documents, but to travel and meet with them and to see in order to find out the truth, is the basic purpose of a researcher. Truth, it is said, is the first causality of war. Behind every war is a long history of struggle, over-ground and peaceful. Hence, it is not surprising that the Indian government denies the very fact of prosecuting a war against its own people (Navalakha 2010: 1).

5.1 Introduction

Among the 30 districts of Odisha, Koraput being the tribal district placed within the Scheduled Areas of the Indian Constitution and remained in news for tribal insurrection either against the British government in colonial period or against the Indian state in the post-independence period. The core issue of the tribals, that is, land problem, has not been solved after seven decades of India's independence and the tribal land alienation in the district of Koraput is going to be precarious day by day. This is not the first tribal movement in the history of Koraput district of Odisha, every decade has witnessed such uprisings and sporadic violent movements on the part of the tribals either on the core issue of land or any other issues but without any solution at the ground level. However, the present movement in the Narayanpatna block of Koraput district has its own importance as it has shaken the state administration and remained in news since 2009–2014. The Narayanpatna tribal movement which is based on land issues, is not less than a popular movement that continues from 2009 to 2014 until forcefully arrested by the coercive state apparatus.

The hill people have organised many uprisings in the past which were known as *fituries* in local tribal language, and therefore it was not smooth for the British to enter into tribal areas. The *savaras* of Gunupur *taluk* killed an inspector and four constables in July 1864. In the murder case, 24 people were arrested and five of them were hanged with the help of the king of Jeypore. In 1865, a similar uprising occurred in that region where three tribal leaders were sent for life. In the Rampa region of Malkangiri district (formerly undivided Koraput district), the *Koya* tribals

S. K. Malik, *Land Alienation and Politics of Tribal Exploitation in India*,
https://doi.org/10.1007/978-981-15-5382-0_5

have protested and captured the Padia police station and had killed the inspector and six constables in April 1980. The leader of the *Koya* tribe, 'Tamma Dora' was killed by the British in July 1880. Similarly, the *Kondhas* of Kalahandi rose against the Odias of the plains (people from coastal Odisha) and murdered several hundreds of them in 1882. The 1910–11 rebellion in the Bastar region also had many repercussions on the tribals of Koraput district. Among all these rebellions of the tribals in the region, the most prominent one was the 'Rampa Rebellion' led by Alluri Sitaram Raju in 1922, and he was murdered in 1924. The 'Rampa Rebellion' in the east Godavari region (now in Andhra Pradesh) inspired the tribal of Koraput district. There was *Kondha* uprising against the British in Narayanpatna area of Koraput district in July1932 which was suppressed by the armed reserved police of the government.

In 1951, under the leadership of Biswanath Pattnaik, popularly known as 'Koraput Gandhi', the first uprising in Gunupur area was organised. He organised the tribals of 35 villages of Gunupur region and started the *bhoodan satyagraha.* A land committee was formed by the tribals under his leadership. The *satyagrahis* used to request the encroachers to leave the tribal land. After the request, they made the whole list of encroached land and filed cases against the land encroachers. They wait for two or three hearings, and if the land problem was not solved, the tribals used to declare and occupy their land forcefully. Bidyut Mohanty and K. Anuradha had cited in their article about the *Savaras* of Koraput district and their peaceful *satyagraha* which were provided in the following paragraph:

> The *Savaras* of Koraput district, who fight for their land had totally followed the path of Mahatma Gandhi's 'non-violence'. During the assembly session in June 1952, the question was raised on the land issue and the then Chief Minister Nabakrushna Choudhury answered; '*Savara*'s tried to occupy their land but they went without arms. Since nobody heard their grievances on land matter they have formed the *Bhoo-Satyagrah* Committee to get their land back'. Some revenue-board officials went and tried to end the dispute by mutual discussion but without success. A few *bhoo-satyagrahis* were also arrested at that time. The core issue remained unsolved because there was no political will to solve the problem. In the 1950s, there was discontent against the Machkund dam in Koraput by the displaced people under the leadership of Gangadhar Jhola. By the end of 1970, the radical communist ideology had started capturing the mind of the poor. Biswanth Das, former Chief Minister of that time maintains, if the problem had been solved with genuineness, then tribals would have never adopt violent tactics.[1]

There was a violent movement by the tribals against Hari Misra (the exploiter landlord) in the village Balikhamar in Rayagda subdivision in 1961.[2] All the tribal lands were under the possession of Hari Mishra because he was the *dewan* of Kashipur *raja* who belonged from the coastal Odisha. Before the violent uprising, the tribals in different time invoked him to return their land, but without any positive consequences.

> From 1952 to 1960, the matter was discussed in the court but without any solution at the ground level. The tribals forcefully occupied their land and when Hari Misra opposed it,

[1]Mohanty and Anuradha (2009). *Failure of non-violent methods responsible for Narayanpatna uprising.* http://www.newsweb.co.in/news_article_en.php?article=1076. Accessed 8 June 2018.
[2]ibid.

> they killed him in 1961. There were uprisings against the powerful landlords in the area in 1967, 1999, 2000 and 2004.[3]

The response of the administration and the government towards the uprisings of tribals was to suppress them forcefully. This trend has been continued since the British period and is still followed today after 70 years of India's independence. Regarding the exploitation of tribals in the Koraput district by the outsider migrants and by the state administration, there is a nice report extracted from the article of Bidyut Mohanty and K. Anuradha and quoted in the following paragraph for a clear understanding of the land alienation process:

> They engaged the tribes in their own land as labourers and duped them in the process. They also established political supremacy over the poor tribes and began to increase their landed property by exploiting the tribes. There is 'regulation 2' of the Orissa Scheduled Areas Transfer of Immovable Property (by Scheduled Tribes) Regulation, 1956 Act, that the non-tribes cannot take away tribal land. But this law is not being strictly enforced. In the wake of the tribal agitation launched by the *Chasi Mulia Samiti* (CMS) in 1998, the government declared that it would strictly implement the law. But in that year (1998), eight tribes of Mandrabaju village in the district of Gajapati while fighting over land problems were shot dead by the government agents. The government completely changed the tribal land transfer law in 2002 and empowered the district Collector to deal with the matters concerning with transfer of tribal land thereby depriving the tribes of their rights over the land. It was business as usual.[4]

Vinoba Bhave's *bhoodan* and *gramdan* philosophy some extent impacted the people of Koraput region. In 1955, the *bhoodan yajna* movement was started in Koraput district. Through the *bhoodan yajna* movement, near about 165260 acres of land were donated in the district.[5] In 1971, the "Odisha *Bhoodan Yajna* Act, 1953" was ameliorated and renamed as the "Odisha *Bhoodan & Gramdan* Act". But, the noble thought failed to solve the land issues in Koraput region, because the lands which were donated to *bhoodan yajna* were not recorded in the name of the *bhoodan yajna samiti* during the settlement operations in the state. There are instances in some cases that the land have been reoccupied by the donors themselves which were donated in favour of *bhoodan yajna samiti*.

With the above backdrop, the chapter in detail discusses the Narayanpatna tribal movement. The chapter is divided into two parts. The first part discusses about the Koraput district, tribals of Koraput district, their cultural life and socio-economic issues, history of land administration and land alienation in Koraput district, a brief account of the study area and about the *Chasi Mulia Adivasi Sangha* (CMAS) which spearheaded the movement. The second part of the chapter discusses about the Narayanpatna movement, its nature, phases, causes and impact of the movement.

---

[3]Mohanty and Anuradha (2009). *Failure of non-violent methods responsible for Narayanpatna uprising*. http://www.newsweb.co.in/news_article_en.php?article=1076. Accessed 8 June 2018.

[4]ibid.

[5]Administrative setup, Koraput district, Government of Odisha. https://koraput.nic.in/Administrative-setup/. Accessed 15 December 2019.

5.2 The Koraput District

Koraput is a tribal-dominated district in the Eastern *Ghat* region of southern Odisha. The district is encircled by the Malkangiri district (Odisha) in the southwest, Bastar district (Chhattisgarh) in the west, Srikakulam (Andhra Pradesh) in the southeast, Visakhapatnam (Andhra Pradesh) to the south, Nabarangpur district (Odisha) in the north and Rayagada and Kalahandi district (Odisha) in the northeast.

> The district has two sub-divisions; Jeypore and Koraput, and fourteen blocks; Koraput, Bandhugaon, Laxmipur, Kundra, Nandapur, Pottangi, Semliguda, Jeypore, Boipariguda, Kotpad, Lamtaput, Boriguma, Dasmantpur and Narayanpatna. There are 1,922, inhabited villages, 106 uninhabited villages, and 226 *panchayats*.[6]

Koraput is the part of southern Odisha's tribal belt. The aboriginal and indigenous tribals called themselves as "*adivasis*" but they are recognised as Scheduled Tribes and Primitive Tribal Groups (PTGs*)* in government parlance. The district is well known for its steep hills and dense forest. The dense forest in the district is a part of the famous *dandakaranya*[7] area of the epic *Ramayana*. The district is part of the Koraput–Bolangir–Kalahandi (KBK) region. As per the 2011 Census report, the following data about the district were provided:

> The total population of the district as per the 2011 Census is 13, 79,647 having 699,070 female and 677,864 male population. The population density of the district is 156 having a total area of 8,807 km^2 in the state. In 2011, the average literacy rate of the district stood to 49.87%. As per the gender analysis, female and male literacy were 38.92 and 61.29% respectively. According to 20011 census figure, the male-female sex ratio is 1031 female per 1000 male which is positive towards gender index.[8]

It is noteworthy to mention that the average national sex ratio in India is 940 as per 2011 census. Koraput is a tribal-dominated district which comes under Schedule V Areas of the Indian Constitution and have 49.62% of tribal population against the total population of the district. The rural areas of the district show more tribal proportion having more than 56% as compared to the urban areas.

For the people of Koraput, agriculture is the primary occupation and acts as life-sustaining role in the district and its economy. More than 64% of STs and SCs directly and indirectly depend on agriculture.[9] The district is situated in remote areas of the

---

[6]Administrative setup, Koraput district, Government of Odisha. https://koraput.nic.in/Administrative-setup/. Accessed 15 December 2019.

[7]The '*dandakaranya*' region covers an area of 92,300 km^2. It borders the *Eastern Ghats* and in the west it includes the 'Abujhmar Hills'. It extends to the part of Odisha, Chhattisgarh, Andhra Pradesh and Telangana.

[8]Census 2011, Office of the Registrar (General and Census Commissioner), Ministry of Home Affairs, 2/A, Mansingh Road, New Delhi. http://censusindia.gov.in/2011census/dchb/2129_PART_B_DCHB_KORAPUT.pdf. Accessed 18 August 2019.

[9]Administrative setup, Koraput district, Government of Odisha. https://koraput.nic.in/Administrative-setup/, https://koraput.nic.in/about-district/. Accessed 15 December 2019. https://koraput.nic.in/about-district/.

state with poor communication. In undivided Koraput district, before independence, it was more than 70% of forest cover, and owing to disforestation, industrialisation and development projects, the density of forest in the district slowly diminish to only 21.34%.[10]

5.3 Tribals of Koraput

In Koraput, 50% of the total population in the district are tribals, accounting for 23% of Odisha's total tribal population.[11] Among the 62 tribal communities dwelling in Odisha, there are 51 tribal communities are only available in the district.[12] These 51 tribal communities are divided into three types: (i) *Kolarian* or *Munda* race (*Gadaba, Savara),* (ii) Dravidian race (*Poraja, Kondh, Koya* and *Gond*) and (iii) Austro-Asian race (*Bondas,* one of the most primitive tribes). Dravidian race (*Poraja, Kondh, Koya* and *Gond*) constitute the largest of the total tribal population. Other than these major types and categories, many others tribes are there, i.e. *Llhunia* and *Qlnathio* where the origin of these tribes is not known. Among the 51 tribal communities living in Koraput district, the major tribal groups are *Gadaba, Munda, Kondh, Paroja, Saura, Omanatya, Bhumias, Bondas, Gonds, Bhottadas, Duruas*, etc.

The *Gadabas and Mundas* speak *Desia* and *Gutab* dialect of the Austro-Asiatic language family and practice shifting cultivation. They live in Koraput and Jeypore region. *Omanatya* is another major tribal group of Koraput district and largely found in Jeypore, Boriguma, Kundra and Kotpad block. For livelihood, they depend on agriculture. *Parojas* are other major tribal groups found in Koraput district. They are basically engaged in collection of charcoal, firewood and practices goat breeding. They are largely found in Semiliguda, Koraput, Laxmipur, Pottangi, Nandapur, Dashmantpur, Lamataput, Boipariguda, Jeypore, Borigumma and Kundra block of the district. In Koraput district, the *Parojas* live with the *Paika, Mali, Rana, Domb, Kondh* and *Gadaba.* The *Sauras* who live in Koraput are the oldest tribes of Odisha and are also mentioned in *Hindu* myths and *purans* like *Ramayan* and are known as in different names such as *Sora, Sabara, soura*, etc. They speak *Mundari* dialect called *Sora.* The society of *Saura* is further divided into 25 sub-divisions based on food habit, traditions, customs, occupation and social status. The *Bhumias* are mostly well known for their skill in agriculture, and basically present in, Boipariguda, Jeypore and Kundra block of Koraput district.

Kondhs or *Khonds* are major tribe in Koraput. The word '*Kondh*' is derived from the word '*Konda*' meaning 'hill'. They are mostly shifting cultivators and a migratory race. Traditionally, they were hunter-gatherers and for Census purposes, they are

---

[10]Administrative setup, Koraput district, Government of Odisha. https://koraput.nic.in/Administrative-setup/. Accessed 15 December 2019. https://koraput.nic.in/district-at-a-glance/.

[11]Tribes of Koraput. https://koraput.nic.in/tribes/, https://koraput.nic.in/district-at-a-glance/. Accessed 21 December 2019.

[12]ibid.

categorised as plain-dwelling *Khonds* and hill-dwelling *Khonds*. Another primitive tribe is the *Bonda*. The name *Bonda* means naked because the female *Bondas* are barely clothed. They are divided as lower and upper *Bondas*. The upper *Bondas* live in high hills and are maintaining their culture and tradition. The lower *Bondas* live in foothills and blend with other tribes. The *Gonds* are the settled cultivators and live in Jeypore zone especially Umerkote areas. They are largely open to new cultures, ideas and are changing themselves to altering circumstances. Collection of forest produce is the chief occupation of the *Gonds*. They also prepared intoxicating liquors out of mahua flower, jackfruit, palmyra palms, mango and other millets.

5.3.1 Cultural Life

For the tribals, life is nothing but culture and traditions which embodies their way of life, philosophy and worldview. In order to know about any tribal communities, the study of the cultural history of that community is very significant, because the base of the tribal history lies in their culture. Any one deeply engaged in studying the cultural history of primitive tribes must visit the 'hub of tribals', that is 'South Odisha' in general and Koraput region in particular. The Koraput region became the arena of tribals and the centre of study and research for them, where the Council of Analytical Tribal Studies (COATS) is situated. Debashis Patra in his article, *the Cultural History of the Tribals of the Koraput Region,* has mentioned the following about the cultural life of the tribals of Koraput:

> The cultural history of tribals of the district have special importance all over India. This aboriginal tribes are divided into three communities' viz. Austro-Asiatic, Dravidian and Indo-Asian. They have their culture of own which is linked to their ambiance and language. Literally, the definition of their culture is so broad that one appreciate and accept every aspect of their life style which is associated with culture from different perspective such as social and religious milieu, village system, folk literature, dance and song, fairs and festivals, way of life and folk art (Patra 2011: 46).

The tribals embody their identity and culture through their tradition, customs, festivals, taboos, ornaments and dress. From the name of a tribe, one can have a clear view of their cultural characteristics and identity, because a particular tribe's name is coined especially for the identity of that tribe. Every tribe has a certain place of origin, own written and oral language and that language or dialect helps them for the interaction within the member of the communities. Marriage among the tribes is arranged within its own community and they oppose matrimonial relation beyond the particular community. The particular tribe maintains its own social relations, group administration, own belief and tradition and also respect their community judicial system. These belief in tradition and community helps in preserving the tribal customs, law, collection of food, hunting, shifting agriculture, worship, handicraft, economic policy and the whole tribal worldview.

On account of industrialisation, urbanisation and deforestation, the tribals of Koraput like other parts of the state have adopted new ways of life and the principles of modernity. The weekly market called '*haat*' or '*haat poda*' plays significant role in preserving tribal identity. The district administration organised the festival called the '*Parab*' or the '*Dongar* festival', a famous festival of the tribals is being organised to exhibit the life of tribals of Koraput district in every year, particularly, in the month of November. Nowadays, due to loss of tribal culture, identities and their way of life, the tribals are being exhibited as 'museum specimen' in different tribal fares or *adivasi melas*. The '*Sabara Srikhetra*' (other name of Koraput) is famous for lord Jagannath temple (Mohanty et al. 2008: 4). It is called *Sabara Srikhetra* because the *Sabara* tribes had worshiped lord Jagannath there, before the Puri temple was made, whereas the Puri temple (Jagannath temple) is popularly known as '*Srikhetra*'.

5.3.2 Socio-Economic Issues

Koraput district which remain a part of the 'Koraput–Bolangir–Kalahandi' long-term action plan is considered as a backward region both in the state and in the country. The people in the district, particularly, the Scheduled Tribes are living in an execrable condition. Among other causes for the deplorable situation of the tribals in the district, the major factor is landlessness. Most of the tribal families either have small patches of land or are landless. In this situation, it is very difficult to feed the family throughout the whole year. The pace of development in the district is very slow owing to lack of implementation of government programmes and lot of corruptions. There are health service problems, where the tribals and other marginal segments of people find it very difficult to access them. In the district, food insecurity is raising day by day owing to displacement, inaccessibility of work, loss of land and forest resources. The exacerbating condition of the tribals has forced them to migrate to out of state to sustain their lives. Livelihood was one of the major issues in the district which leads towards chronic poverty and food insecurity. In Koraput region, agriculture is the primary source of livelihood. Other than displacement, decline of forest resources is another factor for loss of livelihood. In the tribal areas of Koraput, encroachment of outsider migrant and also migration due to displacement are common factors which lead to poverty. Migration in the district is a non-voluntary tactic for survival. Migration has far-reaching results, affecting both the life of the tribal labourers and their family. Migration in the Koraput district has happened due to the following reasons:

- Inaccessible of work, late payment of wages and very low earnings
- Landlessness due to displacement, encroachment and alienation
- Lack of natural and forest resources due to deforestation
- Insufficient food or food insecurity
- Low production due to drought and lack of irrigation
- Chronic poverty and indebtedness.

5.4 History of Koraput

Koraput district has a pretty old history that goes back to 3rd century B.C. Regarding the origin of the name 'Koraput', there are several theories but none of these seems true. In view of Mr. R. C. S. Bell,

> The name of the district came from the name of the town 'Kora-Putti' or the hamlet of the 'nux-vomica'. The word 'nux-vomica' came from the name of the tree that must at one time have been prominent near the place (Bell 1945: 171).

The view of Mr. Bell is open to criticise because there is not a single tree of such variety is found near the town today. Another theory regarding the origin of the name 'Koraput' is that during the time of Nandapur kings, one 'Khora Naiko' laid the foundation of the village and later named after him as 'Khora Putu' and subsequently abridged to 'Koraput' after long time.

The present district was a former hill country of Jeypore. There is some evidence from the inscriptions that bear witness for the beingness of a kingdom since the year 1061 A.D (Bell 1945: 21–22). During the fourteen centuries, there is also a historical evidence of a kingdom in the region. A line of kings ruled over the region from the fifteenth century till the British period. As the historians view, a feudal king of Kashmir, who originated from the Solar Race was the ruler of that region during the said period. There are some other accounts regarding the origin which depict that the ruler of Jeypore was the servant of descended of ancient king of *Jagarnath* (ibid.: 22). Other theories have also confirmed that the kings who ruled the area for centuries were from the other regions and especially from the coastal regions of Odisha. In 1 April 1936, with the creation of the new province 'Odisha' on the basis of Odia language, Koraput was added to it.

5.5 History of Land Administration in the Koraput District

Permanent settlement was enacted in the whole district of Vizagapatam under Regulation XXV of 1802 on the lines of the Bengal permanent Settlement Regulation of 1793.[13] Since the introduction of the permanent settlement in Vizagapatam, until the Jeypore commotions in 1848, the officers of Vizagapatam district remained unaware about the functions of Jeypore *zamindary*[14] Regarding the tyranny and stupidity of Shri Vikram Deo and the misrule of his managers, a great complain reached to Vizagapatam in 1848 (Bell 1945: 33). Then, the old *raja* (king) has decided to allow his son to handle the administration and all affairs of the Jeypore *zamindary* remained in Narayanpatna.

[13]Odisha State Archives, Orissa District Gazetteers. http://www.odishaarchives.nic.in/node/169213. Accessed 22 December 2019.

[14]ibid.

Once again, the Jeypore matter appealed to public attention in 1855, due to the practices of *meriah* sacrifices (the ritual of *Khond* tribes of sacrificing human to appease their Gods for the purpose of good harvest) and *sati* (widow sacrifices herself by sitting atop her deceased husband's funeral pyre) which were accepted by the *raja* (king) (Padel 1995, Bell 1945: 38). The *meriah* agency that was constituted by Act XXI of 1845, to inhibit *meriah* sacrifices within Bengal and Madras Territories had visited Jeypore many times and finally succeeded in prohibiting it (Bell 1945: 38). From 1713 to 1752, Biswambara Deo, who ruled Jeypore (the present Koraput district was a part of the former Jeypore *zamindary*) established Narayanpatna as the capital of the kingdom. The British government assumed direct administration of the areas held under Jeypore *maharaja* with effect from January 1863 where Captain Galbaraith was appointed as Assistant Superintendent of Police and Leiutenant Smith was appointed as the Assistant Agent.[15]

5.5.1 Land Administration During the Regime of the Kings

The ancient feudal system of land revenue administration prevailed in the Koraput region during the regime of the *rajas* (kings). It was not possible to know exactly the extent of the land with each *ryot* hold at that time because there was no survey and settlement of land during the *raja* (king) period.[16] The amount of revenue land was accounted in terms of seed capacity. The land was administered either by the village system called mustajari or by ryotwari system. Like the *gaonti* system of tenure in Sambalpur, the *mustajari* arrangement is almost the same.[17] By this system, the land revenue is collected by an agent of the landlord called *mustajari* who is compensated either through some part of the collections or by a piece of free land. The office of the *mustajari* was normally held by a brawny and influential individual in the village and the post was ancestral. They were not asked to possess any land records of the village land holdings. In contrary, the *ryotwari* system was based on an accord between the tenants and the landlords. Each village has a register under the revenue *naik* who was appointed by the estate. Nevertheless, very few villages have this kind of system at that time.

To perform various services like defence, religious rituals and revenue collections, the king had appointed people from the coastal areas as the king himself was from the coastal plains. Therefore, the *amins* and *mustajaris* who were appointed by the kings were not tribals and were outsiders to the area who later became the immediate exploiters of the tribal land. There was exploitation by the *amins* and *mustajaris* who exploit and forced many tribals to deeper dense forest through displacing them from their land. The system of *dana* (land grants) by the king to the upper castes people for

[15] Odisha State Archives, Orissa District Gazetteers. http://www.odishaarchives.nic.in/node/169213. Accessed 22 December 2019.

[16] ibid.

[17] ibid.

religious purpose was prevalent there which facilitated the land alienation problem in the area. For this purpose, large extent of land was given to the outsiders by the king in the area. The system of *goti/bethi* (forced unpaid labour) was practiced at that time by the landlords and dominants in the tribal areas.

5.5.2 Land Administration During the Period of British Rule

The collection of land revenue and the exploitation of natural and forest resources were the only interest of the British in tribal areas. The British government introduced many acts for increasing the revenue but did not do anything to modify the system of land revenue. The feudal estate became more powerful under the provisions of the permanent settlement. There was more pressure on the tribals with the increase in rent to pay more under the new provisions. On 1 July 1908, the Madras Estate Land Act came into force in Koraput (Bell 1945). The Act governed the relationship between the tenants and the land holders. As far as the problem of the tenants is concerned, the act was not much beneficial. The British did not do anything, or intend to set up any principles as far as the rights of the tribals over the land were concerned. In 14 August, 1917, 'The Agency Tracts Interest and Land Transfer Act' was enacted to safeguard the interests of the tribals for the first time (ibid.). The spirit and purpose of the said act was not implemented properly where the principal aim was to prevent transfer of land from tribals to non-tribals. Before this Act was implemented, a bulk of tribal land has already been transferred. Bidyut Mohanty and K Anuradha in their article have highlighted the loopholes of the act in the following paragraph:

> People could not take advantage of the passing of this act as they were uneducated and ignorant, even transfers were made after the date. The officials remained completely indifferent in the matter and muted the names of the transferees in the estate records. This left practically no documentary evidence for proving transfer of the land of tribals to non-tribals. Further, this act did not affect the relinquishment of land by tribals in favour of the land holder. So, in several cases, the act was dodged by the tribals relinquishing his land in favour of Jeypore estate and the shrewd non-tribals find an opportunity in obtaining the same from the estate employees.[18]

Under the Government of India Act 1919, the area was first treated as backward tract and then demarcated as partially excluded area for the first time under the Government of India Act 1935. But in the Koraput region, the commercial autocrat and the imperialistic ambitions were salient despite all these acts which made the tribal condition sorrier. On 1 April 1936, when the Koraput district was formed and integrated in the new Odisha Province, a new episode in the history of Jeypore Country was begun.

> The survey and settlement in Koraput were carried out in 1938–1964. The survey and settlement covered an area of 6740 sq. miles (17254.40 sq. km) out of a total area of 25320.96

[18]Mohanty and Anuradha (2009). *Failure of non-violent methods responsible for Narayanpatna uprising*. http://www.newsweb.co.in/news_article_en.php?article=1076. Accessed 8 June 2018.

sq. km. Almost half of the total area of the undivided Koraput district was not surveyed and settled (Kumar et al. 2005: 52)

As Koraput was declared as Scheduled Area by the Indian Constitution, which means the legislation passed by the union and the state will be imposed automatically otherwise debarred by the legislature or the government. After the Constitution of India came into force, the laws which were in force in the state of Odisha and in the country, in general, and land administration laws, in particular, were automatically applied to the district of Koraput.

5.5.3 *Land Administration During Post-independence Period*

The second phase of survey and settlement process started from the year 1951 during the post-independence period.[19] Due to unsuitable technique, hill slopes greater than 10° (the traditional land of the tribals) were not recorded in their name. Because of their proximity to the surveyors and better knowledge, the landlords, feudal heads, *mustajaris* and *amins* in the district recorded the majority of land in their name. Through offering bribe to the survey officers, they have recorded the tribal land in their name. Due to their shy nature and lack of knowledge about the system, the tribals became marginalised again. As there was no end of exploitation of tribals, the euphoria of independence faded away and melted down very soon. The consequence resulted with different form of tribal uprisings, some non-violent and some violent as the issue of land again cropped up in the area.

5.6 The History of Koraput Land Alienation

The first wave of tribal land alienation in Koraput region started by the *amins* and *mustajaris* and the mediator of the kings who were appointed by the kings, mostly outsiders to the area, who later became the immediate exploiters of the tribal land. The second wave of land alienation happened with the survey and settlement procedure of 1960s. The tribals were left out of the whole process of survey and settlement. Lands above 10° slope were not surveyed and settled with the tribals and declared as forest land. The third wave of land alienation in Koraput started in 1970. The non-tribal 'men of affairs' and landlords migrated to Koraput district in 1970 due to the armed revolution in Srikakulam (Andhra Pradesh) (Bannerjee 1986: 214). After settling there, they joined hand with the outsider coastal people of Odisha and unitedly encroached the tribal land. The fourth wave of land alienation and displacement started with the four mega-dams (Kolab, Machhkund, Indrabati and Chitrakonda)

[19] Koraput Survey and Settlement report (1956). Government of Orissa. https://indiacode.nic.in/Bitstream/123456789/5918/1/the_gunjam-koraput_survey%2C_record-ofright_and_settlement_operations.pdf. Accessed 22 June 2019.

and two projects (NALCO-National Aluminium Corporation and HAL-Hindustan Aeronautics Limited) which added to the existing land issues of the tribals of Koraput in contemporary time. The recent commercial plantations on the common property resources and on the so-called 'encroached land' (the tribal lands which were declared as encroached by the government due to lack of land record on the part of the tribals) add to their excruciations.

With this backcloth, the tribals of Narayanpatna block of Koraput district are now being exploited by the outsider encroachers. The non-tribals are enticing the tribals with liquor and keeping them indebted using liquor as bait. The encroachers/landlords/businessmen, etc., commonly known as 'exploiters' or '*dikus*' (outsider exploiters in tribal language), always try that the tribes should not muster enough courage to raise their voice against the exploiters. The bootleggers and the contractors are constantly attempting to intoxicate the tribals by providing hootch to them and jeopardising their life, livelihood and land.

Before discussing the Narayanpatna tribal movement in Koraput district in detail, it is pertinent here to provide a social-demographic account about the study area 'Narayanpatna block'. The researcher has conducted the fieldwork in Narayanpatna block through questionnaire and direct interview method in order to get a complete picture regarding the land problem and about the Narayanpatna movement (2009–14). A social-demographic account of Narayanpatna block in Koraput district of Odisha was discussed below for the easy understanding of the backdrop of the problem and the movement.

5.7 A Brief Account of the Study Area

> Narayanpatna is a block among the total 14 blocks of the Koraput district in Odisha. It is situated in the valley between the hills of Laxmipur and Potangi on two sides, the vast tracts of river irrigated agricultural land of Rayagda on the third side and the plains of Andhra Pradesh on a fourth side. The block has 9 Gram *Panchayats* and 127 villages.[20]

It was a region inhabited by tribal populations consisting of *Kuis* (*Kondh* tribe speaks *kui* language), *Praja* and *Jatapu* who remain isolated till recent times. The number of total families in Narayanpatna block are 9,560 having a total population of 43,575.[21] There are 8,517 BPL families which constitute 89.08% of the total families among which dalit constitute 7.13% and tribals are 81.95%.[22]

[20]Administrative setup, Koraput district, Government of Odisha. https://koraput.nic.in/Administrative-setup/. Accessed 15 December 2019.

[21]Census 2011, Office of the Registrar (General and Census Commissioner), Indian Ministry of Home Affairs 2/A, Mansingh Road, New Delhi. http://censusindia.gov.in/2011census/dchb/2129_PART_B_DCHB_KORAPUT.pdf. Accessed 18 August 2019.

[22]ibid.

The report by the 'Fact Finding Committee on Narayanpatna' constituted by Kuldeep and others have provided the social profile of the Narayanpatna block which was provided in the following paragraph:

> Narayanpatna block is inhabited by sixteen tribal communities including *Kui, Praja, Jarka, Matia, Doria* and others, of whom the *Kuis* are numerically predominant. The tribals who constitute more than 80% people of Narayanpatna block, are interspersed with dalit communities such as *Dombo, Forga, Paiko, Rilli,* etc. Dominant caste such as *Sundis* (local liquor traders/vendors) and *Brahmins* are numerically small but are powerful and influential. Though the incursion of non-tribals has a long history going back to the establishment of the 'Narayanpatna *raj*' since centuries back, the *Sundis* have entered the district after they were driven away from coastal areas of Andhra Pradesh during the Srikakulam armed struggle in the 1960s. The *Sundis* as well as the small section of dalits from the *Dombo* and *Rilli* castes too have made money by exploiting the tribals and selling them liquor (Kuldeep et al. 2011: 1).

The ruling elite of Narayanpatna belongs to this dominant group who are non-tribals exploiters. Moneylenders, landlords, liquor vendors, businessmen and politicians are not separate but belong to the same identity of 'exploiters' in the eyes of the tribals. Primitive accumulation of capital in Narayanpatna region started with the arrival of the liquor dealers called *sundis* in the local language. In the beginning, the tribals had prepared booze from home-based items like fruits, trees, grains, etc. The concept of licensed liquor was introduced and country liquor was banned to punish the tribals. In this way, from *desi* (home) liquor to license foreign liquor took place.

Now, after the ban of home-made liquor and penalisation of the tribals, the traders became the only possessor of liquor which the tribals have to exchange something for consuming liquor, because the tribals are habituated with the consumption of liquor. What mattered to the trader was only the mass of value that could be extracted from the region and for that exchange had to take place in monetary form.

For consumption of liquor, the only possession that the tribals had with them is their land produce or a piece of fertile land. The value that the liquor trader had to extract had to be in the form of money because of two reasons. Firstly, the liquor trader was part of the larger market where money was the only medium of exchange. Secondly, the liquor trader needed the money to prevail in Narayanpatna, so that his market was expanded not only for liquor but for the consumer goods that he sell as part of his expanded business. This was the compulsion to extract value in the form of money, which excluded consumption of forest products by the capitalist. So the tribals were left to bet their land because of the refusal of the capitalist to exchange with the produce (Kuldeep et al. 2011: 2).

Regulation 2 of the OSATIP Act, 1956 directs that tribal land cannot be transferred, purchased or alienated by the non-tribals in the Scheduled Areas or in the areas having more than 50% tribal populations.[23] But, in the case of Narayanpatna, the state's executive did not properly implement the said regulation and never try to forbid non-tribals' acquisition of tribal land. The landlords from the coastal areas of Andhra Pradesh have joined with the liquor vendors of Narayanpatna area and exploited the

[23]The Odisha Scheduled Areas Transfer of Immovable Property (OSATIP) (by Scheduled Tribes) Regulation, 1956. http://www.igrodisha.gov.in/pdf/regulation2.pdf. Accessed 9 November 2019.

tribal situation there and functioned as a class of capitalists. These capitalist migrants from coastal Andhra Pradesh and Odisha have joined hand and alienated the tribal land. The situation in Narayanpatna was made such that for survival, the tribals had nothing to sell but their power of labour. In this way, the tribals of Narayanpatna became wage labourers in their own land. During this period, the population of tribals in Narayanpatna were 85%, whereas, the actual land the tribals possessed was about 10–15% (Satyabrata 2009a: 3). This was the condition till the Narayanpatna movement began in 2006 by the CMAS (Patnaik 2009: 4). In order to understand the nature and objectives of the Narayanpatna movement, it is imperative to provide a short background about the 'CMAS', the organisation which organised the movement in Narayanpatna block.

5.8 *Chasi Mulia Adivasi Sangha* (CMAS); Genesis and Development

The tribal movement in Narayanpatna was organised and led by the *Chasi Mulia Adivasi Sangh* (CMAS). Anshuman Behera in his article has provided an account regarding the origin of the CMAS. The narrative was quoted in the following paragraph:

> The origin of the CMAS goes back to the *Rythu Coolie Sangham* (RCS), an Andhra Pradesh based peasant organisation which founded by the pro-Maoist peasant leaders in the Vizian-gram district of the state. A branch of RCS was opened in Odisha by 'Bhaskar Rao' alias 'Basa' in Almonda of Bandhugaon block of Koraput district in 1995. The RCS, once active in Koraput, was successful in garnering support of the local tribals, peasants and the bonded labourers, mainly from Bandhugaon and Narayanpatna blocks of Koraput district. There had been a close association between the RCS branch of Odisha and its parent organisation in Andhra Pradesh. Some of the important leaders of Communist Party of India–Marxist-Leninist (CPI-ML) such as Gananatha Patra were actively involved in the activities of the RCS (both in Andhra Pradesh and Koraput) (Behera 2013: 2).

In 1990s, some members of the RCS, Koraput had also participated throughout the anti-*arak* (local liquor) movement in Andhra Pradesh (Behera 2013: 2). It influences the activities of the RCS, Koraput. In 1995, Kondagiri Paidamma from Baba Bankidi village started the anti-liquor movement in Koraput (ibid.). Due to spearheading violent activities, she was arrested by the police but released later finding no evidence against her. With the active support from the leaders of the CPI-ML, i.e., Gananath Patra, Srikanta Mohanty, Bhaskar Rao and Brahamananda Muli, the RCS-Koraput organised mass rallies demanding land to the landless tribals; effective and welfare administration in their areas, and a ban on consumption and selling of liquor through mass rallies and protest with the help of some active members like Nachika Linga, Wadeka Singana, Nachika Chamara, and Arjun Kendruka etc. (ibid.: 2–3). Before Nachika Linga, Kondagiri Paidamma had emerged as the leader of the RCS branch in the Koraput district by 2001 (ibid.: 2). Gananath Patra remains as the advisor of the RCS Koraput. The organisation carried out regular activities and rallies which demanded '*jamin, jal and jungle*' (land, water and forest) for the tribals.

The RCS in Koraput, in the meantime, has changed its name as '*Chasi Mulia Adivasi Sangh*' (CMAS) due to certain compulsions which were quoted from Anshuman Behera and given in the following paragraph:

> The RCS was banned in Andhra Pradesh on August 17, 2005, following a ban on the CPI (Maoist) and its frontal organisations. In anticipation of a similar ban by the Odisha government, the RCS-Koraput changed its name to *Chasi Mulia Adivasi Sangh* in 2006. The first ever rally under the banner of the CMAS was organised on October 10, 2006 demanding registration of land in the names of the tribal and release of their members arrested by the police. The activities of the CMAS, however, were not all that altruistic and peaceful. The CMAS activists in different times were engaged in violent activities during the mobilisation of the people and during the rallies. During 2006–2008, the CMAS members were involved in grabbing land from the non-tribal exploiters; giving veiled threat to the 'corrupt government officers', mobilising the people to join the CMAS and organising rallies against liquor consumption (Behera 2013: 3).

While collecting the data during the fieldwork, it was informed that the *Chasi Mulia Adivasi Sangh* (earlier recognised as RCS), though functioning in the district for last 15 years had took its organisational work only in 2004.[24] Since then, with the leadership of the CMAS, the people of Narayanpatna have been protesting on various issues. Under the banner of CMAS, the people launched scathing attacks on the illegal and licensed country made and Indian manufactured foreign liquor and brandy shops operating under the jurisdiction of Narayanpatna block in January, 2009.[25] The illegal manufacturing units of the country liquor and the vehicles transporting them had been destroyed by them. During the first 4 months of the agitation, the tribals were able to stop the transporting and manufacturing of the 'hooch' illegally distilled and usually substandard alcoholic booze. After that, the tribal began their protest against the landlords who were illegally grabbing their land and exploiting them.

> On 12 June 2008, thousands of people belonging to hundreds of villages under six *Gram Panchayats* (GPs) of Narayanpatna block walked to the land of the landlords shouting slogans on demanding the right of the people over the land and posted red flags there occupying the land, and ploughed the land collectively.[26]

They also distributed the pieces of land among the landless poor tribals during 5 July to 10 July, 2008.[27] Through this movement, they took possession of around 3000 acres of land (Patnaik 2009: 3). The exploiting groups of Narayanpatna, mostly the

[24]Data compiled on 20 December 2015 during the interview with the people of Bhaliaput village of Narayanpatna block of Koraput district (Odisha). The interview was in Odia language and it was translated to English by the researcher.

[25]Data compiled on 21 December 2015 during the interview with the people of Gatigura village of Narayanpatna block of Koraput district (Odisha). The interview was in Odia language and it was translated to English by the researcher.

[26]Data compiled on 21 December 2015 during the interview with the people of Gatigura village of Narayanpatna block of Koraput district (Odisha). The interview was in Odia language and it was translated to English by the researcher.

[27]ibid.

landlords and hooch traders, were driven away from the villages by the tribal people. The rest of the moneylenders gave the land back to the tribals by conforming to the demands of the CMAS. The fact that people's force can conquer any force, whatsoever it may be, is now realised by the tribals. The hooch traders and the landlords reinvigorated their efforts through conspiracies and had tried in different ways to suppress the Narayanpatna movement.

The government never sorted out the land issues of the people although they are asking for rights over the land through lawful agitation and had brought it to the notice of the government many times in the past (Kar 2012: 2). So, the tribals under the banner of CMAS boycotted the false democracy and farcical elections propounded by the ruling class. They also had decided to give up the way of appealing to the government and the state agents. Finally, the tribals of Narayanpatna under the banner of the CMAS launched the movement to drive the moneylenders and landlords out of the Narayanpatna area and posted red flags on the land occupied by the CMAS.

5.9 The Narayanpatna Movement

The landless poor tribals of Narayanpatna have organised themselves and fought back their tormentors the '*Sundi-Sahukar-Sarkar*' (liquor vendor-landlord-government) nexus over the last few years, under the banner of CMAS" (Patnaik 2009: 2). The CMAS' land and anti-liquor movement took a decisive turn in the year 2009 though the CMAS was working in the region for more than 15 years. It reached a flashpoint in January 2009, when the tribals of Narayanpatna block not only chased away the liquor vendors from the villages, but rallied themselves in thousands to prosecute them to their stronghold (ibid.). The CMAS activists destroyed the wine shops in Narayanpatna town. In the villages like Bhaliaput, *Mahua* trees from which cheap liquor was produces were destroyed by the *Biplabi Adivasi Mahila Sangha* (BAMS)[28] with the cooperation of the CMAS, and therefore, now, there is not a single *mahua* tree in the Narayanpatna block.[29] The inhibition in the sale and ingestion of liquor was almost checked by 2009. The liquor traders and landlords fled from the region and the parasitic trade collapsed due to the mass movement led by the CMAS. The mass success against the liquor traders and landlords encouraged the tribals to heighten the land movement. The lands which were tricked out from the tribals earlier by the landlords and *sahukars* (moneylenders) are now reclaimed by the CMAS. Under the banner of the CMAS, the tribals recaptured more than 3000 acres of such land, and

[28]The *Mahila (women)* organisation of *adivasis* formed in Narayanpatna in line with CMAS to protest and fight against the state and police oppression. The word *adivasi* is used interchangeably with the word tribal in Odisha, though the word *adivasi* specifies for the indigenous aboriginal people of that particular region.

[29]Data collected during the interview with the people of Jhaliagura village of Narayanpatna block in Koraput district of Odisha on 24 December 2015. The interview was in Odia language and it was translated to English by the researcher.

distributed among the landless tribals of Narayanpatna block within a month.[30] As a response to the raising surge of mass struggle, on 4 May 2009, the liquor vendors and the landlords of the area with the active cooperation from the state have formed the peace committee or '*shanti sena*' to counter the tribals' movement in Narayanpatna.[31]

5.9.1 Various Phases of the Movement

With the success of anti-liquor movement, Nachika Linga, the chief leader and president of CMAS (Narayanpatna) went on to forcibly grab land from the landlords, locally known as the sahukars. Linga tried to mobilise people with the slogan 'mada mukti, jami mukti and goti mukti' that means freedom from liquor, capturing tribal lands from the landlords and freedom from bonded labour. Between 2000 and 2006, the initial phase of the Narayanpatna movement started, and near about 180 acres of tribal land were repossessed by *Chasi Mulia Adivasi Sangh* from the clutches of the non-tribal landlords.[32] Nachika Linga was sentenced for imprisonment in 2006, with different charges against him, including the charges of being a Maoist.[33] In 2008, he was exonerated of all charges.[34] Then, the second phase of the Narayanpatna movement gets started. In this phase, the CMAS led the tribal movement and had grown in considerable extent. Prior to the assembly election of Odisha in 2009, Nachika Linga, the chief leader of the movement was released from jail.[35] After Nachika's release from jail, with the support from *Ghenua Bahini* (tribal youth armed with traditional weapon) the CMAS arranged a big rally. After the massive rally, the nature of CMAS' movement has considerably changed and it has acquired a relatively belligerent form with 3000 acres of land being in its control.[36]

---

[30]An interview with the people of Jhaliagura village of Narayanpatna block in Koraput district of Odisha on 24 December 2015. The interview was in Odia language and it was translated to English by the researcher.

[31]ibid.

[32]An interview with the people of Narayanpatna village in Koraput district of Odisha on 25 December 2015. The interview was in Odia language and it was translated to English by the researcher.

[33]An interview with the people of village Mundigura in Narayanpatna block of Koraput district during the fieldwork on 26 December 2015. The interview was in Odia language and it was translated to English by the researcher.

[34]ibid.

[35]ibid.

[36]ibid.

5.9.2 Suppression and Resistance

As far as the state's action towards the Narayanpatna movement is concerned, the state government on 4 May, 2009, formed the '*Shanti* Committee' (peace committee)[37] which carried out protests against the CMAS (Kuldeep et al. 2011: 3). The nexus between the government and the 'peace committee' was revealed in a report by ICAWPI which was quoted in the following paragraph:

> The peace committee submitted a memorandum to the BDO of Narayanpatna demanding the ban of the *Chasi Mulia Adivasi Sangha* (CMAS), arrest of *sangha* leaders and retrieval of land occupied by the *Sangha*. Thereafter, the peace committee went on a rampage, destroyed houses of 10 *Sangha* activists and looted away their all belongings. They also destroyed houses of the *Sangha* leaders. In order to repulse the attack and the 'destructive' spree of the 'peace committee', armed with traditional weapons, people in hundreds of villages led by the *Chasi Mulia Adivasi Sangha* in Narayanpatna area got ready. They boldly faced the goons of the 'peace committee' who were continuously attacking villages one by one. They closely followed the goons of the 'peace committee' and drove them away as far as five kilometres from Narayanpatna. During the clash between the 'peace committee' and the *Sangha,* Nityananda Malik of Gatiguda village, who owed allegiance to the 'peace committee', lost his life. Unable to face the stiff resistance put up by the *Sangha* people, the 'peace committee' had to retreat.[38]

The so-called 'peace committee' failed to check the movement on account of powerful opposition from the tribals led by CMAS. Therefore, the government took efforts to arrange the committee anew. Instead of 'peace committee', in all the blocks of Koraput district, the *Nagarik Suraksha Samiti* were formed.[39] It organised programmes of open public meetings against the CMAS and the Narayanpatna tribal movement by conducting processions (rallies) and *dharna* (strike) in Bandhugaon, Laxmipur, Simliguda, Damanjodi, Kaekori, Nandapur Gumma, and Dasmantpur areas which are adjunct to the Narayanpatna block.[40] The CMAS and its members were depicted as plunderers and unruly by the *Nagarik Suraksha Samiti* to create dissentious feeling and a situation of mass hysteria among the people of the district. Companies like Hindustan Aluminium Corporation (HINDALCO) and National Aluminium Company (NALCO) with the help of the government and landlords of the area have spent brobdingnagian amounts of money for the *Nagarik Suraksha Samiti* to strategically crush the movement of the tribals because the CMAS was influencing the tribals of other areas against the bauxite mining in the Deomali hills which creates problem for both HINDALCO and NALCO.

---

[37]The *shanti* committee was formed on 4 May 2009 by the state to suppress the movement and later identified as *Nagarik Surakshya Samiti.* The members of the committee were the landlords, exploiters, persons from upper castes and mainly the outsiders whose land was captured by the CMAS.

[38]The Flames of Narayanpatna, Orissa, report by International Campaign against War on the People in India (ICAWPI), p. 4. http://www.icawpi.org/resistance/news1/965-the-flames-of-narayanpatna. Accessed 22 October 2018.

[39]In an interview with the people of Narayanpatna village during the fieldwork on 27 December 2015. The interview was in Odia language and it was translated to English by the researcher.

[40]ibid.

So, the total purpose of the *Nagarik Suraksha Samiti* was only to serve the interest of the exploiters including the present government, which went against the tribals of Narayanpatna, and there was nothing called 'peace element' or *Nagarik Surakshya* (citizens' protection) in their agenda. Regarding the combined terror of the *Nagarik Suraksha Samiti* and the police towards CMAS, the villagers of Mundiguda have expressed their views in Odia language (during the fieldwork) which were translated and quoted in the following paragraph:

> The *Chasi Mulia Adivasi Sangha* organised an open meeting at Laxmipur in August, 2009, in protest against series of attacks and oppression of the peace Committees/*Nagarik Surakshya Samiti* and the conspiracy of the government. While the police did not permit the *Sangha* to hold such mega meeting, the *Nagarik Suraksha Samiti* along with the police terrorised the people who were coming to attend the meeting. The police detained the people and the vehicles so as to disrupt the meeting. Despite this hurdles, thousands of people, *Sangha* activists and belligerent '*Ghenua* brigade' (arm militia of CMAS) walked to the place of the meeting at Laxmipur from Narayanpatna holding flags, placards and banners brushing aside all threats and terrors posed by the *Nagarik Suraksha Samiti* and police.[41]

Due to peoples' strength *en masse,* the meeting was a great success despite all the hurdles created by the united force of *Nagarik Surakshya Samiti* and the police. The so-called *Nagarik Surakshya Samiti* and the landlords once again raised their voice against the *Sangha* in the wake of the success of the meeting. The reaction of the *Nagarik Surakshya Samiti* was described in the article written by Amitabha Kar (interview with Dandapani Mohanty on November 18, 2012) which was provided in the following paragraph:

> They submitted a memorandum to the Governor demanding imposition of ban on the CMAS and the arrest of all *Sangha* members and hanging of Nachika Linga to death, restoration of land wrested back by the tribes, led by the *Sangha.* The *Nagarik Suraksha Samiti* have observed a *bandh* (strike) in Koraput on October 21, 2009. The political leaders of the ruling party (BJD), the landlords and the exploiting class of Narayanpatna and its adjunct areas have guided the *Nagarik Surakshya Samiti.* It also tried to conflict between the tribal and non-tribal poor dalits by manipulating them and creating commotions among the two exploited groups (Kar 2012: 4).

With the instruction from the *Nagarik Surakshya Samiti*, in the name of sorting out the problem and for the peoples' security, the police forces were sent by the government to the Narayanpatna block. The Boarder Security Force (BSF), the Special Operation Group (SOG) and the Central Reserved Police Force (CRPF) camped in Narayanpatna with the help of the landlords and *Nagarik Surakshya Samiti.* As per the information collected during the interview at Jhaliagura village in the Narayanpatna block, the villagers have described that These forces visit the villages every day in the name of patrolling and threatening the people. They entered each home and arrested people falsely alleging that they (the people) had links with the Maoists.[42]

---

[41] Data collected during the interview with the people of village Mundigura in Narayanpatna block of Koraput district during the fieldwork on 27 December 2015. The interview was in Odia language and it was translated to English by the researcher.

[42] During an interview with the people of Jhaliagura village in Narayanpatna block of Koraput district during the fieldwork on 28 December 2015. The interview was in Odia language and it was translated to English by the researcher.

10 police personnel were attacked and killed at Palur (near Beharampur, Odisha), by the People's Liberation Guerrilla Army (PLGA) of the Maoists, on 18 June 2009. After this incident, to took avenge, the police get exasperated and arrested the impeccant tribals of Narayanpatna while they were on their way to market. The angry people opposed to the haughtiness and high-handedness of the security forces. ICAWPI in an article 'The flames of Narayanpatna' has accounted the pathetic conditions of the tribals of Narayanpatna which are quoted below in the following paragraph:

> Around 3000 people took their feet to Narayanpatna police station and the building where the CRPF were camping. The angry mob asked the police to stop oppression and attack on the innocent people. The police had to bow down before the united strength and discontentment of the people. Finally, the police begged apology and gave assurance in writing not to repeat the mischief which ultimately helped the people calm down. On the other hand, the people armed with their traditional weapons got ready in the villages to prevent the possible onslaught on them by the police. The people of five/six villages of that area stayed for three days in Palur which was subjected to police high-handedness, extending support to those villagers thereby boosting up the morale of the frightened people. The people blocked all the roads by falling trees so as to prevent entry of the police force into the village of Narayanpatna from Laxmipur, Rayagda, Bandhugaon and Koraput. At last, the situation came to such condition that the government supplied foods stuffs by helicopter to the police force camped at Narayanpatna (The Flames of Narayanpatna, ICAWPI: 5).

Now, the police had targeted the leaders of the CMAS, pasted the posters of Nachika Linga, Ram Padhy and Singhana on the walls of Narayanpatna police station in October 2009. During the interview, it was reported that after seeing the posters of the leaders of CMAS at Narayanpatna police station, people marched to the police station to remove the posters and the police begged to the people on that day. The people of village Podapadar in Narayanpatna block who had witnessed the Narayanpatna police firing on 20 November, 2009, have explained regarding the matter during the interview in the following words which were translated and quoted in the following paragraph:

> Around 200 people walked to the police station on 20 November, 2009, against the police torture and highhandedness. Dissatisfied with the police excesses, the people asked the police why they had gone to Tumbuguda? Why they were committing atrocities on the innocent people? Why they failed to keep up their written promise given to the people? The people demanded answers to these questions from the police through slogans. But the police, without caring for the people, went inside the rooms, locking the gate of the police station which made the people angry. Then, 10 youths of the '*Gehuna* brigade' (peoples' protector comprising youth tribals) along with the *Sangha* leader Singhana entered the police station breaking open the lock of the gate. They asked the police officer about the earlier assurances given to them which triggered heated exchange of words between the *Sangha* leaders and the police. At that time, the police personnel present on both the upper and lower floors of the police station indiscreetly opened fire at the people. One of the bullets heat the head of the leader Andru Nachika (nephew of 'Nachika Linga'-the chief leader of CMAS), who fell down dead on the spot. When *Sangha* leader Kenduraku Singanna (close aid of Nachika) was inside

the police station, a bullet hit him and he came outside injured and fell down near the gate. Singhanna and Andru became martyrs at the police firing and many people were injured.[43]

5.9.3 *Mass Reaction by Different Organisations on the Police Firing in Narayanpatna*

In Odisha, a state wide twelve-hour strike was observed by different organisations on 28 November 2009, to dissent against the police firing on tribals of Narayanpatna and to excoriate the killing of two CMAS leaders (Satyabrata 2009a: 1). Different organisations like *Lok Sangram Manch,* CPI (ML) New Democracy, CPI (ML) Liberation, Malkangiri *Adivasi Sangha,* Odisha Forest *Mazdoor Sangha* and many other progressive organisations participated in the protest. Satyabrata on behalf of *Sanhati* (the online journal) has reported in detail regarding the Odisha *bandh* (Strike) against the police firing and killing of CMAS leaders and the report was quoted below within the following paragraph:

> The protest demanded an immediate withdrawal of CRPF, Cobra and other paramilitary forces from the region and to grant compensation of rupees 10 lakh to the family of those deceased. On the day of 28 November, several demonstrations were organised all over the state, especially in southern Odisha. There were protest rallies in Koraput. In Rayagda, several people organised by CPI (ML) Liberation were arrested for protest and blockade of a road. In Maniguda block, a road blockade was organised by *Lok Sangram Manch.* A protest demonstration was staged in Matili block of Malkangiri where thousands of tribals came out on armed with their traditional weaponry. Four trains, including Rajdhani Express, were halted at Bhubaneswar railway station for three hours due to the down-to-dusk protests (Satyabrata 2009a: 1).

Combing operations in Narayanpatna still continued despite state-wide protests by different organisations. The Cobra battalions were sent to Narayanpatna and its adjunct areas. Media reported the arrest of several 'Naxals' in Narayanpatna and the police accounted that people are no more appealing to the CMAS and peace is being reinstated in the area.[44] The police have also reported that many tribals had given their consent in 'writing' that they won't endorse the CMAS' action any more.[45] Now, the capitalist state has deployed its 'repressive apparatus' to hunt the tribals and trying to forcefully arrest them without solving the land problem.

The state now got the easiest way to arrest the CMAS' activists, because the tribals are now being tagged as Maoists and the CMAS as a frontal Maoists organisation. The opposition parties which have a vibrant role for the safeguard of democracy remained dumb on the Narayanpatna police firing and on the land issues of the tribals. The government of Odisha which had least regard for tribals operates in a tyrannical manner.

---

[43]An interview with the people of Podapadar village of Narayanpatna block in Koraput district on 26 December, 2015. The interview was in Odia language and it was translated to English by the researcher.

[44]The *Dharitri* (2009) (Daily Odia Newspaper, (Bhubaneswar edition) November 30, p. 1.

[45]ibid.

5.9.4 The Situation at the Time of Crop Cutting in the Acquired Land

Due to the united attacks launched on the tribals of Narayanpatna by the peace committee, police and other security forces like CRPF, BSF and SOG; the crops, property and houses of the member and activists of the CMAS had been demolished. Due to police pressure, though few old persons in some villages have surrendered to the police, the '*Ghenua* brigade'[46] and the leaders of the CMAS were convincing the people of Narayanpatna not to give up their struggle. They assure to protect the people and asked the people to prepare for the future course of action.

With such inspiration from their leaders and protection by the '*Ghenua* brigade', the people refused to give half of the crops as share to the landlords while going to the crop fields to cut crops. It is to be noted here that the lands which were produced for crop were forcefully occupied by the CMAS from the landlords during the initial phase of the movement. They challenged to turn down the advice of the police "to leave the land/crop fields". In order to answer the police, all of them say in one voice—If possible and if we have strength, we will harvest crops and if it is not possible, then we may destroy the crops or they may rot, but we will never give a share of the crops to the landlords.[47] With enough courage and confidence, the people plighted to protect their land, property and will never leave the CMAS even at the cost of their blood and lives. The tribals also challenged the police deployed in the villages by saying, We will see, how many of us will you shot to death? If needed, we shall shed our lives in the fields.[48] With all this, the tribals got ready with their traditional weapons (bows and arrows) to face the security and police personnel.

By beating of '*dhampa*' (tribal drum), the tribals announced that no one could eliminate their fight and took the crops from their possession after cutting them from the acquired land and from 23 December, 2009, the tribals of Narayanpatna started to cut the crops.[49] To prevent the tribals from cutting the crops, the police force comes in large numbers to Narayanpatna. While during the clash between the police and the people, one police man was killed and others were injured. One tribal woman namely Mangli was killed during the clash between CMAS and the police forces, and the police had to retreat.[50] The tribals are now again united under the leadership of CMAS, they faced the police boldly, they fought with the security forces and cut crops in spite of police high-handedness and threatening.

---

[46]The youth militant of CMAS, both male and female wearing red shirt with traditional arms and fight with the security personnel during the movement and police oppression.

[47]Narayanpatna Firing and its aftermath (2011). *The New Indian Express*, February 06, p. 3.

[48]The Flames of Narayanpatna, Orissa, report by International Campaign Against War on the People in India (ICAWPI), p. 5. http://www.icawpi.org/resistance/news1/965-the-flames-of-narayanpatna. Accessed 22 October 2018.

[49]An interview with the people of Balipeta village in Narayanpatna block of Koraput district on 2 January 2016. The interview was in Odia language and it was translated to English by the researcher.

[50]ibid.

5.9.5 The Conflict of Tribals and Dalits Within the Movement

The *CMAS* while going for the solution of the land problems of the tribals has done some mistakes. The dealings and attitude of the CMAS towards the encroachers were regarded as its great mistake. In Narayanpatna, though the tribes are majority in number, some non-tribes like *Brahmin, Paidi, Sundhi, Mali, Kumuti and Dombo* also live there. These non-tribals like *Brahmins, Sundhi* and *Kumuti* are the dominant community in the area and have economic and political control over the tribal people. These non-tribal dominant groups in the Narayanpatna area are known as mainly contractors, hooch traders and landlords who exploit the tribals, and therefore known as exploiters in the eyes of the tribals.

But there are some other non-tribal communities belonging to *Dombo, Paidi* and *Reli* castes from the dalit sections who earn their livelihood by small business and daily wage work. Among them, maximum of the dalits in Narayanpatna are poor people and equally exploited by the higher caste people. But few dalits are involved in politics and grabbed the tribal land. These few advanced dalit people are getting the maximum benefits from reservation and the welfare schemes of the state meant for their community. They are the immediate oppressor for the dalit community and also for the tribals who duped the tribals and most of them are involved in 'anti-people' (anti-tribal) activities in the Narayanpatna block.

In order to sort out the conflicts between 'tribals' and 'non-tribals' on the issue of the latter's grab of tribal land, the *CMAS* could not take suitable steps during the Narayanpatna movement. It was not able to convince and unite the non-tribal exploited people, i.e. poor dalits. The *sangha* could not able to attack the exploiting groups distinguishing them from the non-tribal-poor dalits. Considering them as anti-tribes, all non-tribes including the poor dalits of the Narayanpatna block were attacked by the CMAS during the movement. In the attack, some dalits lost their property and houses. As a result, all the families belonging to *Paidi* and *Dombo* caste of the village Podapadar and other villages (under Narayanpatna block) had left their villages and they are now staying in the colonies in Koraput town provided by the district administration and some other dalit households staying at the roadside of the Koraput town without any protection and shelter.[51]

Due to the mistake of the CMAS, the conflict among the exploited and the exploiter turned to be the dispute between the tribes and dalits which facilitate the government to create conspiracy to divide people on this line. The government and the statist media projected the Narayanpatna movement as nothing but the Maoist and the tribals' attack on poor dalits. The dalits and other oppressed people who were driven by the CMAS from Narayanpatna had sheltered in the relief camp at Bhubaneswar and Koraput. The government swayed them with the allurement of jobs to help

[51] Data collected on 27 December 2015, during an interview with the dalit people of Narayanpatna block of Koraput district (Odisha) who were driven by the CMAS and were staying with their family at the district relief camp in Koraput town. The interview was conducted in the relief camp in Koraput town and the pictures were provided in the annexure. The interview was in Odia language and it was translated to English by the researcher.

the 'peace committee' which later renamed as *Nagarik Surakshya Samiti* and to work against the CMAS (Kuldeep et al. 2011: 3). The mass media highlighted the misinformation that CMAS which is a '*sangha* of looters' and run by the Maoists, has attacked the poor dalits of Narayanpatna (which was already planned by the government), and the news creates a mass hysteria towards CMAS and Narayanpatna movement among the public.[52]

Later, the CMAS realised its mistake, but it was too late. The *sangha* changed its *modus operandi* after identifying its faults and took steps to bring back the poor dalits who had left their home. The *sangha* tried its best to consult with them and discuss the matter, but the exploiters played cunning role by taking the support of the poor dalits who have left their villages, through different means. In this regard, the International Campaign Against War on the People in India (ICAWPI) has reported in an article which is pertinent to quote here and was provided in the following paragraph:

> Each step of the CMAS in this connection was thwarted by the government, exploiting landlords and by the vested interest groups who tried their best not to allow any peaceful solution to the problems. They also tried not to allow the exploited people to get them united. In the aftermath of the police firing on 20 November, the dalit people were being kept in the forefront while launching attacks on the villagers. The situation had come to such a position that if somebody was shot dead by the police, he or she was proclaimed as either a tribal or a dalit. The dalit people did not understand the gimmicks played by the government and the moneylenders and did not come forward to sort out the problem through discussions with the *Sangha*. Keeping the greater interests of the people in view, the *Chasi Mulia Adivasi Sangha* had called upon the exploited tribal and non-tribal people to come closer and unite peacefully to sort out the problems they had been facing. It also earnestly asked the people, both tribals and exploited non-tribes, to unitedly participate in the fight against the exploiters, government and landlords foiling their evil designs.[53]

To produce a counter-revolutionary situation and a repressive action, tribal-dalit divide was deliberately created by the exploiters with the help of the state. Now, CMAS was postulated as a militant and terrorist organisation where the Narayanpatna movement was posited by the government as a menace to 'common people' and creating chaos in place of peace. The state with its deliberative propaganda has produced a hysterical milieu and attracted the masses into the counter-revolutionary bloc created by it, to prevent the Narayanpatna movement.

---

[52]An interview with the people of Tentulipadar village in Narayanpatna block of Koraput district on 28 December 2015. The interview was in Odia language and it was translated to English by the researcher.

[53]The Flames of Narayanpatna, Orissa, report by International Campaign against War on the People in India (ICAWPI), p. 8. http://www.icawpi.org/resistance/news1/965-the-flames-of-narayanpatna. Accessed 22 October 2018.

5.9.6 *Role of* Nagrik Surakshya Samiti *or* Shanti Sena *(the Counter-Revolutionary Bloc)*

The state with its deliberative propaganda has produced a situation for the third necessary component for counter-revolution and has created the *shanti sena*' (peace troops) or *Nagarik Surakshya Samiti*.[54] The 'peace' part of the *Nagrik Surakshya Samiti* was nothing else, but constitutes the exploitatory *status quo*. It was in fact a militant outfit of the capitalist landlords and the exploiters of the area which try to save capitalism from its juncture. It portrayed and characterise the CMAS as a Maoist organisation and the CMAS activists are Maoist sympathisers. The *shanti sena* with the support from the administration and police has organised demonstrations against the Narayanpatna movement and demanded for the ban of the CMAS. In Narayanpatna, there was an encounter between the *shanti sena* and CMAS where one person from *shanti sena* group was killed which motivated police intervention and security operation in the area.[55] A CMAS leader was also killed in the fight between the two groups in 2009.[56] The *shanti sena* has projected before the media and the administration that the violence in the area is due to the presence of CPI (Maoists) and its sister organisation, the CMAS, which should be banned and its leaders like Nachika Linga, Gananatha Patra and Srikan Mohanty should be arrested immediately.

The corporate media, the strongest ideological ally of the state, has produced a hysterical surrounding about the tribal movement in Narayanpatna. There were innumerable TV shows that showed that there was *laal attank* (red terror) in the Narayanpatna region.[57] It also showed that the Narayanpatna movement is a brutal attack of the Maoists over the innocent dalits of that area. The alternative media could not formulate the logic of the Narayanpatna movement and could not support the tribals owing to lack of information, due to the isolation character of the movement and 24-hour security operation in the area. Though the movement was against the exploiters, it has wrongly displaced a large section of dalits from that area which provide an anti-dalit character to the movement. Therefore, the civil society and intellectuals of the state generally felt soreness towards Narayanpatna movement.

---

[54] ibid.

[55] The Flames of Narayanpatna, Orissa, report by International Campaign against War on the People in India (ICAWPI), p. 6. http://www.icawpi.org/resistance/news1/965-the-flames-of-narayanpatna. Accessed 22 October 2018.

[56] ibid.

[57] Orissa: Narayanpatna on the boil again over land grabbing (2010). NDTV News, October 17. http://www.ndtv.com/video/player/news/orissa-narayanpatna-on-the-boil-again-over-land-grabbing/170018&cp. Accessed 22 June 2016.

5.9.7 *Role of Women in Narayanpatna Movement*

During the movement, whether it is against arrack business or against the land alienation, the tribal women of Narayanpatna have kept themselves in the forefront of the fight always. They fought against the *Nagrik Surakshya Samiti* and with the police using the home-made chilli powder and traditional weapons. They had also played key role during the fight against liquor and hooch traders in 2004 in the Narayanpatna areas. The organised mass and cooperative efforts of the women in Narayanpatna have proved successful in making Narayanpatna as liquor-free region. In many cases, women in most of the villages of Narayanpatna have pushed men behind and come forward at the time of police attack on the villages. They ask their male members to remain in behind and they will go to face the police. Regarding the role of the women in Narayanpatna movement, ICAWPI has mentioned in an article that they faced the police unitedly and boldly and also attack the police making them injured during the police encounter. The detailed ICAWPI report regarding the role of women during the movement was quoted in the following paragraph:

> In the month of June 2009, 50 policemen entered the houses in the village of Lalisahi under Barigi *panchayat*, threw around the belongings and tried to arrest the male members of the families. At that time, the women unitedly caught one policemen and beat him up. Thinking that the women may kill him, the remaining police force restored to blank firing there, freed their colleague from the clutches of the women and ran away. On 3 August, 2009, the gray-hound police numbering 35 had entered the village of Jangadi Balasa under Kerubadi panchayat in Bandhugaon block. On that day, the woman also encircled the police force, clashed with them and sent message about the entry of police into the village to the male members of the village, who were then outside the village. The message was also circulated to other villages. As a result, armed with traditional weapons, the men and women rushed to the spot from all sides and snatched away mobile phone sets, kit bags and arms from the grey-hound police. They tied some of the police force and asked them why the police had come? The frightened police, finding no other way, begged the villagers and politely said "We have small kids, please let us off". Then the people paraded them as far as main road and let them off after obtaining assurance from the Block Development Officer and Sub Inspector there.[58]

In some cases, the police were confronted with brick batting and stone pelting by the children and women of the village. In some other instances, when the male members were taken away by the police, the women fought with the police unitedly and courageously and snatched away their male members from the police. During the meetings, rallies, *gherao* (protest by surrounding a building or person until demands are met) and *dharna* (strike), the women always remain in the forefront. Confronting with the police became the day-to-day affairs for the tribal women of Narayanpatna during the movement and aftermath. In October 2009, when the police pasted the photos of Nachika Linga, Ram Padhi and Singhana, (the leaders of the CMAS) describing them as looters and Maoists, during that time, more than 2000 women

---

[58]The Flames of Narayanpatna, Orissa, report by International Campaign against War on the People in India (ICAWPI), p. 7. http://www.icawpi.org/resistance/news1/965-the-flames-of-narayanpatna. Accessed 22 October 2018.

marched to the Narayanpatna police station and dissented against such activity of the police. ICAWPI in an article has revealed the revolutionary role of the tribal women of Narayanpatna regarding the above matter which was quoted in the following paragraph:

> The women had torn the posters. When a group of tribal women tried to barge into the police station, the policemen immediately closed the gate locking it and *lathi*-charged on the irate mob. Despite this, the people entered the police station crossing over the gate and asked the police officer about their inhuman act. After getting assurance from the police, they had let them off. The women also took part in the incident on 20 November, 2009, where police had opened fire at the people. They had also brought the dead bodies of Singhana and Andru from police station for cremation. The women had also offered stiff resistance to the atrocities perpetrated by police on the male members of the village in the wake of the police firing. When the women were preventing police from arresting and beating up the male members, some of them were also injured as police used slang language and attacked on their heads (The Flames of Narayanpatna, ICAWPI: 7).

Despite being injured, the women followed the police and compelled the police to let off some of the male members of their family. The article depicts police repressin and the role of the tribal women during the movement, which were as follows:

> In the wake of police firing on 20 November, 2009, police force arrested Kumudini of Polapat village, a women leader of the *Sangh,* sent her to police custody in order to bring down the resistance put up by women and to frustrate their united strength. The police had also arrested one women leader of the *CMAS* belonging to Paschimagram, when she was returning to home from Narayanpatna market (The Flames of Narayanpatna, ICAWPI: 8)

During the attacks of the united front of BSF, CRPF, SOG and the police on the villages to arrest the male members and leaders of CMAS, all the male members including the *Ghenua* brigade (young armed militia) had left the villages. During that time, the women, children and old women of the villages were engaged in agricultural and other activities. Armed with traditional weapons, they all were ready and vigilant in protecting their house, property, land and villages.

When the tribals of Narayanpatna start cutting crops from the ‘reclaimed land’ (land acquired from the landlords during the movement), the landlords and the police terrorised them, especially the women. The police threatened to shoot (firing), if anyone come to harvest the crops. The data collected from the fieldwork revealed the valorous fight of the tribal women during the uprising were provided below:

> The police and moneylenders are now provoking the women coming to the market by saying, ‘Where did your husband go away’? ‘What happened to your red sarees (cloth) now’? ‘Will you now come to harvest crops’? But the women didn’t care for them; rather they have vowed to occupy the crop-land. They have prepared themselves to sacrifice their lives in the field, but not to give up the land, crops, the *sangha,* and red flags at any cost even in the face of bullets and blood-shed. Despite of such threatening, the tribal women have harvested their crops with ample of courage.[59]

---

[59]In an interview with the people of Narayanpatna village of Koraput district on 2 January 2016. The interview was in Odia language and it was translated to English by the researcher.

5.9.8 Leaders of the Movement

After several appeals to the government by the tribals in the past, the leaders of the CMAS finally realised the fact that fight is the last option in the hand of the exploited people in order to possess their rights over the land. Keeping this ideology in mind, 'Kendruka Singhana' started the movement in the Narayanpatna against the encroacher landlords and became a martyr on 20 November 2009 while protesting against the police high-handedness in Narayanpatna. 30 years ago, he was born to a poor tribal Kui (*Khond*) family in the village of Podapadar.[60] He had experienced the oppression and exploitation meted out to the tribals in his own village 'Podapadr' and neighbouring villages by the exploiters 'non-tribals', mostly the *Sahukars* (moneylenders), *Mahajans* (landlords) and the *Shundis* (liquor producers and traders), since his childhood. He had confronted exploitation with a revolutionary mind from his childhood and became martyr in the Narayanpatna police firing. The villagers of Podapader have described about the leadership of 'Kendruka Singhana' in their own language (Odia) which was translated by the researcher and provided in the following paragraph:

> He took part in the agitation activities taken up by the *Chasi Mulia Adivasi Sangha* in Narayanpatna in 2004. Since then, he moved forward as a belligerent leader among the people. After realising that people can't achieve their rights unless they are armed, he formed '*Lok Raksha Dal*' (group to protect people) and named it '*Ghenua* brigade' and armed the young boys and girls with traditional weapons. He had given leadership to the brigade.[61]

He always encouraged the tribals throughout his lifetime to root out enemies of the tribals through armed fights and remained in the forefront of the people. The tribals had trust in him. They get encouraged and gained confidence if Singhana was in their midst.

> They believe that no bullets could do any harm to Singhana, nor could any force do anything to him. From this innocent feelings of the people, the faith they had reposed on him is understandable.[62]

Nachika Andru, another prominent leader of the movement was born to a poor tribal family in the village of Bhaliaput in Podapadar panchayat of Narayanpatna block.[63] The CMAS started its activities from this village. He also actively worked

---

[60] In an interview with the people of Narayanpatna village in Narayanpatna block of Koraput district on 2 January 2016. The interview was in Odia language and it was translated to English by the researcher.

[61] In an interview with the people of village Podapadar in Narayanpatna block of Koraput district on 2 January 2016. The interview was in Odia language and it was translated to English by the researcher.

[62] In an interview with the people of village Podapadar in Narayanpatna block of Koraput district on 2 January 2016. The interview was in Odia language and it was translated to English by the researcher.

[63] In an interview with the people of village Bhaliaput of Narayanpatna block in Koraput district on 2 January 2016. The interview was in Odia language and it was translated to English by the researcher.

from his childhood with Nachika Linga (president of CMAS) as both were childhood friends and were members of *Ghenua* brigade. He was murdered in a planned way by the police in Narayanpatna police station on 20 November 2009, while participating in the *gherao* (strike) of police station on the issue of police high-handedness in Narayanpatna. At the age of only 25, he became martyr. Both Andru and Singhana sacrificed their life for the sake of social justice and the struggle for their rights and became martyrs in the history of tribal movement and exploited people's fight against oppression. They will remain alive forever in the long list of martyrs not only in the history of tribal movement in Koraput, but also in the tribal history of Odisha and India.

5.9.8.1 Odisha's Most Wanted 'Nachika Linga' (President of CMAS)

On 4 December, 2009, an order was issued for the immediate arrest of Nachika Linga, the leader of CMAS, because he was in the 'Most Wanted List' of the Odisha police (Satyabrata 2009b: 1). The government throughout the regions of southern Odisha have been put up the posters displaying the photo of Nachika Linga with his crimes written below in the poster. The government have also declared a cash award for anyone who will help to arrest Nachika Linga. There are 46 cases of dacoity, murder, attempt to murder and other charges that have been lodged in his name at different police stations.

In this connection, it is pertinent here to provide a short introduction about Nachika Linga who was put under the most wanted list of the Odisha Police. The latest BSF camp (there were three BSF camp existed in Narayanpatna during the field work) in Narayanpatna block has come up at Bhaliaput village in a house that used to be the home of Mr. Nachika Linga's former owner. The owner of the house was Nilkanta Parida, a local landlord of Bhaliaput village of Narayanpatna block, under whom Nachika Linga worked as a bonded labourer with Rs.5 per day, before he became the leader of the CMAS. His fifth generation remains bonded labourer. Nachika Linga is one among the many aboriginal tribals who reside in Narayanpatna. Later, he became the Naib-Sarpanch (*upa-pradhan*) of his area. He joined the CMAS to fight against the non-tribal exploiters who exploit the tribals of that area. He was put on the most wanted list by Odisha police and he finally surrendered to police with his supporters on 28 October, 2014.[64] With this, the CMAS ceased to operate and the popular tribal movement which demanded rights and justice for the tribals came to an end. There are many other leaders and CMAS activists were also arrested by the police as Maoist sympathisers and were now in jail. The state has forcefully arrested the Narayanpatna movement and has banned the CMAS as a frontal Maoist organisation.

[64]The *Dharitri* (2014) (Daily Odia Newspaper). October 29, p. 1. The news was in Odia language and it was translated to English by the researcher.

5.9.9 Significance of the Movement and Its Impact

As far as the significance and impact is concerned, the Narayanpatna movement has inspired and encouraged the people of Deomali hill range to fight against the mining activities carried out by the companies at the behest of the government which lead for the displacement of the tribals. Regarding the impact of the *Chasi Mulia Adivasi Sangha* (CMAS), Narayanpatna, it is very crucial to quote from the leaflet of CMAS, foreword by Nachika Linga (for the purpose to appeal the public towards Narayanpatna issue), translated by Lenin Kumar, was quoted below:

> There are a number of hill p*anchayats* of Kotia, Turia and Kanti under Pattangi block in Koraput district which were also got inspired from Narayanpatna struggle and called a similar agitation against the exploiters. The CMAS of Narayanpatna has installed confidence into these people to stand up against displacement. The *Sangha* has prepared these people to fight for their cause. It has formed '*Deomali Surakshya Samiti*' (an organisation to protect Deomali hill) uniting all the exploited people. The *sangha* convened an open meeting in April, 2009 and gave a call for fight throughout this vast gathering, where 12,000 people joined. The *sangha* called upon the people to fight against the capitalist and colonial forces, who are displacing the tribes for their monetary gains. It asked people to pledge to protect Deomali. The *Sangha* has spread its activities to six blocks in Koraput district. The government tried hard to bring down the agitation with a cruel hand which was launched by the tribes with much courage and patience for land, food and freedom.[65]

5.10 Conclusion

The state has forcefully arrested the tribal movement with the help of the paramilitary forces such as BSF, CRPF, SOGs and the police after declaring the CMAS as a frontal organisation of the Maoist and banning it. The entire movement has gone underground and the vast majority of the CMAS members hide in far within the jungles, often on the move without food, in constant risk of being apprehended and forced to surrender before the police in fear of encounter.

Without achieving any long-term or short-term result, no revolutionary struggle or movement ever fails, to which Narayanpatna movement is not an exception. It has motivated the people of Pattangi block and Deomali areas of Koraput district to fight against the mining activities in that area and also against the displacement. It also influenced other areas of the district and the state. Due to Narayanpatna movement, the tribals have forcefully occupied around 3000 acres of land, which were rightfully theirs. But, the land is going to be repossessed by the non-tribal encroachers again, after the forceful arrest of the movement by the state. The police and the administration are helping the encroachers to reclaim that land from the tribals. Due to the movement and the untiring fight of the tribals, the tribal land alienation problem and the Narayanpatna movement was placed for discussion in the

[65]The Flames of Narayanpatna (2010). Published by *Chasi Mulia Adivasi Sangh* (CMAS), Narayanpatna, Odisha, Foreword by Nachika Linga, and translated by Lenin Kumar (editor of Nishan), 22 December, p. 11. http://sanhati.com/excerpted/3115/. Accessed 8 February 2018.

Odisha Legislative Assembly. The discussion in the Assembly remained unsuccessful because the ruling party projected the problem as Maoist problem and the weak opposition remained silent without any strong move.

Though the Narayanpatna movement is very crucial in the history of the tribals of Odisha, it was least highlighted because the 'corporate media', 'police state' and the 'statist academia' have presented it in a distorted form. One must visit Narayanpatna in order to find the truth which the state wishes to hide, to give a voice to the peoples' concern and to act as a corrective to such media misinformation.

References

Administrative setup, Koraput district, Government of Odisha. https://koraput.nic.in/Administrative-setup/. https://koraput.nic.in/district-at-a-glance/. Accessed 15 December, 2019.

Bannerjee, T. K. (1986). Girijan movements in Srikakulam: 1967–70'. In A. R. Desai (Ed.), *Agrarian struggles in India after independence*. New Delhi: Oxford University Press.

Behera, A. (2013, August 5). *Maoists link in Odisha: Case of the chasi mulia adivasi sangh*. New Delhi: Institute for Defence Studies & Analyses (IDSA). http://www.idsa.in/system/files/IB_MaoistsLinkinOdisha_ABehera.pdf. Accessed 9 October, 2019.

Bell, R. C. S. (1945). *Orissa district Gazetteer, Koraput*. Cuttack: Orissa Government Press.

Census 2011, Office of the Registrar (General and Census Commissioner), Indian Ministry of Home Affairs 2/A, Mansingh Road, New Delhi-110011. http://censusindia.gov.in/2011census/dchb/2129_PART_B_DCHB_KORAPUT.pdf. Accessed 18 August, 2019.

Kar, A. (2012, November 30). The invincible flame of Narayanpatna: An interview with dandapani mohanty. *Sanhati*, (11) (online journal). http://sanhati.com/journal-2012/. Accessed 29 December, 2018.

Koraput Survey and Settlement report (1956). Government of Orissa. https://indiacode.nic.in/Bitstream/123456789/5918/1/the_gunjam-koraput_survey%2C_record-ofright_and_settlement_operations.pdf. Accessed 22 June, 2019.

Kuldeep, et al. (2011, April 27). Narayanpatna: A Report from Ground Zero', a Fact Finding Report by DSU Fact-finding Team. http://www.countercurrents.org/Narayanpatna270411.htm. Accessed 27 July, 2018.

Kumar, K., et al. (2005). *A socio economic and legal study of scheduled tribes' land in Orissa*. Bhubaneswar: Study Supported by World Bank, Washington. http://www.researchgate.net/publication/232062518_A_socioeconomic_and_legal_study_of_scheduled_tribes'_land_in_Orissa. Accessed 10 March, 2020.

Mohanty, B., & Anuradha, K. (2009). *Failure of non-violent methods responsible for Narayanpatna uprising*. http://www.newsweb.co.in/news_article_en.php?article=1076. Accessed 8 June, 2018.

Mohanty G., et al. (Eds.). (2008). *Cultural heritage of odisha* (Vol. XI). Koraput District, Bhubaneswar: SLVFMSS.

Narayanpatna Block, Koraput District, Odisha. http://www.census2011.co.in/data/subdistrict/3204-narayanpatana-koraput-orissa.html. Accessed 22 September, 2019.

Narayanpatna Firing and its aftermath. (2011, February 06). *The new Indian express* (p. 3).

Navalakha Gautam. (2010, April 1). *Days and nights in the heartland of rebellion, sanhati*, (online journal). http://sanhati.com/wp-content/uploads/2010/05/navlakha_daysnights_v3.pdf. Accessed 22 August, 2019.

Odisha State Archives, Orissa District Gazetteers. http://www.odishaarchives.nic.in/node/169213. Accessed 22 December, 2019.

Orissa: Narayanpatna on the boil again over land grabbing. (2010, October 17). NDTV News. http://www.ndtv.com/video/player/news/orissa-narayanpatna-on-the-boil-again-over-land-grabbing/170018&cp. Accessed 22 June, 2016.

Padel, F. (1995). *The sacrifice of human being: British rule and the Kondhs of Orissa*. Delhi: Oxford University Press.

Patnaik, K. S. (2009, September 25). Narayanpatna block in Orissa's Koraput under control of Chasi Mulia Adivasi Sangh. *Indian Vanguard*. https://indianvanguard.wordpress.com/2009/09/25/narayanpatna-block-in-orissas-koraput-under-control-of-chasi-mulia-adivasi-sangh/. Accessed 12 January, 2019.

Patra, D. (2011, December). The cultural history of the tribals of the koraput region. *Orissa Review*.

Satyabrata (2009a, November 29). Odisha *Bandh* (Strike) against the police firing and killing of CMAS leaders. *Sanhati*. http://sanhati.com/narayanpatna/#1, http://sanhati.com/narayanpatna/#sthash.1LkGgc6p.dpuf. Accessed 22 October, 2018.

Satyabrata (2009b, December 7). Odisha's most wanted: On Nachika Linga, leader of the Chasi Mulia Adivasi Sangha (*CMAS)*', *Sanhati* (online Journal). http://sanhati.com/Narayanpatna/#4. Accessed 18 November, 2019.

The Dharitri (2009, November 30). Daily Odia Newspaper (Bhubaneswar edition) (p. 1).

The Dharitri (2014, October 29). Daily Odia Newspaper (Bhubaneswar edition) (p. 1).

The Flames of Narayanpatna. (2010, December 22). Published by *Chasi Mulia Adivasi Sangh* (CMAS), Narayanpatana, Odisha, Foreword by Nachika Linga, and translated by Lenin Kumar (editor of Nishan). http://sanhati.com/excerpted/3115/. Accessed 8 February, 2018.

The Flames of Narayanpatna, Orissa, report by International Campaign against War on the People in India (ICAWPI). http://www.icawpi.org/resistance/news1/965-the-flames-of-narayanpatna. Accessed 22 October, 2018.

The Odisha Scheduled Areas Transfer of Immovable Property (OSATIP) (by Scheduled Tribes) Regulation (1956). http://www.igrodisha.gov.in/pdf/regulation2.pdf. Accessed 9 November, 2019.

Tribes of Koraput. https://koraput.nic.in/tribes/. Accessed 21 December, 2019.

Chapter 6
Role of the State and Different Political Parties Towards Narayanpatna Movement

6.1 State Repression of the Movement

The state has tried in every manner to arrest and forcibly stop the Narayanpatna movement with different tactics. One such tactics was that the state has formed a 'peace committee' to counter the movement and to portray the movement as an attack on poor dalits by the Maoists of Narayanpatna. After the land occupied by the tribals of Narayanpatna, the local bourgeoisie and those instrumentalised in Narayanpatna had fled from the area fearing attack and gathered in adjoining Laxmipur block (an industrial area). There, they mobilised local population and propagandised against the tribal movement at Narayanpatna with the help of the state. In Laxmipur, the bourgeoisie, the ousted landlords, brewers and liquor merchants were used by the state against the tribals. They told the media that they had instrumentalised in Narayanpatna by the tribals in two ways. First, they posited themselves as 'poor people' who suffered from the 'voice of terror' of the Narayanpatna tribal movement.[1] Secondly, they were posited as 'oppressed dalits' that gave an anti-dalit colour to the Narayanpatna movement.[2] All this have happened from the direction of the state and ruling party.

As a result, with the help of the state, the bourgeoisie were able to create a sort of a mass hysteria against the tribal movement in Narayanpatna. All these people who have exploited the tribals, with the help of the state and police, have formed the 'peace committee' later renamed as *Nagarik Surakshya Samiti* (committee for the protection of the citizens) to counter the Narayanpatna tribal movement. The state government formed the *Nagarik Suraksha Samiti* in every block of Koraput district to fight against the tribals and to safeguard the interest of the exploiters in the name

[1] Narayanpatna Firing and its aftermath (2011). *The New Indian Express*, February 06, p. 3.
[2] ibid.

S. K. Malik, *Land Alienation and Politics of Tribal Exploitation in India*,
https://doi.org/10.1007/978-981-15-5382-0_6

of restoring peace in Narayanpatna areas.[3] The Committee constituted comprising the elites of different political parties including the ruling party. The members of the *Nagarik Surakshya Samiti* were the party leaders and members of BJD, BJP and Congress, and the landlords of the area, the contractors, petty business men, the *shundis* (liquor vendors), etc. who had lost their land during the Narayanpatna movement. Regarding the nature and extent of state repression, it is pertinent to quote from the article written by Pramodini Pradhan and published by PUCL which was provided in the following paragraph:

> From the beginning, since 2004, the government has been mounting pressure on the *Chasi Mulia Adivasi Sangha*, and those who participated in the movement against landlords and the hooch-traders. As a result, the *Sangha* leader Nachika Linga along with other agitating people had been arrested and put behind the bars. After the CMAS' successful culmination of the land struggle by 2009, the state repression on the tribals was also scaled up. One such other incident of state repression was the murder of Singana and Nachika Andru at Naryanpatna police station on 20 November 2009, followed by wanton attacks, raids and combing operations in the region, establishing a region of state terror. The entire villagers are often forced to take shelter in the forests and hill as fugitives. The government had virtually imposed a seize of Narayanpatna by deploying more than 5000 paramilitary troops including BSF, IRB, CRPF, and hundreds of Special Operation Group Commandos, Odisha Police, and *shanti* committee vigilante forces and closing off all the important entry and exit points to and from Narayanpatna. It seemed, rather than addressing the demands of the people, the state has mobilised more and more troops to crush the movement forcefully (Pradhan 2009: 2).

6.2 Reaction of the Government

After its formation, the CMAS, though began its agitation against hooch trading but in course of time, spread its agitational agenda quickly towards land issues of the tribals. During the land agitation, the CMAS' activists with ample courage confronted the '*shanti shena*' (the militant brigade of the 'peace committee') and the police.

> Because of the mustered confidence and strength, in November, 2009, they unitedly got ready to cut the crops they had raised in the land occupied by them through agitation. They had raised crops toiling hard, shedding their blood and sweat. When they were cutting crops with much enthusiasm, the police force reached at Thumbuguda village 2 km away from Narayanpatna at 10 A.M. on November 20, 2009 and asked the people working in the field, you are helping the Maoists; tell us where they are now?[4]

As reported from the field, during the interview, the interviewees described the incident on the day when the police firing at Narayanpatna police station caused the death of two CMAS leaders, which was provided in the following paragraphs.

[3]Data collected from an interview with the people of Narayanpatna during the fieldwork in the said block in the Koraput district of Odisha on 22 December 2015. The interview was in Odia language and it was translated to English by the researcher.

[4]Data collected from an interview with the people of village Tentulipadar in Narayanpatna block during the fieldwork in the said block in the Koraput district of Odisha on 29 December 2015. The interview was in Odia language and it was translated to English by the researcher.

The paragraphs depicts the nature of oppression by the state and the intention of the government towards the tribals.

> The police threatened the people and talked in obscene language with the women, besides rebuking the CMAS. Finding no other way, the people immediately brought this matter to the knowledge of Nachika Linga (the president of CMAS). When the matter reached the *sangha*, leaders then advised the people to walk to Narayanpatna in order to raise their voice of protest against police demeanour and high-handedness. At once, 200 villagers along with the *sangha* leaders proceeded to Narayanpatna police station. The people from hilly areas also joined them.[5]
>
> The people asked the police, why they had gone to Tumbuguda? Why they were committing atrocities on the innocent people? Why they failed to keep up their written promise given to the people? The people demanded answers to these questions from the police through slogans. But the police, without caring for the people, went inside the rooms locking the gate of the police station, which made the people angry. Then 10 youths of the *Ghenua* brigade along with the *sangha* leader Singhana entered the police station breaking the lock of the gate.[6]
>
> They asked the police officer about the 'earlier assurances given to them' (as the police will not disturb the people) which triggered heated exchange of words between the *sangha* leaders and the police. At that time the police personnel present on both the upper and lower floors of the police station indiscreetly opened fire at the people. One of the bullets heat the head of the leader Andru Nachika (nephew of Nachika Linga), who fell down dead on the spot. When *sangha* leader Kenduraku Singanna (close aid of Nachika) was inside the police station, a bullet hit him and he came outside injured and fell down near the gate. Singhanna and Andru became martyrs at the police firing and many people were injured. The incident was unexpected in which many people got injured seriously and heavily wounded. The leaders of the CMAS Singhanna and Andru who were spearheading the movement for claiming rights over land, were killed in a planned way. The police sounded high alert and issued prohibitory orders under section 144 over the area, not to allow people to protest against the killing of their leaders.[7]

Immediately, after the firing, the entry of outsiders into Narayanpatna region was blocked by local police. In their evening bulletin, the electronic media have reported that two CMAS members have been killed as police fired upon them in 'self-defence' as they were trying to loot weapons from the Narayanpatna police station. The same story was carried by all large-circulation Odia dailies like, *Dharitri* and *Samaj* in the next day.[8] The next day, there was a television interview with Gananath Patra

---

[5]Data collected in an interview with the people of village Tentulipadar in Narayanpatna block of Koraput district during the fieldwork on 1 January 2016. The interview was in Odia language and it was translated to English by the researcher.

[6]Data collected in an interview with of village Tentulipadar in Narayanpatna block of Koraput district during the fieldwork on 1 January 2016. The interview was in Odia language and it was translated to English by the researcher.

[7]Data collected during the interview with the people of village Tentulipadar in Narayanpatna block of Koraput district during the fieldwork on 1 January 2016. The interview was in Odia language and it was translated to English by the researcher.

[8]The Dharitri (2009) Odia daily Newspaper (Bhubaneswar edition). November 21, p. 1. The Samaj (2009) Odia daily Newspaper (Bhubaneswar edition). November 21, p. 2. The news was in Odia language and was translated to English by the researcher.

(advisor of CMAS and the member of CPI-M) to whom questions were being asked as to whether they had links with Maoists or not? The media had to show that they were 'neutral' and they were giving scope to Narayanpatna CMAS to place its perspective in front of the public. But its nepotism against the tribal movement was clearly visible in the interview where Gananath Patra was harassed with questions that could not have clear answers, which provided fuel to the already propagandised and hegemonies public opinion and created an impression that CMAS was a frontal organisation of the CPI (Maoist). This announced the start of repressive days for the people of Narayanpatna, by the state. Even, The All India Women's Fact Finding Team (consisting of 9 women) were not allowed to meet the police station in charge as they want to meet the people of Narayanpatna. The state has deployed every possible measure to hide the police torture on the tribals and to supress the movement.

A state wide twelve-hour *bandh* (strike) was observed on 28 November 2009, in Odisha, by different organisations to protest against the police firing on tribals and to condemn the killing of two *Chasi Mulia Adivasi Sangh* (CMAS) leaders.[9] In spite of state-wide protests, combing operation still continued in Narayanpatna and adjoining regions through Cobra battalions. The hostels of schools in the area were vacated and police forces were accommodated there. The police destroyed the houses of the *sangha* activists there with the help of 'peace committee' and *shanti sena* members. The goons of the *shanti sena* lead the police to the villages to identify the CMAS members and their houses. The name of the united combating operation carried out was 'Operation Linga' and 'Wanted Linga'. They have pasted posters with photos of Nachika Linga on the walls and announced cash prize on Linga's head (Satyabrata 2009: 2).

Within few days, Gananath Patra (advisor of CMAS and the member of CPI-M) was arrested with several cases slapped against him. On the evening of 27 January 2010, Gananatha Patra, aged 70, was picked up by plain clothes police from the road in Bhubaneswar. He was on his way home from a meeting with members of a proposed fact-finding team to Narayanpatna (Padhi et al. 2010: 24). There are allegations against him that he was the one who had planned the 'Maoist attack' on the Narayanpatna police station. There are public protests but that was limited to a small group whose voice could not be heard by the public, because it was not conveyed to them by the media. Then, Tapan Mishra, a close associate of Gananath Patra, was arrested while on his way to Narayanpatna. Though he had no organisational linkage with the Maoists, still he was arrested and sent to jail and branded as a member of the CPI (Maoist) under the Unlawful Activities Prevention Act (UAPA). 'Nachiika Linga', the chief leader of the Narayanpatna movement was made into a 'most wanted' criminal by the state.

The *shanti sena* which was formed by the government had started their propaganda against the candidate of the CPI (ML) {the CMAS supports the CPI (ML)} during the state Assembly election, 2014. *Shanti sena* functioned as an organ that was to hegemonies the whole public opinion for assembly elections in the Koraput region. The election results were stunning. The ruling party *Biju Janata Dal* (BJD)

[9]Narayanpatna Firing and its aftermath (2011). *The New Indian Express*, 6 February, p. 3.

acquired over 75% of the seats in the assembly election, including that seat of which Narayanpatna was part. The Odisha Legislative Assembly had become a hub of bourgeois politicians and there were no voice that will raise the question of Narayanpatna from the side of opposition. After the BJD's win in assembly election, several CRPF troops were sent into the region and camped inside the Narayanpatna region to search and hunt down the CMAS members in the name of being 'Maoists'. The District Magistrate who was sympathetic to the tribal movement had been transferred and grounds had been prepared for the militant move of the coercive organs of the state to crush the movement.[10]

6.3 The Reign of Arrest and Torture by the State

On the 27 January 2010, Gananath Patra, one of the advisors of *Chasi Mulia Adivasi Sangh* that spearheaded the land movement in Narayanpatna, was arrested as he was stepping out after a meeting with Prof. Manoranjan Mohanty in Bhubaneswar, who is a renowned political scientist and social researcher (Satyabrata 2010: 1). He has been charged with sections pertaining to kidnapping, assault, attempt to murder and murder (ibid.). The views of Prof. Manoranjan Mohanty, who was a professor in political science in University of Delhi, regarding the arrest of Gananath Patra and the report by Satyabrata on behalf of *Sanhati* (online journal) were provided in the following paragraph:

> The arrest was a pre-planned move by the Odisha police as plain cloths policemen were keeping a watch on the meeting. The Odisha government has been regularly attempting, through the media and other sources, to brand the CMAS as a formal organisation of the CPI (Maoist) in spite of denials of this allegations by both CMAS leader and CPI (Maoist) state committee secretary 'Sabyasachi Panda'. The easiest path that the Indian state has found to crush democratic movements is by using the biggest fetish of democracy, 'the law'. The movement of Narayanpatna was never illegal and was aimed at implementing an existing law regarding the distribution of land to tribals. This is why even the collector of the region was sympathetic to it and ended up being accused of backing the Maoists. The best way to suppress an uprising or a movement is to brand it as Maoist or Maoist-backed, as the Maoists have been posited by the Indian state as the single largest threat to 'internal security'. The 'civil society' of Odisha has partially been subsumed by brutal attacks of the state and partially been hegemonies in the typhoon ongoing 'development'. Therefore, a consciousness of a generalised logic of ongoing movement that could force the state back, is not existent. As a result, its response to the arrest of Gananath Patra has been very limited. Gananath Patra's arrest is a slap in the face of all the movements that are potentially revolutionary and also a slap on the face of democracy (Satyabrata 2010: 1).

Advocate Nihar Ranjan Pattnaik of Koraput, who is litigating the case for the Narayanpatna tribals has mentioned that; over 117 people have been arrested so far and those arrested, include 12 children too, who are now facing charges of conspiracy

---

[10]Data collected in an interview with the people of Bhaliaput village in Narayanpatna block of Koraput district during the fieldwork on 2 January 2016. The interview was in Odia language and it was translated to English by the researcher.

to wage war against the state (Padhi et al. 2010: 25). The high-handedness of the police and security personnel, and the random arrests have made the entire Narayanpatna area a region of terror. Even the entry of journalists and investigation teams were not allowed inside the area.

6.4 Role of Different Political Parties and Organisations Towards the Movement

After the police firing at Narayanpatna police station on 20 November 2009, the police and the *goons* of the 'peace committee' created panic to those who took part in the procession of dead bodies of Andru and Singhana.

> The police frightened the people, patrolled on the road with guns and arrested the tribes wherever they managed. Despite this hurdles, thousands of people came walking through forests and hills from many kilometres away to the village of Podapadar to which Singhana belonged and paid their last tribute to their beloved leader. It was reported in the mass media that the village Podapadar reverberated with slogans- *'lal salam'* (red salute), 'Singhana and Andru *Amar Rahe'*, shouted by the people.[11]

Representatives of different left parties, intellectuals and the democracy lovers from different parts of the country have joined the condolence meeting. The leaders who joined the meeting were Prafulla Samantray of *Lok Shakti Abhiyan,* Balachandra Sarangi of CPI (ML) New Democracy, Shivram of *Bastee Suraksha Samiti,* Tapan Mishra, an associate of the *Sangha,* S.P. Satyanarayan, the secretary of Vizianagaram district (Andhra Pradesh) of All India *Kshet Mazdoor Sangh*, Dandapani Mohanty of Odisha Forest *Mazdoor* union and Buddha Gamanga of *Lok Sangram Party.*[12] These leaders and sympathisers of CMAS were terrorised by the police in their way to Narayanpatna and their vehicles were detained in the adjunct road of Semliguda, Laxmipur and Bandhugaon. In spite of all hurdles created by the police, the peoples from adjunct areas, intellectuals, democracy lovers, activists and leaders had walked to the meeting place to pay tributes to Singhana and Andru. The ICAWPI's report regarding the condolence meeting was given in the following paragraph:

> Because of the hurdles posed by the police and peace committee, the condolence meeting was delayed by two days and held on 23 November. Those who attended the meeting and funeral rites condemned the police firing on 20 November, in their speeches. They demanded judicial inquiry into the police firing and punishment to the guilty. The leaders also demanded to immediately stop the police attack on the villages, arrest of innocent people, combing operations, atrocities on the women and withdrawal of additional police force from the area. They also urged the concerned authorities to grant record of rights over the land to those who occupied the land through struggles. When the meeting ended, the leaders interacted with

---

[11]The Flames of Narayanpatna, Orissa (2010). Report by International Campaign against War on the People in India (ICAWPI), 11 October, p. 7. http://www.icawpi.org/resistance/news1/965-the-flames-of-narayanpatna. Accessed 22 October 2018. For detail, visit the youtube video link- https://youtu.be/X8N5-ktURVk.

[12]ibid.

the people about their problems. The people described before the leaders vivid accounts of police atrocities on them including damage of crops and arrest of innocent peoples. They brought to the knowledge of the leaders, about the pressure put on them to surrender before the police and leave the *sangha* and the land they occupied. They also informed the leaders about resale of hooch, which was stopped by the *sangha* in Narayanpatna. The people paid tributes to the departed leaders pledging to follow the revolutionary path shown by Singhana and Andru, and being a part with the *sangha* and their land even in the face of suppression.[13]

The united forum off all mass-organisations of Odisha gave a *bandh* (strike) call in South Odisha on 28 November, in protest against police firing on 20 November.[14] The Maoist party also gave *bandh* call separately protesting against the incident. The people of Koraput, Malkangiri, Kandhamal, Rayagda, Gajapati and Ganjam districts observed *bandh* protesting against the Narayanpatna police firing. The mob condemned the police firing, blocked the roads and brought resolutions against the government. Tapan Mishra (supporter of the CMAS) and his companion were arrested near Bandhugaon by the police and sent to the jail while they had been to Narayanpatna to meet the people. They were arrested as Maoist and false cases were lodged against them. The police wilfully detained and sent back the human rights activists and women representatives coming to Narayanpatna from different parts of the state to understand the nature of attacks and atrocities on the people.

The famous mass-movement leader Medha Patkar has asked the government for protecting the life and property of Nachika Linga as there was impending danger on his life and he was not a criminal.[15] The 'Committee on Freedom of Political Prisoners' put a proposal before the government to accord status of political prisoner to those arrested in connection with solution of land problems.[16] The government, 'peace committee' and the police unitedly took up efforts to stop flow of co-operations, help and moral support to the CMAS from outside. The peace committee or *Nagarik Surakshya Samiti* is all along demanding the arrest of all the leaders of CMAS, and a total ban on the CMAS.

The Narayanpatna movement gained sympathy from the left-wing parties and groups because it was brutally crashed by the state. There were protest rallies by left groups with *Gandhians* and *Lohiaites* against state coercion that had brutally suppressed the Narayanpatna movement. The support of the left groups like CPI (ML) New Democracy, CPI (ML) Liberation, *Samajwadi Jan Parishad, Lok Shakti Abhijan* and other local groups from different parts of Odisha has created a counter-hegemonic space in the civil society towards the CMAS and the Narayanpatna movement targeting the state action.

---

[13]The Flames of Narayanpatna, Orissa (2010). Report by International Campaign against War on the People in India (ICAWPI), 11 October, p. 7. http://www.icawpi.org/resistance/news1/965-the-flames-of-narayanpatna. For detail, visit the youtube video link- https://youtu.be/X8N5-ktURVk. Accessed 22 October 2018.

[14]The Dharitri (2009) Daily Odia Newspaper, Bhubaneswar. 29 November, p. 1.

[15]The Flames of Narayanpatna, Orissa (2010). Report by International Campaign against War on the People in India (ICAWPI), 11 October, p. 8. http://www.icawpi.org/resistance/news1/965-the-flames-of-narayanpatna. Accessed 22 October 2018.

[16]ibid.

Towards the land issue of Narayanpatna, the state response always remained tongue-tied. The present *Biju Janata Dal* (BJD) government vehemently suppressed the movement, to protect the interest of the exploiters, after branding CMAS as a frontal organisation of the Maoist and the movement is Maoist led, without solving the real problem of tribal land alienation. It arrested almost all the leaders in charge of being Maoists with the help of Odisha police, BSF, CRPF and other paramilitary forces and also ultimately banned the CMAS. The state declared Nachika Linga who is the chief leader of the movement in its most wanted list, after firing to other CMAS leaders during the protest in 2009.

The Congress party, which ruled the state for nearly about four decades, adopted a laissez-faire policy towards the tribal problem. During 1990–1995, it was only throughout the Janata Party period (led by Biju Patnaik), the state recognised the problem as a socio-economic and then Chief Minister, Biju Patnaik, divided the large area districts into small ones in 1992. Nevertheless, this administrative reconstituting had not impacted on the activities of the administration and the problem of tribals remains as usual. Neither have the respective regime in Odisha evolve any clear-cut policy on the issue. The leaders of the state have never tried to realise the problem and the government tends to look at the problem as a Maoist problem; the police say it is a law and order problem, while the bureaucrats call it a socio-economic problem.

On the above backcloth, the current Chief Minister's positive move to solve the tribal problems seems receiving. Chief Minister Naveen Patnaik's latest move seems to have given the state government some direction. The Chief Minister has maintained that he has an open mind to talk about the tribal problem. The government had a dialogue with the leaders of the organisations and allowed the tribal people to refrain the extremist line and to participate in the mainstream. In 2019, the state government challenged a High Court judgement that could weaken efforts to restore land to tribals from whom it was fraudulently taken away by others in the past.

> The High Court of Odisha in one of its judgments in April 2019 has made section 3 (B) of Odisha Schedule Area Transfer of Immoveable Property (OSATIP) Regulation ineffective. This section has been designed to restore tribal land which had been taken away from them through clever manipulation, said activist Prafulla Samantara, in his letter to the Chief Minister.[17]

Damodar Rout, the *panchyat raj* minister of Odisha, expressed that "the state government is planning to empower the tribals in remote areas through developmental programmes in order to counter the rising influence of Maoists".[18] He pointed that local self-governing bodies could be utilised in this regard and stated that the centre has agreed to provide financial support for tribal empowerment projects in Odisha. The Naveen Patnaik government seems to tackle the land issues and the left extremism in southern Odisha, in general, and Koraput district, in particular, when he declared

---

[17]The Hindu (2019). English Daily Newspaper (Bhubaneswar Edition) July 7, p. 1. https://www.thehindu.com/news/national/odisha-chief-minister-urged-to-challenge-hc-order-on-tribal-landtransfer/article28313731.ece. Accessed 21 December 2019.

[18]The Dharitri (2015). Odia Daily Newspaper (Bhubaneswar edition), November 12, p. 2. The news was in Odia language and it was translated in English by the researcher.

not to press charges against 156 suspected rebels in 34 cases and to drop 1,513 minor cases against villagers of the tribal-dominated Koraput district and to review the cases relating to land and extremist activities.[19]

6.5 Present Scenario

Since the firing on 20 November 2009, all the tribals of Narayanpatna have seen the slow marginalisation of their lives. Not only have three BSF camps been set up in Narayanpatna block, but Maoist activity has also been on the rise. There is still no guarantee that the paddy that rightfully belongs to the tribals would not be illegally split 50–50 between the tribals and the non-tribals—*sahukars* and 'landlords', as happened in 2014, after the suppression of the *Chasi Mulia Adivasi Shangh.*[20] The entire movement (in Narayanpatna block) of the CMAS has gone underground. 150 CMAS members are in jail, including Gananath Patra, of the CPI (ML) who was the advisor of CMAS and arrested as a Maoist, and his associate Tapan Mishra who has already clashed with officials in the prison after going on numerous hunger strike. After the movement has gone underground, the vast majority of the CMAS live in fear, within the jungles, often on the move, without food and with constant risk of apprehended.

On 20 February, 2013, 113 tribal activists shunned ties with the *Chasi Mulia Adivasi Sangh* (CMAS), declared to be a frontal organisation of the Communist Party of India-Maoist (CPI-Maoist) by the state, surrendered before Narayanpatna police in Koraput district.[21] The surrender process started since 2013, when around 778 CMAS activists of the Nachika Linga-led faction of CMAS from 22 villages, have left the Linga group and expressed their interest to join the mainstream.[22] Among them, there are 62 activists of CMAS from Nachika Linga's own village, 'Bhaliaput' (under Narayanpatna block of Koraput district) who have left him finally.[23] The people who surrendered made it clear that they are now neither supporting CMAS nor Nachika Linga. Is the surrender a sign of down of extremism and violence in the region? Or due to forceful and a feared situation created by the state and its agencies? As reported from the field, during the interview that the CMAS activists after their leaders' arrest have surrendered in fear to the police and the police have been taking the credit by preaching that so many Maoists have surrendered to police and are interested to join the mainstream.

[19]The Dharitri (2015). Odia Daily Newspaper (Bhubaneswar edition), November 12, p. 2. The news was in Odia language and it was translated in English by the researcher.

[20]Data collected in an interview with the people of Bhaliaput village in Narayanpatna block of Koraput district during the fieldwork on 2 January 2016. The interview was in Odia language and it was translated to English by the researcher.

[21]The Samaj (2013). Odia Daily Newspaper (Bhubaneswar edition) February 21, p. 2. The news was in Odia language and was translated to English by the researcher.

[22]ibid.

[23]ibid.

The Maoists' influence over the Narayanpatna CMAS was particularly identified when the *sangha* militant kidnapped Jhina Hika, the Laxmipur MLA. It is said that, under the Maoist influence, the CMAS activists abducted Jhina Hika (MLA of Laxmipur Constituency under which Narayanpatna block is a part), in March, 2012. Jhina Hika was released by the Maoists with some conditions. After that incident, combing operations and patrolling was intensified in the Koraput district and the CMAS activists like Lingama Habika and Kameya Habika were arrested. Nachika Chamara aka Samara, the body guard of Nachika Linga, surrendered to police on January 4, 2013.[24]

Now, it was realised by the tribal people of Narayanpatna that the CMAS is no longer able to protect from police arrest and can't rescue the people it had earlier promised. They also realised that they will not get the benefits of the government's developmental and beneficial schemes, if once they had been accused as CMAS activists. It was a mixed activity of peoples' realisation about the *Sangha's* activity after the arrests of its leaders and also the fear of arrest as once they had been branded as CMAS activists. Then, the surrender process of the CMAS activists in Narayanpatna started. Deepak Kumar Nayak (research officer at IPCS, New Delhi) in his article published by Institute of Peace and Conflict Studies (IPCS) has articulated the surrender process in detail which was quoted in the following paragraph:

> The surrender of Samara on January 4, 2013, was followed by the surrender of 121 CMAS activists on January 11, 12 and 13 respectively. Tribals deserting the CMAS have now become a veritable phenomenon in the area and the number of surrenders has started to swell day by day. All the surrendered CMAS activists are now approaching the administration and want to avail benefits of developmental schemes of the government. Earlier in 2009, when more than 60 CMAS activists had surrendered in Narayanpatna police station after the arrest of hundreds of their activists by the police, the trend did not continue as expected. Nevertheless, the numbers and volume of the present mass surrenders has certainly given a clear indication that the extremist clout is losing its credibility among the peoples of Narayanpatna and if the tribals continue to snap their association with CMAS, it will help the state to weaken the movement and the existence of the CMAS in the region (Nayak 2013: 1).

6.6 Why the Surrender Drama?

There raises a number of questions with the mass surrender, e.g. does it mean the tribals are losing their confidence over the CMAS? Does it mean that the tribals are no longer following the path of violence? Is the left extremism losing its ground in Narayanpatna, in particular, and in the Koraput district, in general? Does the surrender forced Nachika Linga to surrender as well in 2014, which put an end to the CMAS and the movement? It is widely believed that Nachika Linga direct the followers to first surrender to the police, in order to see the state's reaction before his own surrender, as he was put in the most wanted list by the Odisha police with a cash prize of 5 lakh. The police stated that the security persons have generated a

[24]The Dharitri (2013). Odia Daily Newspaper (Bhubaneswar edition), January 5, p. 2. The news was in Odia language and it was translated to English by the researcher.

confidence among the people and that's why finding no way, the CMAS (Maoists) are coming for surrender. The statement of the security forces was reported in IDSA issue briefs by Anshuman Behera and was quoted in the following paragraph:

> The security forces, especially the state police are of the opinion that increasing deployment of security forces, both the central para-military forces and the Special Operation Group (SOG) of the state has generated a sense of security among the people, hence the surrenders of CMAS and Maoists in the area (Behera 2013: 6). This time around, while the police are taking all credits for these surrenders, there is a general feeling that the mass surrender is because the Maoists are losing ground in one strong holds in the state. But, as far as the issue of surrenders and arrests of CMAS members are concerned, it proves the fact that the CMAS is not a frontal organisation of the Maoists which the police spearheading earlier. Because, the president of the CMAS, Nachika Linga, who refutes police allegation and claims that they do not have any links with the Maoists (Behera 2013: 1–2).

6.7 State's War Against Its Own People

Nachika Linga (chief leader and president of the CMAS) belongs to Bhaliaput village of Narayanpatna block, whose five generation remain bonded labour and he himself was also a bonded labour in the house of Nilkantha Parida (local landlord of Bhaliaput village) before becoming the leader of CMAS. He was put on the most wanted list by Odisha police with 43 different cases and the police had also declared 5 lakh cash prize to capture Nachika Linga.[25] Finding no other way, after the surrender of the CMAS activists, Nachika Linga finally surrendered to police with the supporters on 28 October, 2014.[26] The surrender of *Chasi Mulia Adivasi Sangha* leader Nachika Linga brought an end to the movement of the tribals on the issue of tribal land alienation that was launched to voice against the exploitation of tribals. With this, the CMAS ceased to operate and the death of a popular tribal movement happened.

Nachika Linga was alleged with 43 cases and listed as the 'most wanted' by the Odisha police earlier before his surrender. The south western range I.G., Y Jethwa, said:

> Of the 43 cases, there were Non-Bailabe Warrants (NBWs) against Nachika Linga's name in 23 cases. He further added that police was in search of Linga since 2009, after the attack on police station at Narayanpatna which was organised by him on 20 November, 2009. So, cases of murder, attack on police stations, arson and instigating tribals to taking law into their hands were pending in against him in different police stations. Linga, allegedly with the help of the left wing extremists, set up CMAS and become its leader demanding the settlement of land problem of tribals in Narayanpatna block of Koraput district. Though he surrendered before the police on his own, Linga would be produced before the court as several Non-Bailabe Warrants (NBWs) were pending against his name.[27]

[25]The Dharitri (2014). Odia Daily Newspaper (Bhubaneswar edition), October 29, p. 1. The news was in Odia language and was translated to English by the researcher.

[26]ibid.

[27]ibid.

6.8 Conclusion

As far as the importance of the movement is concerned, it can be mentioned that no revolutionary struggle ever fails without any impact and is true in case of Narayanpatna movement. The movement in other way has inspired the people of Deomali areas and Pottangi block in Koraput district against displacement and mining activities. It also has influenced other areas of the district and the state. Due to the movement, the landless tribals have occupied around 3000 acres of land, though the occupied lands are going to be reoccupied by the encroachers with the help of police after the arrest of all CMAS members. The members of the Odisha Legislative Assembly focused on the land issues of the tribals and the causes of the Narayanpatna movement which may result in bringing a new law in future in order to sort out the centuries-old existing land problem.

At the outset, as far as the Narayanpatna movement and the nature of the Indian state is concerned, I generalised that the state apparatus applies coercion to arrest revolutionary forces through the easy and most popular tactics of suppression after declaring the organisation as Maoist generated and proclaiming a war against its own people in the name of law, order, peace, security and development. After 70 years of India's independence, the tribals of Narayanpatna block of Koraput district in particular, and the tribals of Odisha and in the country, in general, are living at the age of 'colonialism' or 'internal colonialism' in their own country.

References

Behera, A. (2013, August 5). *Maoists link in Odisha: Case of the Chasi Mulia Adivasi Sangh.* New Delhi: Institute for Defence Studies & Analyses (IDSA). http://www.idsa.in/system/files/IB_MaoistsLinkinOdisha_ABehera.pdf. Accessed 9 October, 2019.

Narayanpatna Firing and its aftermath. (2011, February 06). *The new Indian express* (p. 3). https://www.newindianexpress.com/.

Nayak, D. K. (2013, March 8). Naxal Violence: Is the Maoist Base Slipping in Odisha? New Delhi: Institute of Peace and Conflict Studies (IPCS). http://www.ipcs.org/article/naxalite-violence/naxal-violence-is-the-maoist-base-slipping-in-odisha-3836.html. Accessed 24 October, 2019.

Padhi, R., Pradhan, P., & Manjit, D. (2010, March 6–12). How Many More Arrests Will Orissa See? *Economic and Political Weekly, 45*(10), pp. 24–26.

Pradhan, P. (2009, December 20). *Police repression of adivasis in Narayanpatna.* Bhubaneswar: Public Union for Civil Liberties (PUCL) Odisha.

Satyabrata. (2009, December 7). Odisha's most wanted: On Nachika Linga, leader of the Chasi Mulia Adivasi Sangha (*CMAS*). *Sanhati* (online Journal). http://sanhati.com/Narayanpatna/#4. Accessed 18 November, 2019.

Satyabrata. (2010, January 31). The Arrest of Gananatha Patra. *Sanhati* (Online Journal). http://sanhati.com/narayanpatna/#12. Accessed 26 December, 2018.

The Flames of Narayanpatna, Orissa. (2010). Report by International Campaign against War on the People in India (ICAWPI), 11 October. http://www.icawpi.org/resistance/news1/965-the-flames-of-narayanpatna. Accessed 22 October, 2018.

The Dharitri. (2009, November 21 & 29). Odia daily newspaper (Bhubaneswar edition, p. 1).

The Dharitri. (2013, January 5). Odia Daily Newspaper (Bhubaneswar edition, p. 2).

The Dharitri. (2014, October 29). Odia Daily Newspaper (Bhubaneswar edition, p. 1).
The Dharitri. (2015, November 12). Odia Daily Newspaper (Bhubaneswar edition, p. 2).
The Hindu. (2019, July 7). English Daily Newspaper (Bhubaneswar Edition, p. 1). https://www.thehindu.com/news/national/odisha-chief-minister-urged-to-challenge-hc-order-on-tribal-land-transfer/article28313731.ece. Accessed 21 December, 2019.
The Samaj. (2009, November 21). Odia Daily Newspaper (Bhubaneswar edition, p. 2).
The Samaj. (2013, February 21). Odia Daily Newspaper (Bhubaneswar edition, p. 2).

Chapter 7
Conclusion

India concedes the special protections for her tribal or indigenous peoples in the Constitution, recognising their distinctive cultural, social and economic identity from that of the mainstream Indian society by admitting the fact that they need some protection from exploitation by the mainstream. However, in spite of these special provisions, the Scheduled Tribes continue to be the most vulnerable and impoverished sections of the Indian population. Despite the centrality of land to the identity, economy and culture of the Scheduled Tribes, the protections for the Scheduled Tribes and Scheduled Areas in the Constitution were fragmented and somewhat contradictory in conception and execution from the time of their inclusion in the Constitution. The creation of these fragmented protections was in turn the product of two factors. First, it arose partly from the reality of the tribal situation that, even at the time of drafting of the Indian Constitution, many tribal communities were no longer located within the geographically isolated Scheduled Areas, while many non-tribal communities were resident there. In the interest of doing justice to all communities, the Constitution makers chose to create safeguards both for the tribal people resident in the Scheduled Areas and those that were residing outside the Scheduled Areas. Second, it arose from the inherent contradiction in creating geographically protected areas for the Scheduled Tribes, while at the same time imposing no limitations on the movement of tribals outside those areas, and no restrictions on the movement of non-tribals to those areas. Indeed, given that the Constitution guaranteed to all citizens the fundamental right to move freely throughout the territory of India, it is not clear how such a limitation could have been imposed by law.

There is a fundamental contradiction between two narratives that have characterised the policies of the British colonial state and the independent Indian state. The first narrative that we call the 'identity-based isolation' narrative identifies the tribals as a 'distinctive group outside the mainstream Hindu society both in terms of their cultural traits and geographical isolation, who are keen to preserve their distinctiveness and their isolation. The second narrative called the 'development through integration' narrative identifies the tribal way of life as backward compared to the

S. K. Malik, *Land Alienation and Politics of Tribal Exploitation in India*,
https://doi.org/10.1007/978-981-15-5382-0_7

mainstream Indian population and seeks to improve their economic and social indicators through integrating or assimilating them within the mainstream population. Both the 'identity-based isolation' and 'development through integration' narratives characterised the drafting of the constitutional protections for the STs, while the post-independence policy making was guided primarily by the latter. However, the Scheduled Tribes have regarded the 'development through integration' narrative as both paternalistic and patronising and alleged that this narrative does not seem to capture the aspirations of the tribal people to 'develop according to their own genius'.

In order to have a coherent strategy for the uplift and protection of the tribal people, we need clarity on how the 'identity-based isolation' and 'development through integration' narratives can be integrated in policy discourse and law-making process, so as to facilitate the design of laws and policies that can safeguard the rights of the tribals. Needless to say, the processes of law making must happen in consultation with the tribal communities and not be a paternalistic imposition on them by the state, where they are not only a minority, but a very special minority.

A contrary legal framework comprising of colonial and postcolonial forest, mining and land acquisition laws has further diluted the constitutional protections for the STs. The land alienation prohibition laws only prohibit the transfer of tribal land to non-tribals. Nothing prevents the state from acquiring land in the Scheduled Areas for its own purposes in the exercise of its power of eminent domain or assertion of its rights over forestland. The 'Samata Judgement' not only prohibited the grant of mining leases in the Scheduled Areas by private companies, but also to the state mining corporations which every state should follow. Based on the intensity of dams and mining in the Scheduled Areas, we can easily infer that land acquired in the Scheduled Areas for the purposes of construction of dams and mining have displaced and impoverished millions of Scheduled Tribes. While 90% of all mineral wealth generated in India comes from the Schedule Area of the states, this wealth is not channelized appropriately for the benefit of the tribal people. This is especially worrying when we find that there are huge shortfalls in expenditure in the special financial allocations made for the welfare of the Scheduled Tribes.

All of the above is not to say that the struggle for safeguarding the rights of tribal peoples has been a total failure. The decriminalisation of criminal tribes, the special constitutional provisions for representation, affirmative action for the tribals, recognising the land rights of tribals in the Scheduled Areas, creation of Tribal Sub-Plan (TSP) for special financial allocations for tribal population, creation of the National Commission for Scheduled Tribes, the Ministry of Tribal Affairs, the enactment of the Panchayat Extension to Scheduled Areas (PESA) Act, 1996, the Forest Rights Act (FRA) and the creation of the District Mineral Foundation under the MMDR Act, 2015 are all important constitutional, legislative and administrative steps that have the potential of going a long way to redress the historic injustices against the tribal communities in India. But only the effective and coordinated functioning of all these mechanisms can truly safeguard the rights of tribals in India.

The nature and typologies of tribal land alienation bring out the complex matrix of policies, laws and local contexts which frames the issue of tribal access to land. In policy circles, land issues have been seen through the simple lens of alienation of tribal land, which provides only a partial picture. It is obvious that the issue of alienation of *patta* land by non-tribals through land mortgages and sale is extremely serious. Historically, this has been the most critical mode of loss of good quality agricultural land by tribal. However, given that, there are strict laws which forbid the land transfer and allow for restoration of tribal land which has been illegally transferred. The major intervention in this regards would be to ensure better implementation of these laws and extension of similar provisions to non-Scheduled Areas. The PESA Act should be extended to municipalities also.

The flaws in the survey and settlements, revenue administration and forest declaration which have led to non-recognition of customary tribal land ownership has meant that cultivation by tribal on such customary land has become criminalised. Often, such lands are diverted by the government for plantations or other activities. Even, where tribals continue to cultivate such land, uncertainty of tenure means that they can't invest on these lands nor can they access formal credit for such development. The tribal households have lost access to such land occupied by them because of government plantations. Lack of secure rights over their customary land has meant that the state has been at liberty to displace the tribals from their livelihoods and resources easily, even without paying any compensation. Hundreds of thousands of tribals have been displaced in this manner by dams, industries and other development projects as well as wildlife sanctuaries. Displacement has a devastating impact on tribal psyche, given their cultural attachment to their land and their clans, and their inability to adjust to new locations. The rehabilitation and resettlement packages have been dismal, even not providing land for land in most situations. From all metrics, the situation of tribals in India remains dismal.

The current situation continues to exist because of many reasons. The tribal communities are held in contempt by the dominant caste-based Hindu society, which holds the reins of power in the state. Evolutionism and negative stereotypes about tribal from the colonial era have merged with the Indian elite's ideas of 'assimilations' to produce a disdain for tribal culture that is almost universal among the non-tribals who live near tribals and have power over them. This contempt and disdain is reflected in the prevalent discourses of 'shifting cultivation' being a 'pernicious and evil' practice, tribals being socially and culturally backward, etc. Any discussion with local officials or local non-tribal elite will bring out these biases that tribals are dirty, superstitious, ignorant, backward, addicted to drinking, loose morals, etc. At the best, they are 'simple, innocent, straightforward people' who need to be protected and whose culture needs to be preserved.

At the same time, a normality of extortion and exploitation has been established, with lower level policemen, forest guards and revenue officers demanding bribes and benefits from tribals in a routine way. The lack of rights on land and the dependence on forests for livelihoods play into the hand of these petty officials, who extract bribes for each and every activity necessary for tribals' survival. Thus, lack of rights over land and other resources not only lead to extraction of rent from tribals, but it also disempowers them vis-à-vis the local officials and non-tribals who are much more familiar and conversant with the laws and procedures of bureaucracy.

The same processes have been repeated time and again in all tribal areas where development projects have been implemented. Such exploitation and dispossession explain the growing disenchantment of tribal communities with current governance processes, as it fails to address these critical issues. Improving tribal access to land and other natural resources is not even a part of the development discourse in tribal areas, even though hundreds of millions of rupees are being spent on tribal development programmes. Even watershed development programmes, with explicit focus on development of natural resources and land on a watershed basis, have nowhere addressed these issues. This raises doubt about the very relevance of these development programmes to tribal situation.

Land alienation is related to the existing socio-economic order and not a mere 'structural-legalist' process and phenomenon. As far as tribal land alienation as a major problem is concerned; at the national level, documents highlighting government plans and policies, decisions and announcements with respect to prevention of tribal land and forest should be analysed on time interval. Odisha having the most tribal infested states and the KBK areas (earlier Koraput–Bolangir–Kalahandi districts, now constituted with eight districts, comes under the Fifth Schedule of the Indian Constitution) should be given special focus in the state plan and policies keeping in mind the prevention of encroachment in tribal land. Keeping the above significant issues in mind, throughout the book, the author attempts to highlight the process of land estrangement among the tribals which has been identified in the Narayanpatna movement. The Narayanpatna movement against tribal land alienation has highlighted the land issues of the tribals which also come under the purview of tribals' rights as well as human rights.

The major issue for the vast majority of the tribals in India, in general, and Koraput district of Odisha, in particular, is the scarcity of land or limited access to land which leads to the problem of backwardness, rural poverty and food insecurity in tribal areas. With the objective of bringing equilibrium and to bridge the difference among the rich landed peasantry and the poor landless, the post-independence state brought some land reform legislations. The central government at different times has brought different laws to prevent tribal land alienation and to restore the already alienated land. Odisha also initiated a number of legislative measures to improve the poor peoples' access to land, especially for the tribal access to land. Although a number of land reform legislations were promulgated, their state of implementations remain a major concern. Additionally, land that has been donated under *bhoodan* movement, initiated by Vinoba Bhave, has been reoccupied by the former owner and in some cases remains either undistributed. However, due to encroachment and alienation of tribal land, the problem of landlessness among the tribals still continues in the country, in general, and Koraput district of Odisha, in particular.

The tribals in the country show a variety of customary land tenure systems which have been often modified and changed by the state-government-imposed tenure systems which facilitate tribal land alienation. Due to reservation of forests, increased pressure on land, imposition of formal land tenure system, interactions with markets, and also due to encroachment by the outsiders, the traditional land tenure system of the tribals has been changed drastically. For example, in Odisha, 74% of the land in the Scheduled Areas are categorised as state land, among which 26% are non-forest land and 48% as forest land. In these Scheduled Areas of the state, most of the tribal are either marginal landowners or landless. In Odisha, among all the Scheduled Tribes land owners, at least 20% are landless and more than 50% of tribals are marginal landholders.

The major factor behind such skewed landownership is that shifting cultivation and communal land were never settled in the name of the concerned tribal communities. But in reality, much of such land is still cultivated by the tribals, and the government is treating them as encroachers. The ineffectiveness of the existing law to prevent tribal land transfer to non-tribals, and due to the notification of vast areas of land as forests or government land, the tribals became landless. These trends have continued even after independence, as customary tribal lands were diverted for conservation and development projects by the state government, because legally most of this land are identified as government land.

In fact, there are legislations protecting tribal rights to land; however, these protective laws were not strictly observed. So, the biggest challenge for the government is to implement the existing legislation more effectively and meaningfully in all parts of the state, and to reframe the legislations in accordance with the needs of the tribals. The 'Narayanpatna movement' on the issue of land alienation may be attributed to the negligence of the state administration and its failure in implementing the land laws rigorously.

As the tribals were depended on forest land for their life and livelihoods, the complexity of laws and procedures by bureaucracy and the unscrupulous activities of the petty officials forced them for the deprivation of rights on land and forests. Due to the ingress of non-tribals into tribal areas and increasing industrial and mining activities, the situation in Scheduled Areas of the country, in general, and Odisha, in particular, continued to decay. Tribal access to land is not even a part of the 'paradigm of the development discourse' where, in the name of tribal development, millions of rupees are being spent. This creates dubiousness about the state's intention and invites sceptic regarding the relevance of the step taken under these development programmes as far as tribal land situation is concerned. After 70 years of India's independence, 'the politics of tribal exploitation' remain as usual like the 'British Period' and the present situation for the tribals may be called as '*internal colonialism*'.

Koraput being the most tribal-dominated district in Odisha with more than 50.6% of tribal population, remains rampant in terms of tribal land alienation and landlessness. It covers the transfer of the tribal land to the hands of non-tribals largely through the means of force, the abuse of law, and through *benami* (illegal) transfers by moneylenders, traders, contractors and landlords. In Koraput, the ongoing land alienation since centuries forced the tribals for extremely low holdings which is the most important factor for their backwardness, extreme poverty and food scarcity.

The above process of land alienation in the Koraput region began during the period of the kings of Jeypore. The colonial state, if not abetted, but permitted the practice of land encroachment in tribal areas either directly or indirectly. Due to lack of proper and regular survey and settlement, tribals have also lost their land on a massive scale in the post-independence period. Sale of land to non-tribals, debt mortgaging, etc. are the main factors of *patta* land alienation and for that reason, in the Koraput district, more than 50% of the Scheduled Tribe landowners are marginal. To that extent, even in the Primitive Tribal Groups (PTGs) outback areas, most lands are owned by the state. Though many of this PTGs practice communal landownership of swidden land, no communal ownership rights have been provided in the Survey and Settlements process and swidden cultivation land have been classified as state land. Land transfer to the non-tribals from the tribal is checked by section 3 of OSATIP Regulation, 1956, in Scheduled V areas and section 22 of the Odisha Land Reforms Act, 1960, for non-Scheduled Areas which remain full of loopholes. Both laws provided for sale of land after obtaining permission of the competent authorities.

The undivided Koraput district alone had lost 7.42% of its land areas to 18 development projects. But the thing which is important is that they received no compensation when such land was taken up for development projects because swidden land, shifting cultivation land and land on communal ownership which were cultivated by Scheduled Tribes were not legally settled in their names. Compensatory afforestation under the Forest Conservation Act, 1980, had displaced the PTGs and other tribals as the lands were not recorded with them. Tribal land alienation in Odisha, in general, and in the Koraput district, in particular, happened in a massive scale due to lack of rigorous execution of the Acts like 'OSATIP Act, 1956', 'OGLS Act, 1962', 'OLR Act, 1960' and 'OPLE Act, 1972'. By December 1999; 8,41,916.50 acres of tribal land were alienated in the state, in which Koraput district has contributed 28,901.55 acres of alienated land and remain highest among all the districts. Concisely, it can be said that among other causes of dispossession and impoverishment of the tribals of Odisha in general, and Koraput district in particular, land alienation remains as the prime factor.

The first phase of the land alienation in Koraput district started during the rule of the king of Jeypore who ruled from the coastal area of Odisha. To help the king, there are *amins, mustajars, inamdars* and landlords who were appointed from the plain areas. They all are 'the outsiders' who had encroached tribal land by cheating them, by exploiting their ignorance and due to the outsiders' proximity to the king and the administration.

The second phase of land alienation in the district began with the survey and settlement process in 1960s. The tribals were left out of the whole process of survey and settlement. So, a large amount of land in Koraput district such as shifting cultivation land and land above 10° slope line remain unsurveyed and without settlement; where the tribals were treated as encroachers in their ancestral land. The land which were declared as 'deemed forest' by the Madras Estate without any notification also forced the tribals to desert from their land.

The third phase of land alienation in Koraput started in 1970. The non-tribal 'men of affairs' and landlords migrated to Koraput district in 1970 due to the 'armed revolution in Srikakulam' (Andhra Pradesh). After settling there, they joined hand with the outsider coastal people of Odisha and unitedly encroached the tribal land. They engaged the tribes in their own land as labourers and duped them in the process. They also established political supremacy over the poor tribes and began to increase their landed property by exploiting the tribes. It may be mentioned here that the Orissa

Scheduled Areas Transfer of Immovable Property (by Scheduled Tribes) Regulation (2), 1956 Act was there, which prevents the non-tribes to take away any tribal land. But, this law was not being strictly enforced. As a result, lands were occupied by these people from coastal Andhra and Odisha which alienated the tribal population from their land. This happened in the Koraput district, in general, and Narayanpatna block, in particular.

The fourth phase of land alienation and displacement started with the four mega-dams (Kolab, Machhkund, Indrabati and Chitrakonda) and two projects (NALCO-National Aluminium Corporation and HAL-Hindustan Aeronautics Limited) in the district which added to the existing land issues of the tribals of Koraput in contemporary time. The recent commercial plantation such as eucalyptus, sisal and cashew on the common property resources and on the so-called 'encroachment land' (the tribal lands which were declared as encroached by the government due to lack of land record on the part of the tribals) adds to their excruciations.

The land issues of the tribal of Koraput district are complex and centuries-old problem which remain unsolved even today. Due to continuous land encroachment and alienation by the outsiders, negligence of the revenue administration and the apathy of the state government, the Koraput tribal land issues became precarious. While there are many who suggest that the state government can make a start to settle the issue by establishing 'special land tribunals' to efficiently sort out the matters relating to land encroachment, land alienation, entitlement and land distribution within a deadline. The state government also needs to seriously review issues of land acquisition, transfer and alienation of land linked with other problems like outside encroachment, industrialisation, mining, development-induced displacement and commercial agriculture as far as tribals land are concerned.

Koraput being the most tribal-dominated district in Odisha has witnessed incessant tribals' agitation against the land encroachment and alienation, but no solution has been visible at the ground level. Revolving around the tribal land issues and alienation, each decade has experienced some kind of violent uprisings and sporadic movements but without any substantial changes at policy level.

Historically speaking, the indigenous people of Koraput district have never retired from their relentless protest against the land-grabbers. Tribal agitations have consistently targeted foreign interventions (called '*dikus*') via expropriation of their land that threaten to culminate in economic distress. The tribal uprisings in Odisha have a definitive historical pattern. The indigenous people have struggled against the colonial government in pre-independence period as well as against the Indian state after independence to the present period. They have violently challenged the land-grabbers and *zamindars*, formed alliance against the kings, conspired to overthrow the British and have demonstrated ample courage in battling against the caste supremacies of the upper caste Hindus.

In 1994, tribal movement reportedly started in Narayanpatna block of Koraput district over land dispute. The tribals demanded that the 'arrack trade' and land grabbing must be stopped because the community of '*sundhis*' (the non-tribal outsiders who are mostly liquor vendors), the arrack businessmen and contractors were entrapping tribals in a debt trap through mortgaging their land and thereafter grabbing it.

Tribals were often being treated as virtually slaves and bonded labourers in their own usurped land. Local officials, the revenue officers and police acted in collusion with the land-grabbers.

Again in 1998, in the wake of the tribal movement in Narayanpatna on the issue of tribal land alienation, organised by the *Chasi Mulia Samiti* (CMS), the government then announced that it would rigorously enforce the land laws. But till now, the government has not implemented the law in its letter and spirit. Once again, the tribals of Narayanpatna have launched the movement against hooch and land grabbing, under the leadership of the *Chasi Mulia Adivasi Sangha* (CMAS).

In order to get back their grabbed land from the clutches of the landlords and encroachers, since 2006, the tribals of Narayanpatna had taken the path of agitation considering it as the only alternative. They had launched an armed agitation against the hooch and land grabbing under the banner of CMAS. But the government had done nothing concretely in this regard; however, the landless tribals of Narayanpatna had been persistently demanding to recoup their land from the possession of the non-tribal owners. The land disputes, which remained unsettled for generations, were tried to be solved by the cooperative efforts of the tribals through Narayanpatna movement under the banner of CMAS and also succeeded in taking their land back which were rightfully theirs, from the encroachers.

Through this movement, by the end of 2009, the tribals of Narayanpatna block reoccupied 3000 acres of land, where the tribal women and the tribal youth (both men and women knows as '*Ghenua Vahini*' or 'the army militia of CMAS') had played a major role. In reaction to the popular movement, on 20 November 2009, the police opened fire at assembled tribals in front of the police station causing the death of two tribal leaders, where the cause of the tribal protest was against police torture and high-handedness in the area. The police and security forces had already arrested more than 200 CMAS members including their leaders. The movement came to an end in 2014 when the chief leader of the movement, Nachika Linga, surrendered to police on 28 October 2014.

Towards the land issue of Narayanpatna, the state response always remained tongue-tied. The present *Biju Janata Dal* (BJD) government vehemently suppressed the movement to protect the interest of the exploiters, after branding CMAS as a frontal organisation of the Maoist and the movement is Maoist led, without solving the real problem of land. It arrested almost all the leaders in charge of being Maoists with the help of Odisha police, BSF, CRPF and other paramilitary forces and also ultimately banned the CMAS. The state declared Nachika Linga (the chief leader of the movement) as the most wanted, after firing two other CMAS leaders during the protest in 2009.

The Congress party, which ruled the state for near about four decades, adopted a laissez-faire policy towards the tribal problem. During 1990–1995, it was only throughout the Janata Party period (led by Biju Ptnaik), the state recognised the problem as a socio-economic, and Biju Patnaik (the then Chief Minister) divided the large area districts into small ones in 1992. Nevertheless, this administrative reconstituting had not impacted on the activities of the administration and the problems of tribals remain as usual. Neither have the respective regime in Odisha evolve any clear-cut policy on the issue. The leaders of the state have never tried to realise the problem, the government tends to look at the problem as a Maoist problem, the police says it is a law and order problem, while the bureaucrats call it a socio-economic problem.

Recently, after the Narayanpatna movement, the Odisha government became very active in implementing the land laws in Koraput district and the Chief Minister has announced such in public. But the centuries-old land problems will not solve by the present initiatives. The land issue of the Narayanpatna will solve by the redistribution of land to the original tribal owners, by taking the land from the encroachers which needs a new law with the intent for strict implementation. There is need to think radically regarding the land issues, because the already existing laws will not solve the issue. Trying to solve the problem with the existing law will like to keep it under the carpet where it will crop up again in the future.

The state forcefully arrests the tribal movement with the help of the paramilitary forces such as BSF, CRPF, SOGs and police after declaring the CMAS as a frontal organisation of the Maoist and banning it. The entire movement has gone underground and the vast majority of the CMAS members hide in fear within the jungles, often on the move without food, in constant risk of being apprehended and forced to surrender before the police in fear of encounter.

The CMAS activists after their leaders' arrest have surrendered in fear to the police and the police have been taking the credit by claiming that so many Maoists have surrendered to police. Since January 2013, from 22 villages of Narayanpatna block, 778 CMAS activists had dissociated from CMAS and declared that they want to join the mainstream politics. Around 113 CMAS members had left Nachika Linga and surrendered before the police of Narayanpatna on February 2013.

The most wanted Nachika Linga from Bhaliaput village of Narayanpatna block, who was put on the most wanted list by Odisha police with 43 cases earlier, surrendered to police with his supporters on 28 October 2014. The surrender of Linga brought an end to the popular tribal movement that was launched by the tribals to raise voice against the exploitation of tribals and peasants. With this, the CMAS ceased to operate. It became the death of the revolutionary force (the Narayanpatna movement) not only in the history of Odisha but also in the history of India too.

There is nothing doubtful that the encroachment by the non-tribal outsiders, negligence of the revenue administration and the non-implementation of the land reform measures have been responsible for the centuries-old land problem, exploitation and underdevelopment in the tribal areas of Narayanpatna. But, the existence of left extremism in one hand and the police high-handedness in the other has aggravated the condition of the innocent tribals of Narayanpatna. The tribals faced double problem; as suspected 'informers' to the police, they are targeted by the Maoists, and vice versa. If they informed the police and cooperate, then the Maoists target them and the reverse. The basic necessities and rights are not available due to left extremism and government apathy where around 80% of development projects and welfare measures of the government remain unimplemented.

Although the state administration has been facing the acute endanger for the last three decades, no consistent strategy was developed yet. Proper understanding of the problem by a sensitive administration with strong political will could help to sort out the problem and also countering the left-wing extremism in the district in particular, and in the state, in general. Now, in the part of the state, a long-term and result-oriented approach is a pressing imperative to solve the tribal problems.

By way of conclusion, it may be said that no revolutionary struggle ever fails without any short-term and long-term result, and this finds true in case of Narayanpatna tribal movement. The movement elsewhere has inspired the people of Deomali areas and Pottangi block in Koraput district while struggling against displacement and mining activities. It also influenced other areas of the district and the state. Due to the movement, the tribals have forcefully occupied around 3000 acres of land, which was rightfully theirs, though the occupied lands are going to be reoccupied by the encroachers with the help of police after the arrest of all CMAS members. The matter during the movement was placed for discussion in the Odisha Legislative Assembly where the ruling party projected it as Maoist problem and the weak opposition remained silent without any strong move.

Though the 'Narayanpatna movement' is very crucial in the history of tribal movement, it was least highlighted because the 'corporate media', 'police state' and the 'statist academia' have presented it in a distorted form. One must visit the tribal areas of Narayanpatna in order to find the truth which the state wishes to hide and to give voice to the peoples' concern, to act as a corrective to such media misinformation.

By addressing all the major issues raised by the present study, the conclusion attempts to offer the following basic arguments: Firstly, land remains central issue and viable for the tribals, as their life, livelihood, freedom and development are concerned. Secondly, the cultural attachment of the tribals and their worldview to the idea of 'place' (land) furnishes crucial perspectives in apprehending the politics of collective resistance. Thirdly, the politicisation of group identity and material interest against the outside authority serve as the basis of the unrest among the tribals. Finally, when the grudges of the people are hardened in an insensitive and tyrannical way, the extent of tribal resistance escalates and the war starts between the state and its own people.

As far as the building of theory is concerned, I generalised the following line in the context of the Narayanpatna movement and the nature of the present Indian state that the state apparatus applies coercion to arrest revolutionary and social forces through the easy and most popular tactics of suppression after declaring the organisation and movement as Maoist generated and proclaiming a war against its own people in the name of law, order, peace, security and development. The easiest path that the Indian state has found to crush democratic movements is by using the biggest fetish of democracy, 'the law'. The tribal movement of Narayanpatna was never illegal and was aimed at implementing an existing law regarding the distribution of land to tribals. The best way to suppress an uprising or revolution is to brand it as Maoist or Maoist-backed as the Maoists have been posited by the Indian state as the single largest threat to 'internal security'. The 'civil society' of Odisha has partially been subsumed by brutal attacks of the state and partially been hegemonies in the typhoon ongoing 'development'. Therefore, after 70 years of India's independence, the tribals of Koraput district (Odisha), in particular, and in case of India, in general, remain poor, backward and underdeveloped.

On the basis of the findings and inferences, however, the present research dares to recommend some suggestions for new policy formulation and government attention which may be accepted for solving the problem of tribals in Narayanpatna of Koraput district, in particular, and improving tribal access and control over land in the country, in general, as tribal land alienation, encroachment and exploitation are concerned. These include the following:

- Effective administration regarding land questions and improving tribal access and control to land should be made the core strategy of development for tribal areas.
- Removing 10 degree slope criteria for settling shifting cultivation land with tribal cultivators.
- Strengthening tribal land protection laws and implementing such laws seriously.
- Transparency and simplification in land administration.
- Creation of tribal land bank.
- Land acquisition/purchase from non-tribals for transfer to tribals.
- Proper recording of occupation rights through survey and settlement.
- Need for proper implementation of Forest Rights Act.
- Cashew nut plantation in the tribal areas should be leased directly to the tribals for developing their economic condition which will indirectly arrest the tribal insurgency as implemented and succeeded in case of rubber plantation in tribal areas by the Tripura government. So the Tripura model should be followed.
- In case of Odisha, the state should strengthen the provisions of the OSATIP Regulation, 1956 on the basis of the *Samata* Judgement (given by the Supreme Court) and the Andhra Pradesh tribal land protection laws.
- 'Special land tribunals' should be formed to expeditiously sort out the land cases within a time bound.
- The existing laws will not solve the issues. There is need for a new law, because the core land issue is the redistribution of land which needs rigorous implementation with strong political and bureaucratic will.

Suggestions with regard to the CMAS and the Narayanpatna Movement:-

- All the CMAS members arrested during the Narayanpatna movement should be released immediately without any condition.
- The land issue of tribals in Koraput district, in particular, and in the state, in general, be immediately settled.
- All the BSF camps in Narayanpatna must be withdrawn.
- The land which was occupied by the tribals during the movement should be recognised by the state.
- The tribals of Odisha, in general, and Koraput district, in particular, be provided the basic facilities such as education, healthcare, electricity, drinking water, communication etc.

- A compensation of Rs. 10 lakh to the family of the person killed by the police during the tribal protest at Narayanpatna, should be paid by the government.
- The government should release the encroached and alienated land from the clutches of non-tribals and hand it over to the tribal to solve the land problem.

Appendix
Questionnaire Section

For the Study of Narayanpatna Movement in Koraput District of Odisha

Date: 18-12-2015 to 03-01-2016
Date: 27-06-2017 to 11-07-2017

NAME: SEX: MALE/FEMALE
RESIDENCE: OCCUPATION:
TRIBAL/NON-TRIBAL
AGE: CASTE:
LITERACY: SUBCASTE:
RELIGION:

Section A: Questionnaire for Members of '*Chasi-Mulia-Adivasi Sangha*' (The Organisation Which Lead the Movement in Narayanpatna)

(1) Are you a member of '*Chasi-Mulia-Adivasi Sangha*'?
(2) For how many years is this organisation functioning?
(3) Who are the members of the organisation?
(4) Who are the leaders of the organisation?
(5) What does the organisation do for your benefit?
(6) What is the basic demand of '*Chasi-Mulia-Adivasi Sangha*'?

S. K. Malik, *Land Alienation and Politics of Tribal Exploitation in India*,
https://doi.org/10.1007/978-981-15-5382-0

(7) Did it work for the benefit of tribals?
(8) Are you getting any kind of help from '*Chasi-Mulia-Adivasi- Sangha*'?

(a) Yes……………..
(b) No………………………
If yes, tell me something about it……………………………

(9) Since when has this tribal movement started?
(10) Which are the villages of Narayanpatna block that have been participating in the movement?
(11) Did you participate in the movement against tribal land alienation?
(12) What is the role of '*Ghinua Vahini*' (arm militia of CMAS, who fought with the police)?
(13) Do the police arrest/torture you being the member of CMAS and participating in the movement?
(14) Who are the members of the 'Peace Committee'/'*Nagarik Surakshya Samiti*'?
(15) Did they oppose the tribals and attack the tribals?
(16) How much of land have the organisation restored from the encroachers?
(17) Was the land re-distributed among the landless tribals?
(18) How many persons have been arrested by the police during the movement?
(19) Why did the police fired upon the leaders of '*Chasi-Mulia-Adivasi Sangha*'?
(20) Do you want to continue the movement?

Yes/No…………?
If No…….why?

(21) What are the major problems in your area?
(22) Are you satisfied with the government plan and policies?
(23) Do the government do anything regarding the land issues of the tribals?
(24) Did the government implement any developmental programme for your community?
(25) Has the government taken any kind of step to stop the movement?

(a) Yes………………
(b) No………………………
If yes, then describe the nature and effect of it…………………………………

(26) After the surrender of Nachika Linga (chief leader of CMAS) to police, what is the course of action of the organisation?
(27) Does the organisation exist today?
(28) Do you think that the movement has any impact for the benefit of the people?
(29) Is there any relationship between Maoists and the CMAS as the police is claiming?

(a) If yes, how…………?
(b) If no…………………
Why……………………………?

Section B: Questionnaire for the Leaders of the Movement

(1) Are you the leader of the movement?
(2) Why are you leading this movement?
(3) Is there any political ideology and structure that the organisation maintains?
(4) What are the basic demands of the movement?
(5) Is the present government in failure to solve the issues?
(6) What are the strategies that the organisation adopts in respect of the people and the government?
(7) What are the possible solutions for the land problems of the tribals?
(8) What steps has the government taken so far to fight the problems?
(9) How can this movement be put to an end?
(10) From where do the funds come for launching the movement and to maintain the organisation?
(11) Have there been any peace talks between the government authorities with the people who led the movement?
(12) How and why did this movement emerge in Narayanpatna area?
(13) Who are the sympathisers of the movement?
(14) What is the attitude of the present government and police towards the movement?
(15) Does the CMAS have any link with the Maoists?
(16) What is the situation that now prevails in the area?
(17) Why has your chief leader Nachika Linga surrendered to the police?
(18) Did you stop this movement after Nachika Linga's surrender to the police?
(19) What are your views on the repressive measures adopted by the government like 'operation green hunt', etc and 'Operation Linga'?
(20) Are peace talks/dialogues between the government and the tribals of Narayanpatna even possible today?
(21) Do you know anything about '*Nagarik Surakshya Samiti*'? If so, what are their roles?

Section C: Questionnaire for the Members of 'Peace Committee'/'*Nagarik Surakshya Samiti*' (Mainly an Organisation of Non-tribal Landlords, Sahukars and Encroachers of Narayanpatna Who Oppose the Tribal Movement)

(1) Are you a member of the *Nagarik Surakshya Samiti*?
(2) What is the role of *Nagarik Surakshya Samiti*?
(3) Why does the *Nagarik Surakshya Samiti* oppose the movement?
(4) What in your opinion are the main problems of this movement?
(5) What are their demands?

(6) Why are they continuing their movement against the State?
(7) Did the CMAS has any link with the Maoists?

Section D: Questionnaire for the Officials, Police, Administrators, Social Activists and Local Politicians of Narayanpatna

(1) Do you know anything about the Narayanpatna movement?
(2) Since when has this movement started?
(3) Which areas are severely affected by the movement?
(4) What in your opinion are the causes of the movement?
(5) Did the CMAS has any link with the Maoists?
(6) Has the government taken any kind of step to stop the movement?

    (a) Yes..................
    (b) No............................
    If yes, then describe it.......................................

(7) Has the government tried to solve the problems of the tribals?
(8) Did the government implement any developmental programme for the tribal communities?
(9) As an administrator and officer, what steps do you suggest to stop the tribal movement and violence?

Annexure

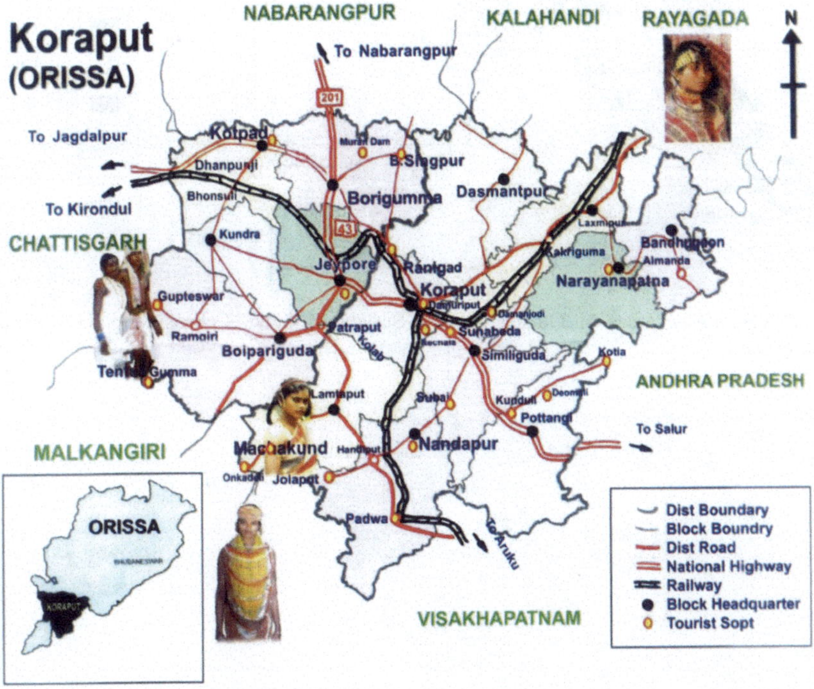

Map 1 Koraput district map (*Source* Survey of India, Census Map, GIS Division Bhubaneswar)

S. K. Malik, *Land Alienation and Politics of Tribal Exploitation in India*,
https://doi.org/10.1007/978-981-15-5382-0

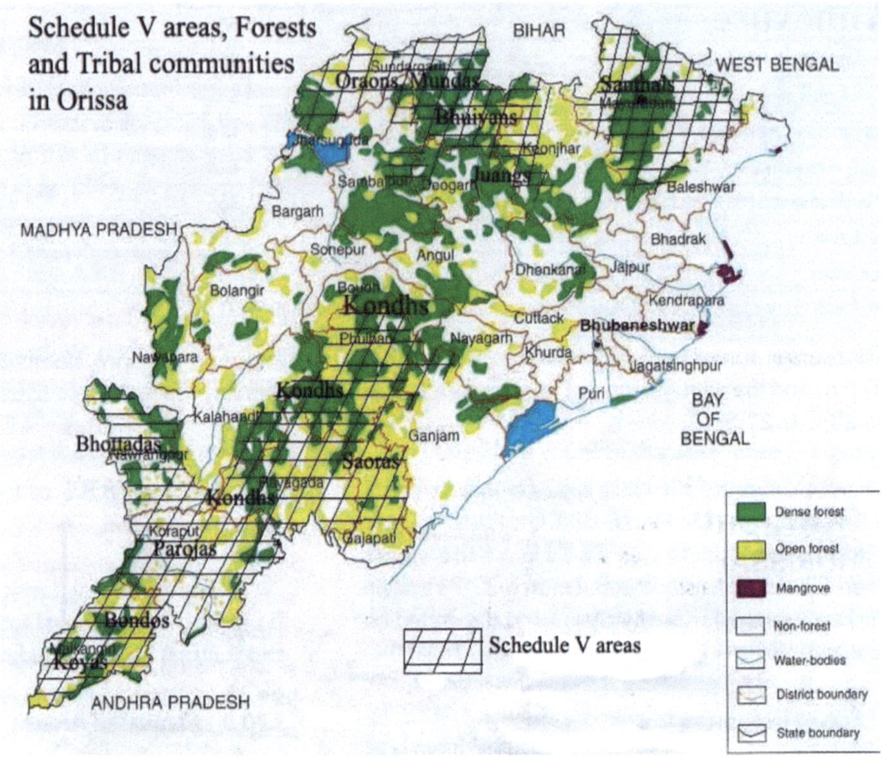

Map 2 Schedule V areas of Odisha (*Source* Survey of India, Census Map, GIS Division Bhubaneswar)

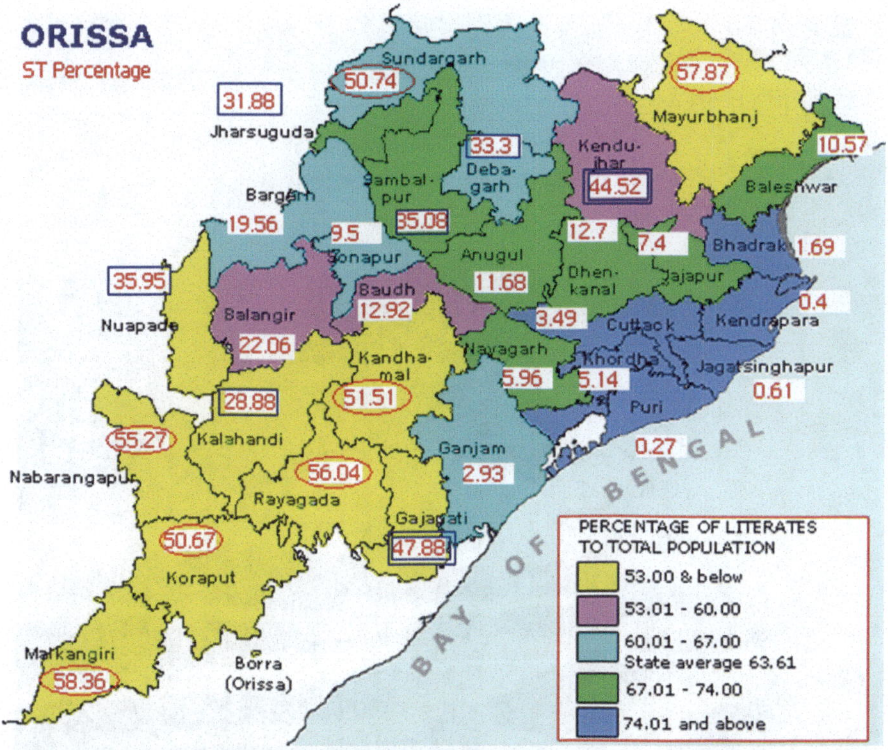

Map 3 Percentage of schedule tribe population in Odisha as per 2011 census (*Source* Survey of India, Census Map, GIS Division Bhubaneswar)

Image 1 (Image taken from—https://www.google.com/search?q=image+of+step+cultivation+in+Koraput+district&tbm). Step cultivation in Koraput district: land up to 30° slope are customarily owned by tribals. But survey and settlement recognised till 10° slope. The land above 10° slope remain unsurveyed and unsettled with the tribals of Koraput district

Image 2 (Image taken from Kumar et al. 2005: 15). A typical landscape in tribal areas of Koraput: valley bottom paddy land and upland are generally under legal ownership. The villagers own only the valley land. The hillsides, though cultivated, are categorised as Government Revenue Land: a major form of land alienation

Image 3 (Image taken from Kumar et al. 2005: 42). The fertile valley bottom land of the tribals in Koraput district are generally mortgaged or sold by tribals through *Benami* (illegal) transaction

Image 4 (Image taken from Kumar et al. 2005: 49). Land claimed customarily by the tribals has been converted to cashew plantations leased out to a government corporation. Tribals have no rights on this land or on the plantations: the other way of land alienation, in the Koraput district

Image 5 (Image taken from Kumar et al. 2005: 69). Tribal women work as daily wage labourer for harvesting of cashew nut from the OSCDC Ltd. plantation leased out to upper caste villagers from Podagarha, Koraput. The tribals claim this land as customarily belonging to them which has been taken away from them by the government for the cashew plantation

Image 6 The community cultivation by the CMAS on the land which it acquired forcefully through the Narayanpatna movement

Image 7 CMAS' rally carrying the dead bodies of Singhana and Andru, the police firing on 20 November, 2009 causes murder of two CMAS leaders at Narayanpatna

Image 8 CMAS's meeting against police firing which causes murder of two CMAS leaders. First image is about the '*Ghinua Vahini*' of the CMAS led by Nachika Linga during the movement

Image 9 Houses burnt by security personnels during the police clash with the CMAS, Narayanpatna

Image 10 Security operation in Narayanpatna area, Koraput. ZEE NEWS Report

Image 11 BSF camp in Narayanpatna block

Democracy' at its worst !

Fact Finding Report on the Police firing on CMAS activists in Narayanpatna, Orissa

Fact Finding Team Members

K Sudhakar Patnaik – Senior Journalist

Manoranjan Routray – Journalist

Sharanya – HumAnE, Koraput

Image 12 Cover page of the fact-finding report on police firing

Fact Finding Report: Narayanpatna Police firing

Prafulla Samantara, Lok Shakti Abhiya, Radhakant Sethy, CPI(ML)(Liberation) Budha Gamanga, Lok Sangram Manch Sivaram CPI-ML

On November 23 a fact-finding team comprising intellectuals and activists from several organisations visited Narayanpatna to inquire about the killing of the adivasis. The team had to face difficulties in entering the region and members of the team were harassed and even beaten up by the police, as one of the team members reported in the press conference held today (November 25). The following is the report of the team released during the press conference.

Image 13 Fact-finding report cover page on Narayanpatna police firing

Image 14 The most wanted Nachika Linga from Bhaliaput Village of Narayanpatna block whose fifth generation remain bonded labourer. He was also a bonded labour in the house of Nilakantha Parida (local landlord of Bhaliaput village) before becoming the leader of CMAS. He was put on the most wanted list by Odisha police and a cash prize of Rs. 5 Lakhs was announced to capture him

Source For Images 6–14. https://www.google.co.in/search?hl=en&site=imghp&tbm=isch&source=hp&biw=1366&bih=667&q=narayanpatna+movement&oq=narayanpatna+movement&gs_l=img. Accessed August 20, 2016.

DHARITRI

Published simultaneously from Bhubaneswar, Sambalpur, D

୪୦ଶ ଭାଗ ୩୩୨ ସଂଖ୍ୟା www.orissakhabar.com/www.dharitri.com ଭୁବନେଶ୍ୱର, ବୁଧବାର, ଅକ୍ଟୋବର ୨୯ /

ନାଚିକାଙ୍କ ଆତ୍ମସମର୍ପଣ

କୋରାପୁଟ/ଲକ୍ଷ୍ମୀପୁର,୨୮।୧୦(ସ୍ୱ.ପ୍ର./ଡି.ଏନ.ଏ.) -ମଙ୍ଗଳବାର ଅପରାହ୍ଣ ୪ଟାରେ ନାରାୟଣପାଟଣା ଆଦିବାସୀ ଚାଷୀମୂଲିଆ ସଂଘ ସଭାପତି ନାଚିକା ଲିଙ୍ଗା ପୋଲିସ ନିକଟରେ ଆତ୍ମସମର୍ପଣ କରିଛନ୍ତି । ନାଚିକା ନାରାୟଣପାଟଣା ପଞ୍ଚାୟତର କେତେ ଜଣ ସଦସ୍ୟଙ୍କ ସହାୟତାରେ ତାଙ୍କ ୪ଜଣ ସହଯୋଗୀଙ୍କ ସହ ପୋଲିସ ନିକଟରେ ଆତ୍ମ ସମର୍ପଣ କରିଛନ୍ତି ବୋଲି ଏକ ଖବରଦାତା ସମ୍ମିଳନୀରେ ଦକ୍ଷିଣ ପଶ୍ଚିମାଞ୍ଚଳ ଆଇଜି ଯଶୱନ୍ତ ଜେଠ୍ୱା ପ୍ରକାଶ କରିଛନ୍ତି ।

କୋରାପୁଟ ଜିଲା ନାରାୟଣପାଟଣା ବ୍ଲକ ପୋଡାପଦର ପଞ୍ଚାୟତ ଭାଲିଆପୁଟ ଗ୍ରାମର ନାଚିକାଙ୍କ ନାମରେ ବିଭିନ୍ନ ଥାନାରେ ୪୩ଟି ମାମଲା ରହିଛି । ଏଥିରୁ ୩୩ଟି ମାମଲା ଜାମିନବିହୀନ । ତାଙ୍କ ନାମରେ ଅଧିକାଂଶ ମାମଲା ଜିଲାର ଲକ୍ଷ୍ମୀପୁର, ବନ୍ଧୁଗାଁ, ନାରାୟଣପାଟଣା ଓ ସେମିଳିଗୁଡା ଥାନାରେ ରହିଛି । ପୋଲିସ ପାଇଁ ନାଚିକା ମୋଷ୍ଟ ୱାଣ୍ଟେଡ ଥିଲେ । ତାଙ୍କୁ ଧରାଇ ଦେବାକୁ ପୋଲିସ ପକ୍ଷରୁ ୫ଲକ୍ଷ ଟଙ୍କାର ପୁରସ୍କାର ଘୋଷଣା କରାଯାଇଥିଲା

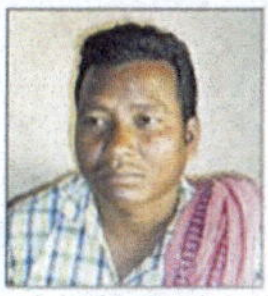

ନାଚିକା ଲିଙ୍ଗା

ବୋଲି ସୂଚନା ଦେଇ ଜେଠ୍ୱା କହିଲେ ଯେ, ତାଙ୍କୁ କୋରାପୁଟ ଆଣିବାକୁ ବିଭାଗ ପକ୍ଷରୁ କର୍ମଚାରୀମାନେ ନାରାୟଣପାଟଣା ଯାଇଛନ୍ତି । ସେ ଏଠାରେ ପହଞ୍ଚିବା ପରେ ତାଙ୍କୁ ପଚରାଉଚରା କରାଯିବ । ବୁଧବାର ତାଙ୍କୁ କୋର୍ଟଚାଲାଣ କରାଯିବ । ସେ ଆତ୍ମ ସମର୍ପଣ କରିଥିବାରୁ ସରକାରଙ୍କ ନିୟମ ଅନୁସାରେ ଥିବା ସହାୟତା ତାଙ୍କୁ ମିଳିବ ବୋଲି ସେ କହିଥିଲେ । ସୂଚାନାଯୋଗ୍ୟ ଯେ, ନାରାୟଣପାଟଣା ଅଞ୍ଚଳରେ ଗୋତି ପ୍ରଥା ଉଚ୍ଛେଦ କରିବା, ଆଦିବାସୀ ମାନଙ୍କଠାରୁ ଜବରଦଖଲ କରି ଅଣଆଦିବାସମାନେ ନେଇଯାଇ ଥିବା ଜମିକୁ ଆଦିବାସୀଙ୍କୁ ଫେରାଇବା, ମଦ କାରବାର ବନ୍ଦ କରିବା ଆଦି ବିଭିନ୍ନ ସମସ୍ୟା ନେଇ ୨୦୦୪ରେ ନାରାୟଣପାଟଣା ଚାଷୀ ମୂଲିଆ ଆଦିବାସୀ ସଂଘ ଜନ୍ମ ନେଇଥିଲା । ପରେ ଏହି ସଂଘର ସଭାପତି ଭାବେ ନାଚିକା ଲିଙ୍ଗା ରହିଥିଲେ । ମାତ୍ର ୨୦୦୬ଠାରୁ ସଂଘର କାର୍ଯ୍ୟକଳାପ ଏହି ଅଞ୍ଚଳରେ ବୃଦ୍ଧି ପାଇଥିଲା । ୨୦୦୯ ନଭେମ୍ବର ୨୦ରେ ନାରାୟଣପାଟଣା ଥାନା ଆକ୍ରମଣ ଘଟଣା ପରେ ସଂଘକୁ ସରକାରଙ୍କ ପକ୍ଷରୁ ବେଆଇନ ଘୋଷଣା କରାଯାଇଥିଲା । ସେହିଦିନଠାରୁ ନାଚିକା ପୋଲିସର ମୋଷ୍ଟ ୱାଣ୍ଟେଡ ତାଲିକାରେ ରହିଥିଲେ ।

Image 15 The most wanted Nachika Linga (leader of the CMAS) has finally surrendered to police with other CMAS members on 28 October 2014. To capture him Odisha government has earlier declared Rs. 5 lakh reward. The news is published in *Dharitri,* the daily Odia newspaper (Bhubaneswar edition) with his photo (*Source* The Daily Odia Newspaper 'Dharitri', October, 29, 2014, p. 1)

Image 16 Way to Narayanpatna: the underdeveloped road from Koraput to Narayanpatna, showing the communication problem. The road has been prepared to easy access of the BSF security forces to the area

Image 17 During the fieldwork. The researcher at the hill road of Narayanpatna

Image 18 Image taken with due permission of the IIC, Narayanpatna (Mr. Suraj Jhankar) and have also a formal conversation with him about the present situation in the area and also about the CMAS

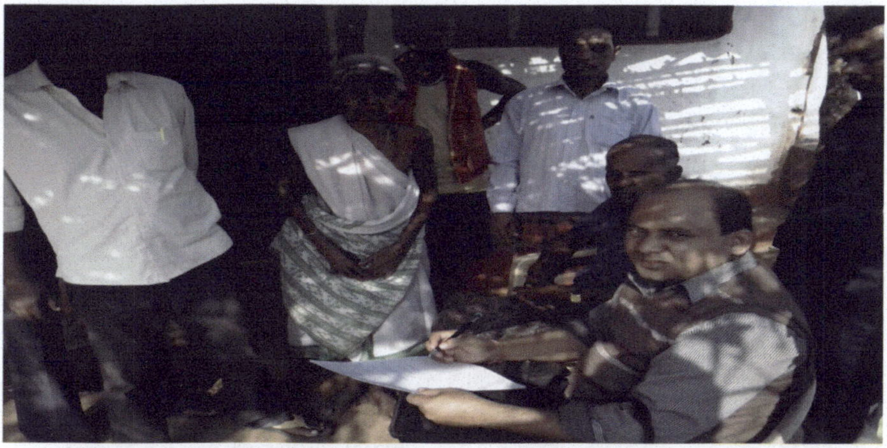

Image 19 Image taken during the interview with the people at Narayanpatna

Image 20 Image taken during the interview with the people at Narayanpatna

Image 21 Image taken during the interview with the people at Narayanpatna

Image 22 Image taken during the interview with the people at Tentulipadar village (G.P) of Narayanpatna block. On my right the Ex-Sarpanch, Tentulipadar G.P. and an old *Kondha* tribal man during the interview

Image 23 Image taken during the interview with the tribal women at Tentulipadar village (G.P) of Narayanpatna block

Image 24 Image taken during the interview with the migrants from Narayanpatna, residing in government colony, Koraput

Image 25 Image taken during the interview with the migrants from Narayanpatna, residing in government colony, Koraput

Image 26 During the fieldwork, I visited the land acquisition office, Koraput and collected the data on land acquisition and displaced persons for the four mega-projects of Machkund Hydro Electric Project (MHEP), Hindustan Aeronautics Limited (HAL), National Aluminium Company (NALCO) and Upper Kolab Hydro Electric Project (UKHEP)

Image 27 During the fieldwork, I visited the land record room, office of the Sub-Collector, Koraput and collected data on transfer/purchase of tribal land by the non-tribals

Glossary

Amin An officer in land department
Bandh Strike
Barga Share-cropping
Benami Illegal
Biplabi Revolutionary
Bonda Naked
Crore Ten million
Dalit Scheduled Caste
Dana Land grants
Dhampa A kind of tribal drum
Diha Homestead land
Dikus Exploitative outsiders
Gharjawae Resident son-in-law
Goonda (goons) Bad character
Goti/Bethi Unpaid labour
Gram Sabha Village council
Haat Weekly Market
Jal Water
Jamin Land
Jotedar Landlord
Jungle Forest
Laal attank Red terror
Lakh One hundred thousand
Lathi Stick used to defend/attack
Lumpen Criminals
Mahua An Indian tree which has fleshy edible flowers and yields oil-rich seeds
Mela A fair or Hindu festival
Mustajari an agent of the landlord for the collection of rent
Naik Leader or Chief
Nux-vomica The seed of the orange like fruit basically used to make medicine
Panchayats Village Council

S. K. Malik, *Land Alienation and Politics of Tribal Exploitation in India*,
https://doi.org/10.1007/978-981-15-5382-0

Patta Deed
Podu Burn and Slash Cultivation (Shifting Cultivation)
Rayatwari One type of revenue system introduced by the British
Ryoti Is a person who held on a permanent tenure on land
Sahukars Moneylender
Samiti A committee, society, or association
Sangha Organisation
Shanti Peace
Sena Army
Shundis Liquor traders/vendors
Subedar A historical rank in the Indian Army
Suo moto On its own motion
Tahasils An administrative area in parts of India (now Tahasil/Block)
Taluk An administrative districts for taxation purpose
Usufruct The legal right to use something
Vahini Brigade
Yozana Plan
Zamindar Landlord

The manufacturer's authorised representative in the EU is Springer Nature Customer Service Centre GmbH, Europaplatz 3, 69115 Heidelberg, Germany. If you have any concerns regarding our products, please contact ProductSafety@springernature.com

Printed and bound by CPI Group (UK) Ltd, Croydon, CR0 4YY
05/10/2026
02228124-0005